THE NAME OF GOD

REVEALING GOD THROUGH HIS NAME

KEVIN J. CONNER

CITYCHRISTIAN
PUBLISHING

www.CITYCHRISTIANPUBLISHING.com

Published by City Christian Publishing
9200 NE Fremont - Portland, Oregon 97220

City Christian Publishing is a ministry of City Bible Church, and is dedicated to serving the local church and its leaders through the production and distribution of quality materials. It is our prayer that these materials, proven in the context of the local church, will equip leaders in exalting the Lord and extending His kingdom.

For a free catalog of additional resources from City Christian Publishing, please call 1-800-777-6057 or visit our web site at www.citychristianpublishing.com.

THE NAME OF GOD

ISBN: 1-59383-030-0

PREFACE

In the days of the Apostles, explicit answers to essential questions of doctrine were available from men to whom the Lord had personally committed "the faith once delivered to the saints." Exact definition of doctrine today is a more difficult problem. The definition lies within the Scriptures but "what saith the Scriptures?" In some important areas of doctrine, sincere men disagree. We cannot appeal to "them that heard Him" for definitions beyond what the Scriptures now afford. Earnest inquiry into the meaning of the Scriptures is therefore imperative.

Few doctrines have been as much the occasion of controversy among Evangelical Christians as the doctrine concerning the name of God. This book by Kevin J. Conner treats that doctrine and is therefore probably going to be viewed as controversial. However, the reader must remember that controversy is not evil in and of itself. It is the servant of truth. Only prejudice is evil and the enemy of understanding.

It is my conviction that this book will bring together opposite poles to a meeting of understanding concerning the great subject of the name of God. If the authority of God is invested in the Name, then obviously the adversary will do anything and everything in his power to hinder the understanding and use of that Name. This book will bring a great enlightenment to its readers on the authority and power of the name of the Lord Jesus Christ, for in Him is invested "the fulness of the Godhead bodily."

I trust that this book will help you as much as it has helped me in understanding the full significance and power of the name of God.

"Therefore will I deliver him: I will set him on high, because he hath known my name" (Psalm 91:14).

Rev. K. R. "Dick" Iverson
Founder and Chairman, Ministers Fellowship International

TABLE OF CONTENTS

SECTION I   THE ETERNAL GODHEAD or THE PERSON OF GOD

Chapter I   1. The Eternal Godhead or The Triunity of God 3
             2. A Statement of Faith 5
             3. Doctrinal Statements 15
             4. Illustration of the Triangle 17
             5. Types of the Triune God 18

Chapter II   1. The Name of God in the Old Testament 25
             2. Is "God" a Name? 25
             3. Has God revealed His Name? 26
             4. The Question of Saints, "What is His Name?" 27
             5. The Name of God in Typical Creations 32

Chapter III 1. The Revelation of "The Name" given to Moses 41
             2. Ministry in "The Name" in the Old Testament 53

SECTION II   THE GODHEAD NAME or THE TRIUNE NAME

Chapter IV   1. The New Testament Name of God, the Triune Name 57
             2. Significance of "The Name" in History 58
             3. The Name in the Four Gospels 62
             4. The Name in the Book of Acts 73
             5. The Name in the Epistles 82
             6. Do all in the Name of the Lord Jesus 86

SECTION III   WHAT ABOUT "THE NAME" IN WATER BAPTISM

Chapter V   1. What about "The Name" in Water Baptism? 91
             2. The N.T. Name of God associated with Three Divine Persons 93
             3. Father, Son and Holy Spirit - Titles or Names 98
             4. The Name of the Father 102
             5. And of the Son 105
             6. And of the Holy Spirit 107

Chapter VI   1. The Dual Application of the Triune Name 119
                 (1) The Name of the Godhead as Father,
                     Son and Holy Spirit
                 (2) The Name of the Godhead Bodily,
                     Godward and Manward aspects
             2. The Revelation of the Triune Name at Pentecost 123

Chapter VII 1. The Great Commission considered in the Book of Acts 133
             2. Water Baptism "In the Name" 137
                 (1) Water Baptism in the Gospels
                 (2) Water Baptism in the Acts
                 (3) Water Baptism in the Epistles
             3. "In or Into The Name" 159
             4. Invoking "The Name" 162
             5. Table of Scriptures on Water Baptism in "The Name" 167

Chapter VIII 1. The Godhead revealed in Baptism 171
              2. A Formula of Scripture 173
              3. Quotable Quotations 177

Summary and Conclusion 185

APPENDIX I   Redemptive Names 187

APPENDIX II   The "I Am's" of Jesus 189

Bibliography 191

DEDICATION

THESE NOTES ARE DEDICATED TO THE FOLLOWING:

"THEN THEY THAT FEARED <u>THE LORD</u>

SPAKE OFTEN ONE TO ANOTHER:

AND <u>THE LORD</u> HEARKENED AND HEARD IT:

AND <u>A BOOK OF REMEMBERANCE</u> WAS WRITTEN

BEFORE HIM FOR THEM THAT FEAR <u>THE LORD</u>

AND THAT THOUGHT UPON <u>HIS NAME</u>."

                                    Malachi 3:16

SECTION I

THE ETERNAL GODHEAD or THE PERSON OF GOD

CHAPTER I

FOREWORD

THE NAME OF GOD is one of the most wonderful and remarkable themes in the Word of God, the Holy Bible. It is a theme which flows through the entire Book, beginning in Genesis (the Book of Beginnings), and consummating in Revelation (the Book of Ultimates).

The value of any Bible theme is seen by the emphasis that God Himself places upon it, hence the Church needs to put value and emphasis where God puts it.

The study of THE NAME OF GOD is inseparable from the study of THE PERSON OF GOD, for, the Name or the Names of God reveal God in all His Glory, Attributes, and Power. The Names of God are a revelation of His very Nature and Being.

The Psalmist tells us that God has magnified HIS WORD even above ALL HIS NAME, Psalm 138:2. And this is rightly so; for, apart from the Word of God, there can be no revelation of the Name of God. It is the Word of God that unveils, unfolds and reveals the glories of the Name of God in all of its wonder, glory, beauty and majesty.

The WORD OF GOD and the NAME OF GOD are absolutely inseparable in the Plan and Purpose of God in His REDEMPTIVE manifestation and revelation to HIS creatures.

All of the great Doctrines in the Bible, clearly seen and defined for us in the New Testament, have been shadowed forth in the Old Testament. Truths were hidden, veiled and concealed in types and shadows, signs and symbols, figures and allegory, prophetic places, persons, events and structures. The Old Testament was indeed "The Age of the Shadow," and as we follow the Shadow, we eventually come to THE PERSON whose Shadow it was, even to the Person of our LORD JESUS CHRIST.

The same is true concerning the Doctrine of the Name of God. The teaching pertaining to God's Name in the Old Testament is particularly shadowed forth in types and symbols, as well as clear revelation in part.

However, it is in the New Testament that we are given the fullest, clearest, richest, and most comprehensive revelation of the Name of God. No words of man can adequately explain or express the Glory of God and His Name.

The purpose of this Compilation of Notes is an endeavor to show the relationship between GOD and HIS NAME; that is, "The LORD JESUS CHRIST" being the Name of the Eternal Godhead.

These Notes are not written for the biased or skeptical, who may approach the subject ready to "strain at a gnat and swallow a camel" (Matthew 23:24). Nor are they written for those who would, as in the days of the Prophet Isaiah, "Make a man an offender for a word" (Isaiah 29:21).

They are written for those who sincerely and earnestly desire to know and understand that portion of truth as concerns God and His NAME.

The writer suggests that the study be completely read, and the Scriptures meditated upon, remembering the words of King Solomon, "He that answereth a matter before he heareth it, it is a shame and folly unto him" (Proverbs 18:13).

The Early Church suffered opposition and persecution over "The Name" to the extent that the Council charged them saying,

> "Did not we straightly command you that ye should not teach in THIS NAME? and behold ye have filled Jerusalem with your doctrine" (Acts 5:28).

Jesus Himself said to His Disciples, "And ye shall be hated of all Nations for My NAME'S sake" (Matthew 24:9).

The Prophet Micah declares, "The Lord's voice crieth unto the city, and the man of wisdom shall see Thy Name" (Micah 6:9).

The fear of the Lord is the beginning of wisdom.

Let us turn to the Word of the Lord. The Word of God is the test of all things and it is in the Scriptures that we seek and find the glorious truth of THE NAME OF GOD.

> "To the Law and the Testimony: if they speak not according to this Word, it is because there is no light in them"
>> (Isaiah 8:20)

These study Notes were originally printed in duplicated form for Bible Class Students in New Zealand and Australia. About 1000 copies were circulated. Upon request for a more permanent form of the same, these Notes are now printed. They are not written from any literary scholarship, but with an honest desire to help believers to appreciate the glory of the Triune Name of the Triune God.

A cursory glance over Church History will show the decline of the Church from the faith once delivered to the saints (Jude 3). Since the period of the reformation God, by His Spirit, has been recovering many truths to His people. One of these truths is "The Name of God." Over the years of meditation and research into "The Name of the Lord Jesus Christ," the writer has found that the interpretation of this Triune Name shows it to be indeed the greatest Compound Redemptive Name of God ever to be revealed. It is a Name which is above every Name, not only in this world, but also in that world which is to come! (Ephesians 1:21)

May the Lord bless the truth concerning His own Name.

Kevin John Conner
7626 N.E. Glisan Street
Portland, Oregon 97213
U.S.A.

Author's Note: All capitals, underlines and emphases are mine throughout. All quotations of Scripture are taken from King James Version unless otherwise stated.

THE ETERNAL GODHEAD

The study of THE NAME OF GOD is inseparable from a study of THE PERSON OF GOD. Therefore this treatise falls into two main sections.

The two main sections will be considered under:

    1. The Eternal Godhead - The Person of God.
    2. The Godhead Name   - The Name of God.

(1) GOD IS.

The Bible nowhere attempts to prove the existence of God - it simply declares it.

"In the Beginning GOD ......" Genesis 1:1.

Belief in the existence of God is absolutely foundational. If a person rejects the fact of the existence of God, there is absolutely no point of commencement.

"For without faith it is impossible to please Him: he that cometh to GOD must believe that He is and that He is a rewarder of them that diligently seek Him" Hebrews 11:6.

This Scripture tells us, "GOD IS." That is to say, God exists. It also tells us, "GOD REWARDS." That is, God reveals Himself to those who diligently seek Him.

This is faith's beginning. Nothing can be known of or received from God unless we believe that He is. Faith is the connecting link between Creator and Creature, between God and Man.

(2) GOD IS A REWARDER.

The next important thing to be recognized is the fact that He has revealed Himself.

If God is, and He is, then how is man to know God? The answer is that God must reveal Himself. If God does not reveal Himself to man, then it is absolutely impossible for man to discover God or find out God for Himself.

Man with all his searching cannot find God. God Himself must take the initiative (Job 11:7; Matthew 11:25-27).

This He has done in His Word, the Holy Bible.

The Word of God is the revelation of God. Without the Word of God we would have no revelation of God in His very Essence, in His inner Nature and Being.

"For the Lord revealed Himself to Samuel in Shiloh by the Word of the Lord" I Samuel 3:21.

4

Unless man accepts this Self-revelation of God, then man stumbles along in the darkness of human thought, reason and intellectualism. Human wisdom is utter foolishness before God (I Corinthians 1:18-25).

God **has** revealed Himself in His Word, and man must accept God's revelation of Himself or else he cannot know God.

(3) THE GODHEAD.

The Scriptures speak of "The Mystery of God" (Colossians 2:2).

The Scriptures speak also of "The Mystery of Godliness - God manifest in the flesh" (I Timothy 3:16).

It is well to note here at the beginning of this section that no human pen or tongue can define God by mere words, and no man can fully explain the Mystery of God.

The Scriptures do not attempt to explain it, but they do declare it!

Much misunderstanding relative to the Person of God has come into the Church over terminology and a theological phraseology or a religious jargon which has developed over the centuries.

It is worthy to remember the words of Isaiah the Prophet which he spoke to those of his own time that it is possible to "make a man an offender for a word" (Isaiah 29:21).

A word used in the New Testament relative to God is "Godhead." The word refers to that which is Divine, to Deity, involving God's revelation of His own mode of Being, His own mode of existence.

> "...we ought not to think that the Godhead is like unto gold, or silver or stone, graven by art and man's device"(Acts 17:29).

> "For in Him dwelleth all the fulness of the Godhead bodily" (Col. 2:9).

> "The invisible things of the world are clearly seen, being understood by the things that are made, even His Eternal Power and Godhead..." (Romans 1:19, 20).

In the Early Church, one of the Church Fathers called Tertullian, introduced the word "Trinity" as the most suitable word to define the teaching concerning God or the Godhead.

The Latin word "Trinitas" is that which comes from the adjective "Trinus." The word simply means "Three-fold," or "Three in One."

However, the word "Trinity" is not used in the Scriptures and for that reason it will not generally be used. But the words "Three," and "One" are used and these will be the words emphasized in this section on the Person of God, or the Godhead.

A STATEMENT OF FAITH

"That is to say, we believe in the Eternal Godhead, who has revealed Himself as ONE GOD existing in THREE PERSONS, even the Father, the Son and the Holy Spirit; distinguishable but indivisible in Essence; co-eternal, co-equal and co-existent in attributes, power, nature and glory." (Statement of faith by the writer as taught in Systematic Theology Class.)

This is God's revelation of His own mode of Being. The Eternal Godhead is the Father, the Son and the Holy Spirit.

The GOD of the Bible is revealed as TRIUNE in Nature and Being. From Genesis to Revelation, whether it be by type or symbol, pattern or created things, shadows or theophanic revelation and manifestation, or whether it be by clear declaration, Scriptures show that GOD is always revealed as One in Three and Three in One -- that is, TRI-UNITY!

Father, Son and Holy Spirit is the Bible definition of God.

> "Baptizing them in the Name of the Father, and of the Son,
> and of the Holy Spirit" (Matthew 28:19).

The following statements cannot be overemphasized as pertaining to the revelation of the Person and Nature of God in His very Essence and Nature or Mode of Being.

In the Scriptural revelation of God, we find there are two streams of truth concerning His Person, and that is, God is One, God is Three.

> The Bible teaches us that GOD IS ONE.
> The Bible teaches us that GOD IS THREE.

Let us group one stream of Scriptures which clearly and unmistakably reveal that God is ONE. Then let us group the other stream of Scriptures which also clearly and unmistakably reveal that God is THREE.

It is important to remember relative to these statements, that if the stream of Scriptures is overemphasized concerning the fact that GOD IS ONE, then it results in the heresy of Unitarianism, that is, a numerical or number one God.

On the other hand, if the stream of Scriptures is overemphasized concerning the fact that GOD IS THREE, then it results in the heresy of Tritheism, that is, the worship of three separate Gods.

It is well to remember the phrase previously used in the Statement of Faith, that "we believe in ONE GOD, existing in THREE PERSONS, distinguishable, but indivisable.

> God is One -- that is, indivisible -- His Unity!
> God is Three -- that is, distinguishable -- His Tri-Unity!

The study of the Oneness of God must always be in connection with the Threeness of God, and the study of the Threeness of God must always be in conjunction with the revelation of the Oneness of God. Otherwise, either extreme can become heresy. There is a great need for Scriptural balance.

```
God is One     )
                )  Tri-Unity
God is Three   )
```

Let us consider the two streams of Scripture which reveal the Tri-Unity of God.

---The Unity of God - God is One - Indivisible---

The God of the Bible, the God whom we worship, is revealed as ONE GOD.

Both Old Testament and New Testament confirm the fact that there is but One God. Both Testaments declare the Unity of God.

Old Testament Scriptures:

1. "The Lord He is God, there is none beside Him" Deut. 4:35,39.
2. "Thou shalt have no other gods before Me" Ex. 20:3
3. "There is none beside Thee" I Sam. 2:2; (II Sam. 7:22).
4. "Thou art God alone" Psa. 86:10; 83:18.
5. "Beside Me there is no God" Isa. 44:6,8; 43:10; 45:18.
6. "Hear O Israel, the Lord our God is one Lord" Deut. 6:4.

Each of these verses show clearly that there is but ONE God, or, that GOD IS ONE, that he is the one and only True God, the one True object of worship.

Heathen Religions make gods and idols out of created things, but God alone is the Creator. Many heathen Religions are Polytheistic, that is, the worship of many gods.

The Scriptures teach that there is ONE God, speaking of God in His Unity, as "Him, His Face, His Voice, His Hand," etc.

New Testament Scriptures:

The New Testament also confirms the fact that there is but One God.

1. "The Lord our God is One God" Mark 12:29.
2. "There is none other God but one" I Cor. 8:4.
3. "For there is one God, and there is none other but He" Mark 12:32.
4. "God is one" Gal. 3:20.
5. "One God and Father of all" Eph. 4:6.
6. "Thou believest there is one God, thou doest well" James 2:19.
7. "For there is one God" I Tim. 2:5; I Tim. 1:17.

Thus Old and New Testament definitely declare the Unity of God, that there is ONE God, not many Gods. The Christian believes in One God, the One True object of worship. God is one. The Unity of God is forever settled by Scripture.

---The Threeness of God - God is Three - Distinguishable---

The next grouping of Scripture as set forth here declare to us the fact that GOD IS THREE. As clearly as the Scriptures teach that God is One, so clearly do the same Scriptures teach that God is Three.

This is to say, in this ONE GOD there are THREE PERSONS, distinguishable but indivisible, and these are spoken to us as being "The Father, The Son and The Holy Spirit," co-equal, co-eternal, co-existing in power, majesty, glory and Essence. One God in Three Persons.

In other words, the Bible teaches the TRI-UNITY of God. The Union of Three in One. One God manifested in Three Persons.

This Union in Deity is defined by the word "Godhead," as already noted. Refer again to these Scriptures. Rom. 1:20; Col. 2:9; Acts 17:29.

The Bible speaks of two kinds of unity or oneness. This is seen in the use of two Hebrew and Greek words translated by the word "one," but each having a different meaning.

The two Hebrew words are: (1) Yachead, and (2) Echad.

(1) YACHEAD - (or YACHID) -- speaks of Absolute Unity - a mathematical or numerical number one.

It is used about twelve times in the Old Testament, but not to describe the Unity of God.

Following are several examples of its use.

Abraham offered up "his only (Yachead) son, Isaac" Gen. 22:2,12.
"Deliver my darling (i.e., My Only one)" Psa. 22:20.
"They shall mourn for Him, as one mourneth for his only (Yachead) son" Zech. 12:10.
Refer also to Jer. 6:26 and Judges 11:34.

This word is significant of the fact that there is only ONE way to God, ONE Son of God, man's one and only Hope of Salvation, and this is through the Lord Jesus Christ. John 14:1,6.

(2) ECHAD -- speaks of a Compound or Collective unity, often a unity which comprises more than one person.

i.e., One crowd, one people, one nation.

Following are several examples of this unity.

"These two shall be one (echad) flesh" Gen. 2:24.
"People gathered together as one" Ezra 3:1.
"All the rest of Israel were of one heart to make David king" I Chron. 12:38.

This Hebrew word, "Echad," is used hundreds of times in the Old Testament and is often significant of a Compound Unity; the unity of more than one. And it is the word "Echad" which is used concerning the ONE GOD!

The two Greek words which carry the same thought as these two Hebrew words are the following.

(1) HEIS -- Metaphorically, Union and Concord. That is, a compound unity.

(2) MONOS -- Alone, solitary. Or, "Monogenes," "Only Begotten" Heb. 11:17.
Numerical number one. (Refer to W. E. Vine's Expository Dictionary.)

"As the Body is one (Greek, Heis) and hath many members, so also is
Christ" I Cor. 12:12.
"That they all may be one (Greek, Heis), as Thou, Father, art in Me, and
I in Thee, that they also may be one in Us." John 17:21-23.

Whenever Scripture speaks of the fact that God is One, it never means the
mathematical or number One God but always a Compound Unity; the unity of more
than One Person.

It speaks of plurality of Divine Persons in the One. God. This Unity is a compound Unity, which unity is revealed as TRI-UNITY, the Union of Three in One.

Israel's National Tenet of Faith for centuries says, "The LORD our GOD is ONE
(Echad) LORD" Deut. 6:4.

This very scripture tells us that the Lord God is a compound Unity. It states
that "Jehovah Elohim" is a United One, or, Uni-Plural in Nature and Being.

The word "Elohim" is a Hebrew uni-plural word implying plurality of Divine
Persons.

The word "Echad" is the Hebrew word for the unity of more than one, or, a compound unity.

It was this which preserved Israel from total lapse into heathen and polytheistic religions, the worship of many gods.

"In that Day, there shall be ONE (Echad) LORD, and His Name ONE (Echad)"
Zech. 14:9.

The Hebrew word for a compound Unity is again revealed in this text. The "Oneness" of God, or "The Unity of God" is thus a Compound Unity, which Unity is
Three Persons, existing in essential and eternal Being.

This plurality of Divine Persons is seen in both Old and New Testaments, in
Divine names and titles of God, as also in Divine conversations and prophecies.

The Oneness of God is NOT numerical. From Genesis to Revelation, the God of
the Bible is never manifested as the singular, solitary numeral, or number
one. The Oneness of God is a Compound Unity.

MAN was made in the image of God. Man himself is a Tri-Unity, or a Triune
Being.

God is the Creator, and Man the Creature, yet the very Nature and Being of man
reflects the fact that God is One and God is Three.

Within man's Nature and Being there are Three Centers of Consciousness spoken
of as Spirit, Soul and Body.

Man is One.   )   Man is Tri-Une. Man is a Tri-Unity. I Thess. 5:23.
Man is Three.)

Spirit -- The God-conscious part of man.
Soul   -- The Self-conscious part of man.
Body   -- The Sense or World-conscious part of man.

> Thus, within man, in his very Nature and Being, that which makes man a
> man, there are three centers of consciousness, spirit, soul and body. Man
> is the union of Three in One, and One in Three. This is the image of God
> that man was made in which man - as creature - dimly reflects.

Thus in the Eternal Godhead there are Three Centers of Consciousness, spoken
of as the Father, the Son and The Holy Spirit. The Union Three in One, and One
in Three.

There are not Three separate Gods, but Three Persons in One God, distinguishable, but indivisible.

All Pagan religions and false religions in Christendom clamor for a numerical
or number One God, rejecting the Deity of the Blessed Son of God and rejecting
the personality of the Holy Spirit.

The Unity of God involves Plurality. Never ever is God revealed as a Number
One God, but always as Three-in-One and One-in-Three Being, or, Tri-Unity!

GOD IS TRI-UNE! The Father, The Son, and the Holy Spirit is the clear Bible
definition of God. Note the following Scriptures.

Old Testament Scriptures:

1. "In the Beginning GOD ... and the Spirit of GOD moved on the face of
   the waters" Gen. 1:1-2; cf. John 1:1-3.
   The word for "God" is "Elohim," plural of the Hebrew word "El," and
   it is a Hebrew uni-plural word, denoting plurality of Divine Persons
   without stating the number, but which subsequent Scriptures show to
   be Three Divine Persons, even the Father, the Son and the Holy Spirit
   each active in Creation.
2. GOD (Elohim, Plurality of Divine Persons) made man in HIS (Singular
   possessive) own image, after HIS (Unity) likeness. Genesis 1:26.
   Plurality of Divine Persons.
3. GOD (Elohim, Plurality of Divine Persons) made man in HIS (Unity) own
   image, after HIS (Unity) likeness. Genesis 1:27.
   Here we have Plurality and Unity of God expressed.
4. "And GOD (Elohim) said: Man is become as one of US, to know good and
   evil" Gen. 3:22.
   Plurality expressed again here.
5. "The Voice of the Lord saying, Who will go for US?" Isa. 6:8. Unity
   and Plurality of Divine Persons. cf. John 12:41.

All of these verses speak of the plurality of Divine Persons in the One God,
and generally this Hebrew uni-plural word "Elohim" is used in the Old Testament to speak of the Eternal Godhead. It is the Old Testament equivalent for
the New Testament definition of God as Father, Son and Holy Spirit, or, the
Godhead.

However, it must also be remembered that the word "Elohim" is used of the gods of the Canaanites, meaning "God, gods, or objects of worship." This is why it is stated the word involves plurality. Deuteronomy 10:17; Exodus 23:13; Judges 2:3. It is also used of rulers of the people. Exodus 22:28; Psalm 82:6.

When it is used of the True God, it implies Plurality of Divine Persons.

Following are several further Scriptures which clearly show plurality of Divine Persons in the Old Testament.

1. "The Lord God (The Father) and His Spirit (The Holy Spirit) hath sent Me (The Son)" Isa. 48:16.
   Three Divine Persons spoken of here.
2. "The Spirit (The Holy Spirit) of the Lord (The Father) is upon Me, because He hath anointed Me" Isa. 61:1. cf. Luke 4:18.
   Three Divine Persons here.
3. "The Lord (The Father) said unto my Lord (The Son), sit Thou at My Right Hand until I make Thine enemies Thy footstool" Psa. 110:1.
   Two Divine Persons here.
4. "Then the Lord (The Son) rained fire and brimstone from the Lord (The Father) out of heaven" Gen. 19:24.
5. "Thy throne O God (The Son, cf. Heb. 1:8-9) is forever...therefore God, Thy God (The Father) hath anointed Thee" Psa. 45:6-7.
   The Son and The Father God mentioned here.

There are numerous Scriptures in the Old Testament which bring out clearly the plurality of Divine Persons in God.

Several others may be referred to in the following:

Psa. 2:7; Isa. 63:16; 7:14; 9:6-7; Zech. 6:12-13; 3:8.

However, the fullest and clearest revelation of the Three Divine Persons is given for us in the New Testament, and we will list a number of Scriptures to confirm this.

New Testament Scriptures:

The New Testament is specific in the revelation of God in His Tri-Unity.
   The Scriptures speak of   The Father
                                The Son
                                The Holy Spirit. .

Each Person is declared to be GOD, yet there are not three Gods, but ONE GOD.

The revelation of God in Three Persons is the distinctive ministry of the Blessed Son of God. The only way God could be become known to man in His inner Nature and Being of Tri-Unity was by revelation. God must reveal Himself. Who could bring or give this revelation? What Patriarch, what Prophet, what Saint could reveal God to mankind? No Angel, no created Being could unveil God in His Glory, in the truth of His Eternal Godhead as Father, Son and Holy Spirit?

The Patriarchs, Prophets and Old Testament Saints all received but fragmentary revelation of God themselves and communicated it to others and to the people of God in the Sacred Scriptures.

The Only One, the Only Person who could reveal God to man was the very One who dwelt in the bosom of the Father.

It had to be One of the Persons in Elohim, One in the Eternal Godhead who alone could reveal God to man. In the Counsels of the Eternal Godhead, it was The Eternal Son (THE WORD) who was to come and declare GOD in HIS TRI-UNITY of Being.

> "God who at sundry times and in divers manners spake unto the fathers by the Prophets hath in these Last Days spoken unto us in the Person of HIS SON..." Heb. 1:1-2.

> "No man knoweth the Son, but the Father; neither knoweth any man the father, save the Son, and he to whomsoever the Son will reveal Him" Matthew 11:27.

> "No man hath seen GOD at any time; the Only Begotten Son, who is in the bosom of the Father, He hath declared Him" John 1:18, cf 14-18.

> The Amplified New Testament says, "No man has ever seen God at any time; the only unique Son, the only-begotten God, Who is in the bosom (that is, in the intimate presence) of the Father, He has declared Him - He has revealed Him, brought Him out where He can be seen: He has interpreted Him, and He has made Him known" John 1:18.

Thus the clearest revelation of God as Triune of necessity had to come through One of these Divine Persons. It is here we have one of the fundamental reasons for the Incarnation. The only way God could be revealed to man was by GOD becoming a MAN.

All of this was prophesied and then fulfilled in the Virgin Birth of the Son of God. God manifest in the flesh. God in human form. God incarnate. Isa. 7:14; 9:6-9; Gen. 3:15; Matt. 1:21-23. John 1:1-3; 14-18.

It is the New Testament which plainly declares the number of Divine Persons to be THREE, no more and no less. The whole of the New Testament abounds with clear references to Three distinct, Divine Persons, who are revealed as God or the Eternal Godhead.

The Lord Jesus Christ is the One who gives us the fullest revelation of God in His tri-unity, and this is the clearest revelation which man will ever be given.

The Old Testament veiled the revelation of God. Being the "Age of the shadow," when all things pertaining to the inner Nature and Being of God were veiled in types, shadows, and Divine Names and Titles, it remained for the Son of God in the fullness of time to unveil God in His Fullness.

Following is a set of Scriptures from the Gospels and Epistles which show the distinction in the Godhead, as Father, Son and Holy Spirit.

These verses tell of THREE distinct Persons, each having distinct ministry and function, yet ONE in mind and will, One in Essence, and One in the purpose, plan and operation of redemption.

Always THREE in manifestation, always ONE in operation!

1. Matthew 3:16-17.
    The Father's Voice which spoke from heaven.
    The Son of God in Jordan's waters of baptism.
    The Holy Spirit descending bodily in the shape of a dove.

2. Matthew 28:19.
    Baptizing them into The Name
            Of the Father,
            And of the Son,
            And of the Holy Spirit.
    Matthew's Gospel opens and closes with specific revelation of the God-
    head, as Father, Son and Holy Spirit.

3. John 14:16-17.
    The Father hears the prayer of the Son.
    The Son prays to the Father.
    The Holy Spirit as the Comforter will be given.
            Three distinct Divine Persons here.

4. I Corinthians 12:4-6.
    Diversities of Gifts, but the same Spirit (Holy Spirit).
    Differences of Ministrations but the same Lord (The Son).
    Diversities of Operations but the same God (The Father).
            The Godhead as Three distinguished again here.

5. Ephesians 2:18.
    Access unto - The Father
    Through Him - The Son
    By one Spirit - The Holy Spirit
            Revelation of the Godhead here also.

6. Ephesians 4:4-6.
    There is one Lord - The Son
    There is one Spirit - The Holy Spirit
    There is one God - The Father
            Three Divine Persons distinguished here.

7. II Corinthians 13:14.
    The Grace of our Lord Jesus Christ - The Son
    The Love of God   - The Father
    The Communion of the Holy Spirit   - The Spirit
            The Benediction for the Church declares the Eternal Godhead,
            distinguishable as Father, Son and Holy Spirit.

8. I John 5:7-8.
    There are Three that bear record in heaven:
            The Father
            The Word (The Son)
            And the Holy Spirit,
                And these THREE are ONE.
    That is, Tri-Unity. One God, manifested and distinguished in Three
    Persons.

The Lord Jesus, in John's Gospel, Chapters 15, 16 and 17 clearly brings to view the Divine Persons in the Godhead. The SON prays to the Father to send the HOLY SPIRIT.

He prays that the disciples may be "one, as WE are one," and that they may be "one in US." John 17:21-23. The "oneness" here is certainly not a numerical oneness, but a compound unity, the unity of more than one person.

Many other Scriptures could be quoted or referred to, but enough verses have been given to show that the GOD OF THE BIBLE, the God whom we worship is always revealed as THREE fold in Essence, Nature and Being.

Jesus said, "Ye believe in God (The Father), believe also in ME (The Son)" John 14:1.

He continued by saying, "I AM the way, the truth and the life; no man cometh unto the Father but by ME" John 14:6.

Paul says, "For there is ONE GOD (the Father) and ONE MEDIATOR between God and men, THE MAN (Son of God) Christ Jesus" I Tim. 2:5.

It is Jesus Christ, the Son of the Living God, who speaks so expressly and specifically of the Person of the Holy Spirit.

False and pagan religions which accept God the Father, reject Jesus the Son as "God manifest in the flesh" (I Tim. 3:16), rejecting His Deity, which rejection leads to the rejection of the Deity and personality of the Holy Spirit, the Third Person in the Eternal Godhead.

The issue of all heresies is not concerning God the Father, but evolve around the Son and the Holy Spirit.

God has declared that "in the mouth of two or three witnesses shall every Word be established" Deut. 19:15. Matt. 18:16-20.

If GOD were not THREE in ONE (Triune), He could never fulfill His own Word. It would mean that God would have given to man a law to fulfill which He himself cannot fulfill.

The Father, the Son and the Holy Spirit are THREE WITNESSES, a perfect, full and complete witness and testimony. God has put this seal of THREE throughout His Word and in the revelation of His own Being. These Three are co-eternal, co-equal and co-existent and for the order and purpose of Redemption's plan,

> THE FATHER is the First Person,
> THE SON is the Second Person,
> THE HOLY SPIRIT is the Third Person.

Wherever we look in the revelation of the ONE GOD, the number THREE is sealed thereon.

> God is ONE)
> God is THREE) Or, God is a TRI-UNE Being, a Compound Unity.

In Summary:

God's revelation of Himself in the Scripture is One God in Three Persons, Eternal, Self-existent; Father, Son and Holy Spirit, distinguishable but indivisible.

Scriptures relative to the Godhead as Father, Son, and Holy Spirit.

THE FATHER.

The Father is God, a distinct person.
The Father is Eternal, Self-existent, Invisible and Immortal, dwelling in light which no man can approach unto; whom no man hath seen, nor can see. I Timothy 6:16.

I Tim. 2:5; I Cor. 8:4; John 6:27; I Pet. 1:2; Deut. 32:4; II Sam. 7:14; Psa. 89:26; Mal. 2:10; Matt. 6:9; Mark 11:25; Luke 12:30; John 4:21-24; II Cor. 6:18; Phil. 4:19; James 1:17; I John 2:15-16.

THE SON.

The Son is God, a distinct Person, co-equal with the Father and with the Holy Spirit. A distinct Personality made visible by the Incarnation.

The Son was Pre-existent. That is, He existed before the world was. He was eternally existent with the Father and with the Holy Spirit.

Mic. 5:2; John 8:56-58; John 17:5; I Cor. 15:47; Phil. 2:6-7; Col. 1:17; John 1:1-3, 14; Rev. 22:13, 16.

The Son not only Pre-existent, but Pre-eminent above all things except the Father.

Matt. 11:27; Matt. 28:18; Luke 20:41-44; John 3:13,31; Acts 10:36; Eph. 1:20-22; Heb. 1:5-6, 4; I Pet. 3:22; Rev. 1:5; Rev. 3:14.

The Son is to be worshipped as God. This would be blasphemy and idolatry if the Son were not God, co-equal and co-eternal with the Father and the Holy Spirit.

Matt. 2:11; Matt. 14:33; Luke 24:52; John 5:23; Acts 7:59-60; Gal. 1:5; Heb. 1:6; II Pet. 3:18; Rev. 5:11-14.

The Son is God manifest in the flesh. I Tim. 3:16; John 1:14-18.

HOLY SPIRIT.

The Holy Spirit is God, a distinct Personality. He is not merely an influence, but a Divine PERSON, co-equal and co-eternal with the Father and the Son.

Gen. 1:2; Gen. 6:3; Isa. 63:10; Joel 2:28; Matt. 10:20; Luke 12:12; John 14:16-17; John 15:26; Acts 2:4; Acts 5:3-4; Rom. 8:14; I Cor. 3:16; Gal. 4:6; Eph. 1:13; Heb. 2:4; Eph. 4:30; I Cor. 6:19.

> Praise GOD from Whom all blessings flow,
> Praise HIM all creatures here below,
> Praise HIM above ye heavenly host,
> Praise FATHER, SON, and HOLY GHOST.

This very benediction declares ONE GOD manifested in THREE PERSONS!

DOCTRINAL STATEMENTS

"The Athanasian Creed," formulated about the 5th Century to combat the heresies concerning the Godhead, and to preserve from the two extremes of Unitarianism and Tritheism, undoubtedly is one of the greatest Creeds of Early Church History. We quote it fully here.

THE ATHANASIAN CREED. A.D. 500.

The Eternal Power and Godhead is a Trinity. Romans 1:20; Matthew 28:19.

The true Christian Faith is this, that we worship One God in Trinity and Trinity in Unity, neither confounding the Persons nor dividing the Substance.

For there is One Person of the Father, another of the Son, another of the Holy Ghost.

But the Godhead of the Father, of the Son, of the Holy Ghost, is all One, the Glory equal, the Majesty co-eternal. Such as the Father is, such is the Son, such is the Holy Ghost.

The Father uncreated, the Son uncreated, the Holy Ghost uncreated. The Father incomprehensible, the Son incomprehensible, the Holy Ghost incomprehensible.

The Father Eternal, the Son Eternal, the Holy Ghost Eternal. And yet there are not three Eternals (or infinities) nor three uncreated, nor three Incomprehensibles, but One Eternal and One Incomprehensible.

So likewise the Father is Almighty, the Son Almighty, and the Holy Ghost almighty; and yet there are not three Almighties, but One Almighty or Omnipotent.

So the Father is God, the Son is God, the Holy Ghost is God, yet there are not three Gods but One God.

For like as we are compelled by the Christian verity to acknowledge every Person by Himself to be God or Lord; so we are forbidden by the Christian faith to say, that there be three Gods or three Lords.

The Father is made of none, neither created not begotten. The Son is of the Father alone, not made, nor created, but begotten.

The Holy Ghost is of the Father and the Son; neither made, nor created, nor begotten, nor proceeding.

So there is One Father, not three Fathers; and there is One Son, not three Sons; and there is One Holy Ghost, not three Holy Ghosts.

And in this Trinity, none is afore or after the Other, none is first and last, none is greater or less than another; but the whole Three Persons are co-eternal together, and co-equal; so that in all things, as aforesaid:
"The UNITY IN TRINITY, and the TRINITY IN UNITY
is to be worshipped."

Dr. Dale in the 19th Century makes the following statements.

"From Eternity to Eternity GOD is FATHER, SON and HOLY SPIRIT. The Father is God, but not apart from the Son or the Holy Spirit. The Son is God, but not apart from the Father and the Holy Spirit. The Holy Spirit is God, but not apart from the Father and the Son.

There is but ONE GOD but in the GODHEAD there are THREE PERSONS. There are not three Gods, but in the Life and Being of the One God, there are three centers of consciousness, volition and activity, and these are known to us as THE FATHER, THE SON, AND THE HOLY SPIRIT."

So that we may say:

THE FATHER is all the Fulness of the Godhead, invisible, without form, whom no man hath seen or can see.
THE SON is all the Fulness of the Godhead, manifested, made visible.
THE HOLY SPIRIT is all the Fulness of the Godhead, acting immediately upon the creature, and thus making manifest, or revealing, the Father and the Son.

The Father planned redemption.
The Son affected redemption.
The Holy Spirit applies redemption.

Thus GOD eternally has been present everywhere, always is present everywhere, always will be present everywhere.

The Father is always the Father. The Father is not the Son, nor the Holy Spirit.

The Son is always the Son. The Son is not the Father, nor the Holy Spirit.

The Holy Spirit is always the Holy Spirit. The Holy Spirit is not the Father nor the Son.

GOD is eternally FATHER, SON and HOLY SPIRIT. ONE GOD in THREE PERSONS.

Illustration of the Tri-angle.

An illustration of the above statements is found suitable in the Tri-angle.

A tri-angle is ONE complete object, composed of THREE co-equals. It would be impossible to have a tri-angle without the three co-equal sides, and each side is always and ever its proper side.

So in the Eternal Godhead, God is ONE, co-existing in THREE co-equals, even the Father, the Son, and the Holy Spirit. This is the Tri-Unity of God, even as illustrated in the Tri-angle which is Tri-une.

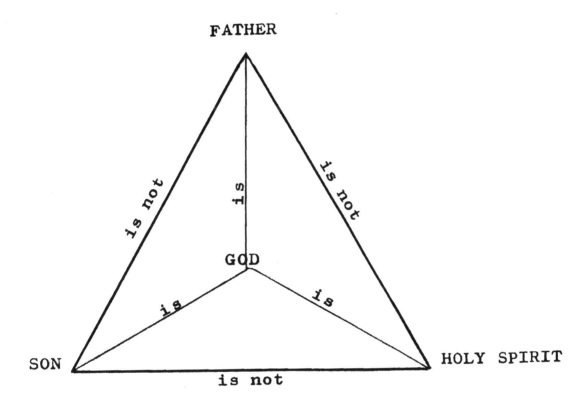

TYPES OF THE TRI-UNE GOD

One of the richest fields of study in the Old Testament concerning the truth of the Eternal Godhead, One God in Three Persons, is that which is seen in typical creations.

Each of these typical creations set forth the Tri-unity of God in His Nature and Being. Let it be noted, that all these things are God-ordained revelations of His own Person and Nature.

Romans 1:20 declares that "the invisible things of Him (that is, the invisible Persons of God) from the creation of the world are clearly seen, being understood by the things that are made (created types, or typical creations), even His eternal power and Godhead, so that they are without excuse."

Scripture abounds with these glorious types of the Godhead as Father, Son, and Holy Spirit, setting forth the Tri-unity of God. Each of the following will be seen to have the impress of God upon them.

The visible reveals the invisible. Col. 1:15-16; II Cor. 4:18.

1. The Sun, Moon and Stars. Gen. 1:14.

    The Sun, Moon and Stars are the source of our light and life, and these are the first manifested three in the Bible.
    These show forth the characteristics of the Godhead.

    The Sun   -- Source of Light and Life, Type of the Father.
    The Moon   -- Becomes as Blood, Type of the Son. Rev. 6:12.
    The Stars -- Multitudinous, Type of the Holy Spirit in the Saints.

2. The Ark of Noah. Gen. 6:14-22.

    God commanded Noah to make an Ark according to specifications which He Himself gave. It was made with "lower, second and third stories." This One Ark with Three stories is a marvellous type of God. One God who is Three Persons, the Father, the Son and the Holy Spirit. It took a tri-une Ark to bring salvation to Noah and his family from the waters of judgment, and it is the ministry of the Tri-une God to bring salvation to mankind from the coming judgment upon sin and all ungodly flesh. Matt. 24:27-42.

    | | (First Story ... Type of the Father, Foundation, Beginning |
    | One Ark | (Second Story ... Type of the Son, the Door, the Way. Jn. 10:9 |
    | | (Third Story ... The Holy Spirit, the Window, the Illuminator. |
    | | Jn. 14:26 |

3. The Rod, the Rock, the Waters. Ex. 17:1-8.

    Another wonderful shadowing forth is that which is found in the history of Israel. Israel thirsted for the living waters in the wilderness. God heard their cry and instructed Moses to smite the Rock and the water gushed forth.

The Rod -- Type of the Father God. He smote the Son on Calvary. It pleased the Father to bruise His Son. Isa. 53:10. God gave His Son an offering for sin. John 3:16.

The Rock -- Type of the Son. Smitten for us. They drank of that Rock which followed them. I Cor. 10:4.

The Waters -- The Type of the Holy Spirit. John 7:37-39. The Holy Spirit flows from the Son as refreshing, life-giving waters. The thirsty may come and drink.

4. The Ark of the Covenant. Ex. 25:10-22. 37:6-9.

The Ark of the Covenant was covered by a Mercy-Seat with two over-shadowing Cherubims of Glory. All Three were fashioned out of One piece of gold. Ex. 25:17-22. Heb. 9:5.

```
                (One Cherub ... type of the Father.
One piece of (Mercy Seat ... type of the Son, Blood-sprinkled.
    gold       (One Cherub ... type of the Holy Spirit. (Rom. 3:25)
```

Between the Cherubim and over the Blood-sprinkled Mercy-Seat was the Glory of the Lord, the very Presence of God. In the midst of that triune typical creation, God communed with His people. Num. 7:89. A most magnificent representation and created, God-ordained type of One God in Three Persons. The revelation of God in His Tri-unity.

5. The Rod of Aaron. Num. 17.

Aaron's Rod that budded is another marvelous typical creation of the Tri-Unity of God. A God-ordained testimony and miracle. One Rod but a manifestation of Three.

```
            (The Bud    ... Type of the Father, Source, Beginning.
One Rod     (The Flower ... Type of the Son, Crushed, Fragrance.
            (The Almond ... Type of the Holy Spirit, Fruitfulness.
```

6. The Burning Bush. Ex. 3:1-6.

The Call of Moses at the Burning Bush was indeed a revelation of God Himself in Tri-unity.

One Bush yet a manifestation of Three.

```
            (The Voice ... Type of the Father God. Ex. 3:4-6.
One Bush    (The Bush  ... Type of the Son, the Root, Branch. Isa. 11:1-2
            (The Fire  ... Type of the Holy Spirit. Heb. 12:29.
```

7. The God of Abraham, Isaac and Jacob. Ex. 3:14-16.

The Three Men show forth the characteristics and ministrations of The Godhead, as Father, Son and Holy Spirit.

```
              (Abraham ... Type of the Father God, Promise, Covenant.
The God of    (Isaac   ... Type of the Son, Only Begotten, Sacrifice.
              (Jacob   ... Type of Holy Spirit, Anointer, Fruitfulness.
```

Only Three Men which God has been pleased to call Himself the God of. A-braham (as the Father) offered up His Only Begotten Son, Isaac (as Jesus), and Jacob, proceeded from the Father Abraham, through the Son Isaac, and was the third Person of that triunity of men, the Anointer of the Rock Bethel, "The House of God."

We quote from James Pluver ("Israel's Triune God"), in the Pentecostal Evangel, January 27, 1963:

"Another approach to the triune God of Israel is found in the third chapter of Exodus, verses 13 to 15, where Moses asks God what His name is. God answers by saying, "The God of A-braham, the God of Isaac, the God of Jacob: this is my name and this is my memorial unto all generations."

By posing a question, this passage may be used to point out the triune nature of God of Israel. The question: If God likened Himself to three earthly persons, as He did here, what was there in these persons or their lives or names that reflected the personality of God?

Then by outlining these names and their meanings we arrive at the Christian idea of God the Father, God the Son, and God the Holy Ghost:
GOD of Abraham - from Abram, meaning "Exalted Father"-GOD the Father.
GOD of Isaac - Isaac was "a seed of promise"; (Jesus was a seed of promise - Gen. 3:15) - GOD the Son.
GOD of Jacob - Supplanter, meaning "one in place of another" - GOD the Holy Ghost.
Jesus said, "And I will pray the Father, and he shall give you another (one in place of myself) Comforter, that he may abide with you for ever" (John 14:16).

Thus when God gave to Moses His name, He revealed His triune nature - that He was an "Echod," a compound unity!"

"Deut. 33:4. The Hebrew word for Lord here is "Echod," and means literally 'a unity.'"

8. The Contents of the Ark. Heb. 9:4.

Beneath the Bloodstained Mercy Seat of the Cherubimed Ark were three arti-cles, which again set forth the characteristics of God in type.

The Tables of the Law ... Type of the Father God.
The Golden Pot of manna ... Type of the Son. John 6:32-36.
The Rod that budded ... Type of the Holy Spirit, Life, Fruitful-ness.

9. The High Priest, Urim and Thummin. Ex. 28.

Again, in the garments of the High Priest we have a glorious prophecy in type of the Godhead Bodily. Aaron, as High Priest, had the Breastplate of

Judgment upon him, and within the Breastplate the two mysterious stones, called Urim and Thummin, by which he received and communicated the mind of the Lord to the Nation of Israel.

```
                     (Urim, "Lights" ... Type of the Father. James 1:17
One High Priest (High Priest    ... Type of the Son, Mediator, Sacrifice
                     (Thummin, "Perfections" ... Type of the Holy Spirit.
```

As all Israel was represented before God in the High Priest, so is the whole church of God represented in the Lord Jesus Christ, our Great High Priest, after the Order of Melchisedek, in whom dwells all the Fulness of the Godhead Bodily.

10. <u>The Three Feasts of the Lord</u>. Lev. 23.

The Three Feasts of Israel set forth the ministrations of the Godhead also. Three yet One.

```
Passover    ... Type of the Son of God, the Lamb. Ex. 12. I Cor. 5:7.
Pentecost   ... Type of the Holy Spirit, the Wave Loaves.  II Cor. 3.
Tabernacles ... Type of the Father, Fulness, Completeness of Redemp-
                tion. Heb. 6:1-2. Matt. 5:48.
```

11. <u>The Three Coverings of the Tabernacle</u>. Ex. 36:18-19.

```
               (Covering of Badger's Skins ... Type of God the Father over
               (                                all.
One Taber-     (Ram's Skins dyed RED       ... Type of the Son, Blood atone-
     nacle     (                                ment.
               (Fine Linen Inwrought       ... Type of the Holy Spirit, in-
               (           Curtains              wrought workings and opera-
                                                 tions.
```

It took the THREE Coverings for the ONE Tabernacle, so it is the Godhead who becomes the true Coverings for the Church, His Tabernacle.

12. <u>The Voice, the Son, the Dove</u>. Matthew 3:16-17.

```
            (The Voice ... The Father
One God     (The Son   ... In the Waters of Baptism in Jordan
            (The Dove  ... The Holy Spirit
```

The Old Testament abounds with these wonderful truths illustrated by types of the Tri-unity of God. Many times God's people are robbed of truth because of rejection of God-ordained types. It is true that no doctrine of Scripture can be established on types only, but it is equally true that God has given numerous types to illustrate the doctrine so clearly expressed in the New Testament revelation.

Many other illustrations could be given but these will suffice. All have the Seal of God upon them. The impress of the THREE and ONE and the central one is always associated with Sacrifice, Blood, Death and Life, while the other two attest to and witness.
The study of the oneness of God must always be in harmony with the study of the threeness of God.

God is ONE. God is THREE.

CHAPTER II

IS "GOD" A NAME?

It is well to note at the beginning the fact that "GOD" is not a proper Name. The word "GOD" (ELOHIM) simply means "an object or objects of worship."

The Scriptures use this word of the True God, of Angels, of men, or Idols, and of Devils. The following Scriptures will be sufficient evidence of this statement.

1. **Of The True God:**

    "In the beginning God created the heaven and the earth" Gen. 1:1. Speaking of the One True God, the Creator of all things.

2. **Of Men or Angels:**

    "God standeth in the congregation of the mighty; He judgeth among the gods" Psa. 82:1.

    Moses was to be "as god before Pharaoh" Ex. 7:1.

    The Scripture saith, "Ye (men) are gods" John 10:34-35.

3. **Of Idols:**

    "Put away the strange gods from among you" Gen. 35:2. Speaking of household idols.

4. **Of Satan:**

    Satan is called "the god of this world" II Cor. 4:4.

Thus "GOD" is not a Name.   All the Nations with their religions, worship some form or concept of a God or Gods, but not necessarily the True God, the God of Creation, the God of the Bible.

DOES GOD HAVE A NAME?

If "GOD" is not a Name, does God have a Name? Yes! God has a Name!

Let the Scriptures speak for themselves from the Old Testament and the New Testament.

THE OLD TESTAMENT:

"Neither shalt thou profane the Name of thy God" Lev. 18:21.
"Thou shalt not take the Name of the Lord thy God in vain" Ex. 20:7.
"Save me O God by Thy Name" Psa. 54:1.
"Sing unto God, sing praises to His Name" Psa. 68:4.
"In the Name of God we will set up our banners" Psa. 20:5.

THE NEW TESTAMENT:

"The <u>Name</u> of <u>God</u> is blasphemed amongst the Gentiles" Rom. 2:24.
"The <u>Name</u> of <u>God</u> and His Doctrine" I Tim. 6:1.
"I will write upon Him the <u>Name</u> of My <u>God</u>" Rev. 3:12.
"And he opened his mouth in blasphemy against <u>God</u>, to blaspheme His
 <u>Name</u>, and His Tabernacle" Rev. 13:6, 16:9.
"Hallowed be Thy <u>Name</u>" Luke 11:2.

Let the student take a Concordance and add other Scriptures from both Testaments.

There are numerous references to this expression concerning "The Name" in both Testaments. We emphasize that which God emphasizes.

HAS GOD REVEALED HIS NAME?

Again the answer is in the affirmative. God not only has a Name but He has chosen to reveal His Name.

God has promised blessing to His people in knowing His Name. Several Scriptures from the Old and New Testament will suffice to answer the question.

OLD TESTAMENT:

"Therefore My people shall <u>know My Name</u>" Isa. 52:6.
"I will set him on high because he hath <u>known My Name</u>" Psa. 91:14.
"The man of wisdom shall <u>see Thy Name</u>" Micah 6:9.
"And a Book of Remembrance was written before Him for them that
 feared the Lord, and that <u>thought upon His Name</u>" Mal. 3:16.
"They that <u>know Thy Name</u> will put their trust in Thee" Psa. 9:10.

NEW TESTAMENT:

"I have <u>manifested Thy Name</u>" John 17:6.
"I have <u>declared Thy Name</u> and will declare it" John 17:26.
"I will <u>declare Thy Name</u> unto My brethren" Heb. 2:12. cf. Psa. 22:22.
"Keep through <u>Thine own Name</u> those whom Thou hast given Me ... I kept
 them in <u>Thy Name</u>" John 17:11,12.

Thus Old Testament and New Testament confirm the fact that God has a Name and that He has revealed or made known this Name to His people.

False gods, strange gods, and idols of heathen religions all have their particular names, and these names are according to their nature and characteristics and that which they represent.

The god of this world, the Devil himself, is also known by many and various names, each and all expressing some aspect of his Satanic nature and being and activities.

How much more shall the true God be known in His very Nature and Being and Characteristics by His many and various Names, and especially in THE NAME which is above "every Name that is Named, not only in this world, but also in that world which is to come" Eph. 1:21.

The Lord writes a Book of Remembrance for those who think upon His Name. Mal. 3:16.

The word "think" means "to regard, value, compute." Let us continue to THINK upon the Name of the Lord.

THE QUESTION OF THE SAINTS

WHAT IS HIS NAME?

The Saints of Bible days desired to know the Name of God. If "God" was a proper Name, then their questions would be meaningless and in vain; but the heart hunger of these Saints was to know God Himself and to know His Name.

1. <u>THE QUESTION OF JACOB</u>: Genesis 32:24-32.

Jacob is returning back to his home land and Bethel (Gen.31:13), and is about to meet his brother Esau from whom he fled 20 years previously after purchasing the Birthright from him, and obtaining the Birthright Blessings from his father Isaac by deception.

As he is left alone, there wrestled a Man with him until the breaking of the day. It was a long weary night .

The Mysterious Visitor that wrestled with Jacob is spoken of as A MAN, AN ANGEL, and GOD.

Neither prevail in the struggle until the hollow of Jacob's thigh - the seat of his strength - is touched.   After this the matter of Names is brought up.

The Heavenly Visitor asks Jacob, "What is thy Name?" And Jacob rightly answered, "My Name is JACOB," which being interpreted means, "Supplanter."

His Name was significant of His Nature. When he confessed his Name, he confessed what or who he was.

However Jacob longs for the Blessing which he realizes the Heavenly Person can bring to him. He will not let go although his thigh is out of joint.

Jacob turns to the Mysterious Person and says: <u>"Tell me, I pray Thee THY NAME</u>?" But the Angel replies with a question: "Wherefore is it that thou does't ask after <u>MY NAME</u>?" And He blessed him there.

Jacob called the Name of that place "Peniel" which being interpreted means "The Face of God."

His Name is changed from Jacob to Israel which means "A Prince having power with God and with men and prevailing."

The New Name was prophetic of the New Nature.

But The Name of this Heavenly Visitor still remains a secret. Jacob's question remains unanswered.

2. THE QUESTION OF MANOAH: Judges 13:2-23.

Israel as a Nation is in bondage and captivity. The Angel of the Lord, who appeared to Jacob years before the Nation existed, now appears to Manoah's wife, and once again the question of Names is brought in.

The Angel tells Manoah's wife that she would bare a son and his Name would be called Samson.

The Angel disappears. She tells her husband that A MAN of God, an ANGEL of God came and appeared to her, but she did not know whence He came, neither did she know His NAME.

After prayer, the Angel returns in visitation to Manoah and his wife.

"And Manoah said unto the Angel of the Lord, WHAT IS THY NAME, that when Thy sayings come to pass we may do Thee honour?"

What was the reply? Simply another question!

The Angel of the Lord said to Manoah, "Why askest thou thus after MY NAME, seeing it is secret?"

The marginal References read, "Why askest thou thus after My Name seeing it is 'Wonderful', 'A Secret', or 'A Wonderful Secret'?"

Once again the Angel disappears. The scene here closes with the question concerning The Name unanswered. Why? Who was this Angel of the Lord?

Why did they want to know His Name?
Why was the question not answered?
Who was this Angel whose Name was secret, wonderful, a wonderful secret?

As to Jacob, now to Manoah, the Mysterious Visitor had appeared, and both had asked after His Name, and both received no answer.

3. THE PROPHETIC QUESTION OF AGUR: Proverbs 30:1-4.

In the Book of Proverbs, we have a most remarkable prophecy which involves the questions of Agur concerning the Name of God.

"The words of Agur the Son of Jaketh, even the prophecy ..." Prov. 30:1.

In verse 4 Agur asks a seven-fold question, and these questions are prophetic, to be answered in due time, in the fulness of time.

For clarity of thought, we set the verse out in question form as follows:

1. Who hath ascended up into heaven?
2. Or descended?
3. Who hath gathered the wind in His fists?
4. Who hath bound the waters in a garment?
5. Who hath established all the ends of the earth?
6. WHAT IS HIS NAME?
7. AND WHAT IS HIS SON'S NAME, if thou canst tell?

This is the same question as previously asked by Jacob and Manoah, with an additional question.

Here TWO DIVINE PERSONS and the question of Names is brought to view.

> The Person of God the Father -- "What is HIS Name?"
> The Person of the Son of God -- "What is His SON's Name?"

The Name of God, ELOHIM YAHWEH, (Deut. 6:4) had been revealed to Moses (as will be seen in due course), under the Old Testament Dispensation, but the Son's Name could not and would not be revealed in its fulness until the fulness of time when the Son would become incarnate by the Virgin Birth, Begotten of God and born of Mary.

Hence we have three of the Old Testament Saints who specifically desired to know the Name of God.

If the Saints of early times desired to ask questions concerning God's Name, may not the believer today ask the same questions and receive an answer from the Book of God? The answer is "Yes."

"The SECRET THINGS belong unto the Lord our God: but the THINGS WHICH ARE REVEALED belong unto us and to our children for ever" Deut. 29:29.

God will and has answered the questions of His Saints.

Agur's questions were rhetorical, as well as having a prophetic strain in them. In verse 9 he talks about the Name of the LORD, that is, YAHWEH, and the danger of taking the Name of God in vain. The question of the Son's Name was not answered.

The Name of the Son would be revealed in the fulness of time. This would be the answer to Agur's prophetic question. This would come when He descended and ascended, as seen in New Testament revelation. Eph. 4:8-10.

4. THE QUESTION OF MOSES:

We come now to the experience of Moses relative to the Name of God. We have placed the question and experience of Moses last because of that which is revealed to him concerning God and His Name.

The Nation of Israel had been in bondage and a strange land for several hundreds of years. That bondage is about to end.

GOD, THE GOD OF ABRAHAM, THE GOD OF ISAAC, AND THE GOD OF JACOB is about to visit His people.

He appears to Moses in the backside of the desert in the Burning Bush. The Bush was burning yet not consumed. The Voice of God calls to Moses as he turns aside to see this great sight.

He is told that he is to remove his shoes for the place where he was standing is "holy ground," made holy by the very manifestation of the Presence and Shekinah Glory of God in that bush.

The Voice calls to Moses, telling him that he is to be equipped and sent to be the deliverer of the enslaved Nation of Israel, by mighty signs and wonders.

The Voice of this Angel of the Lord calls Himself:

> "The ELOHIM (GOD) of Abraham,
> The ELOHIM (GOD) of Isaac, and
> The ELOHIM (GOD) of Jacob."

Moses is filled with excuses first, then questions. The greatest thing that must be settled in His mind and heart is that question pertaining to THE NAME OF GOD.

Moses speaks to God in the Bush saying, "Behold, when I come unto the children of Israel and shall say unto them, The GOD of your fathers hath sent me unto you, and they shall say unto me, WHAT IS HIS NAME? What shall I say unto them?"

If "God" were a proper Name, then this question would be meaningless. It was not enough for Moses to tell the Children of Israel that "GOD" had sent him, or even try and distinguish this "God" by saying "The GOD of your fathers hath sent me."

This God must have A NAME!

After all, Egypt had hundreds of "gods" and worshipped and deified all manner of reptiles, creatures and created things under multiplied names.

This "GOD of Abraham, God of Isaac, God of Jacob" would be classified as another "God," alongside of the many gods of Egypt, Assyria, Babylonia and the gods of the Canaanites. Or else, He would be classed as another of the "Tribal Gods." But this was not to be!

Moses must have the Name of God, the Name of the TRUE God. He must go in this Name. The people must be delivered by the mighty and powerful Name of God. Signs and wonders and plagues of judgment must be done in the power of this Name. It must be a Name different from all the names of the gods of Egypt, and all the other heathen and tribal gods. It must be a Name that none other could possibly and truly declare. It must be an all-powerful Name to deliver Israel as a Nation from the greatest Nation and World-Kingdom of that day.

The very purpose of the True God revealing Himself and His Name to Moses was declared to Moses and Pharoah.

"And in very deed for this cause have I raised thee (Pharoah) up, for to show in thee My power; and that MY NAME may be declared throughout all the earth" Exodus 9:16. Romans 9:17.

"And against all the gods of Egypt I will execute judgment: I am the LORD" Exodus 12:12.

Hence, it is clearly seen that the express purpose of God revealing Himself and His Name to Moses was to show to Pharoah and the whole earth that He alone was the TRUE GOD and HIS NAME is the greatest Name, the Name above all NAMES.

Did God reveal His Name to Moses?
Did He answer the question of Moses?

Yes! To Moses in particular, of these Saints who asked the question, was an answer given concerning the revelation of God and His Name; especially as it pertains to redemption.

This revelation of the Name of God to Moses will be taken up in a subsequent section.

We summarize this section by setting out the questions asked by these Old Testament Saints of God.

1. The Question of Jacob. Gen. 32:29.
   "Tell me, I pray Thee, THY NAME."

2. The Question of Manoah. Judges 13:17,18.
   "What is THY NAME?"
   "Wherefore askest thou thus after MY NAME, seeing it is secret?"

3. The Question of Agur. Proverbs 30:4.
   "What is HIS NAME?"
   "What is HIS SON'S NAME, if thou canst tell?"

4. The Question of Moses. Exodus 3:13.
   "What is HIS NAME? What shall I say unto them?"

Moses specifically receives revelation and answer to his question.

THE NAME OF GOD IN TYPICAL CREATIONS

One of the richest fields of study in the Old Testament, The Age of the Shadow, is that which is found in the Old Testament Habitations of God.

It is only possible to take several of the most important and prominent typical creations as pertaining to the Name of God.

God has always desired A PLACE where He could RECORD HIS NAME!

Old Testament Typical Places and Structures:

1. The Tabernacle of Moses:

   The Tabernacle was a typical and prophetical structure foreshadowing Christ and His Church.

   The express purpose of its erection was that God might dwell amongst His redeemed people, Israel, and that He might record His Name there. His Name signified His Person, His Presence in the midst of His people.

   "Let them make ME A SANCTUARY that I may dwell among them" Ex. 25:8.

   Note these Scriptures also pertaining to the Tabernacle as a Habitation for God and His Name to dwell.

   "In all Places, where I record MY NAME I will come unto thee, and I will bless thee" Ex. 20:24.

   "But unto the Place which the Lord your God shall choose out of all your Tribes to put HIS NAME there, even unto His Habitation shall ye seek, and thither shalt thou come" Deut. 12:5.

   "Then there shall be a Place which the Lord your God shall choose to cause HIS NAME to dwell there" Deut. 12:11.

   "The Place which the Lord thy God hath chosen to put HIS NAME there" Deut. 12:21.

   "In the Place which He shall choose to place HIS NAME there" Deut. 14:23 and 24. 16:2, 6, 7, 11, 15, 16.

   Thus the Tabernacle was the Place, the Habitation, the Dwelling Place of God "in the midst" of Israel. Here God recorded, put, placed and caused His Name to dwell. His Name was there because His Presence was there.

2. The Tabernacle at Shiloh:

   Read these Scriptures. Joshua 18:1-10. 22:9-12. Judges 21:18-21. Psalm 78:60. Jeremiah 7:1-16,30.

   When Israel as a Nation entered the Promised Land, the Tabernacle of Moses was set in a place called "Shiloh", meaning, "Rest". Ultimately, it pointed to Messiah, the True Rest of God.

Shiloh became an important place in the time of Joshua, and on until the time of Samuel the Prophet.

However, in due time, because of sin and apostasy in the Nation, God brought judgment on the Place where He had recorded His Name.

He declares through the mouth of the Prophet Jeremiah, "But go ye now unto My Place which was in Shiloh, where I set MY NAME at the first, and see what I did to it for the wickedness of My people Israel." Jer. 7:12, 14.

God could not dwell amongst His people in the place where sin and iniquity and idolatry abounded. He forsook that place.

God's Name is significant of God Himself, of His own Person, of His own Presence.

3. The Tabernacle of David:

After the apostasy which took place at Shiloh, God allowed the Ark of the Covenant to be taken into captivity for a period of time to the land of the Philistines.

In due time, after Divine judgments on the Philistines, the Ark was sent back to the land of Judah. From here it was taken, and after being in the house of Obededom for three months, it was brought and set in the Tabernacle of David.

Note these Scriptures.

"And they brought in the Ark of the Lord, and set it in his Place, in the midst of the Tabernacle that David had pitched for it" II Sam. 6:17.

"So they brought the Ark of God, and set it in the midst of the Tent that David had pitched for it" I Chronicles 16:1.

The thing that is worthy to note here is that the Ark of God never ever returned to the Tabernacle of Moses, but was taken into the Tabernacle of David for a number of years, and from thence it was taken into the Temple of Solomon.

The important fact about all of this is that it was the Ark of the Covenant which was the actual PLACE where THE NAME of God dwelt. Here His Person, His Presence, His Glory, His Name, dwelt, between the Cherubimed Blood-stained Mercy Seat.

Note these Scriptures which confirm the statements above, and which speak of the Name of God being upon the Ark of the Covenant, the most important piece of furniture in the Habitation of God.

"To bring up thence the Ark of God the Lord, that dwelleth between the Cherubims, whose NAME is called upon it" I Chronicles 13:6.

"To bring up from thence the Ark of God, whose NAME is called by THE NAME of the Lord of Hosts that dwelleth between the Cherubims" II Samuel 6:2.

It was in the Tabernacle of David that many of the "Zion-Psalms" were given and recorded. These "Zion-Psalms" abound with references to "THE NAME."

Several of these are noted here. Let the Student check the Concordance for others.

"The Name of the God of Jacob defend thee" Psa. 20:1.
"In the Name of God we will set up our banners" Psa. 20:5.
"Quicken us, and we will call upon Thy Name" Psa. 80:18.
"To declare the Name of the Lord in Zion" Psa. 102:21.
"To give thanks unto the Name of the Lord" Psa. 122:4.

The Ark of the Covenant, upon which was called THE NAME of God, now finds its resting place in the Tabernacle of David.

4. The Temple of Solomon:

Please read these Scriptures carefully. I Kings 5:3-5, 8:16-48, 9:1-7.
II Chron. 7:20. Neh. 1:9. Jer. 7:1-16.

The final typical structure and Habitation of God in the Old Covenant economy is that found in the Temple of Solomon.

The Ark of God is taken from the Tabernacle of David and set in the Temple of Solomon in the Feast of the Seventh Month, the Feast of Tabernacles. I Kings 8:1-11.

Again we note that the express purpose of the building of the Temple was to be a Habitation of God, a Place where God could cause HIS NAME to dwell.

God gave the revelation of the Temple to King David while the Tabernacle of David was still in function. Solomon is the one who built the Temple according to the Divine pattern given to David. I Chronicles 28:11-21.

Consider these Scriptures in the light of the above statements:

"Built an House for The Name of the Lord God of Israel" I Kings 8:20.
"That Thine eyes may be open toward this House night and day, even toward the Place of which Thou hast said, My Name shall be there" I Kings 8:29.
"That they may know that this House, which I have builded, is called by Thy Name" I Kings 8:43.
"Hallowed this House, which thou hast built, to put My Name there forever" I Kings 9:3.
"This House which I have hallowed for My Name" I Kings 9:7.
"This House, which I have sanctified for My Name" II Chronicles 7:20.
"This House, which is called by My Name" Jeremiah 7:2,14.

The Temple was the last place and structure where God caused His Name to dwell. It was hallowed, sanctified for the Name of God to dwell therein, upon that Blood-stained Mercy Seat.

Thus: Tabernacle of Moses   ) God placed His Name therein upon the Ark
         Tabernacle of David   )   of the Covenant
         Temple of Solomon   )

5. Typical Persons in the Old Testament:

Beside the typical structures mentioned above which were places where God recorded His Name, God also impressed upon various persons that which pertained to His Name.

The Nation of Israel realized the importance and significance in the naming of their children.   Because of this, numerous persons were actually partakers of "The Name of God." This is seen by the Law of Interpretation of Names. "The Name," in the Old Testament, pointed to "The Nature." Hence it will be seen that many many persons under the Old Covenant had "The Name" or incorporated part or parts of "The Name" in their personal names.

Each of these shadow forth "The Name" as it would be seen in Christ and in the Church; bearing and being partakers of the Name of God.

Several examples, with their names interpreted, will suffice to illustrate this truth.

1. "SAMUEL" Samuel's name literally means, "The Name of God" or, "The Name of EL." I Samuel 1:20. Some interpret it as "Asked of God" or, "Heard of God."

    Samuel was indeed "asked of God" by his mother, Hannah, but in the interpretation of his name as "The Name of God", he himself was a living example of that Name.

    As he lived, walked, and existed, Samuel bore the Name of God.   He typified the Son of God who would be born and bear that name in its fulness.

2. "Dani-EL", which means "EL is my Judge." Daniel 1:7. Daniel was partaker of the Name of God, the Name of Elohim.

3. "Beth-EL", which being interpreted means "The House of EL," or "The House of God." Thus this place is impressed with the Name of Elohim. Genesis 28:19.

4. "EL-imelech", by interpretation, "EL (God) is King." Ruth 1:2.

5. "EL-i-JAH", being interpreted means, "EL, the Strong YAHWEH." I Kings 18:1. Elijah was thus partaker of the Name of God, both Elehistic and Jehovahistic Names involved.

    A Bible Dictionary of Interpretation of Names will afford many more examples which show how persons were sharers and partakers of the Names of God; sometimes the Elohistic (Creator) Names, and sometimes Jehovahistic (Redemptive) Names.

New Testament Antitype and Fulfilment:

These Old Testament dwelling places of God under the Old Covenant pointed to the New Testament or New Covenant dwelling place of God.

These Old Covenant Saints, who were sharers and partakers of the Name of God, also pointed to the New Testament Saints who would become partakers of the Name of God.

Thus Tabernacle and Temple, Old Testament Saints, shadowed forth:

(1) Christ, and
(2) The Church, which is His Body.

The Name of God is now to be found in Christ and His Church. If God was so particular about having a place for His Name to dwell in before the Cross, and under the OLD Covenant Dispensation the Saints were partakers of that Name, much more is this true after the Cross and under the NEW Covenant Dispensation.

Typical structures and typical persons had the impress of the Name of God upon them.

If Old Testament Habitations of God housed His Name, so shall the New Testament Habitation.

If Old Testament Saints partook of His Name, so shall the New Testament Saints.

The New Testament Habitation finds fulfilment in Christ and His Church.

1. The Person of Christ Jesus:

Jesus Christ, the Eternal Son of God is the TRUE Tabernacle, and the TRUE Temple. God's Habitation indeed. Col. 1:19, 2:9.

(1) The Tabernacle:

"The WORD was made flesh and DWELT (Grk. Tabernacle) among us, and we beheld His GLORY, the Glory as of the Only Begotten of the Father, full of grace and truth." John 1:14, 1-3.

(2) The Temple:

"Destroy this Temple and in three days I will raise it up. But He spake of the Temple of His body." John 2:18-21.

Thus The Lord Jesus Christ, the Son of God, is indeed God's Tabernacle, God's Temple, God's Habitation in whom dwells the Divine fulness.

"God was in Christ." II Cor. 5:19.
"God manifest in the flesh." I Tim. 3:16.
"Immanu-EL, God with us." Matt. 1:23. Isa. 9:6, 7:14.

2. The Church which is His Body:

The Church is the Body of Christ, the Fulness (Completeness) of Him that filleth all in all. Eph. 1:22-23. Col. 1:17-19.

The Church is clearly spoken of as being God's Temple, His dwelling place, and Jesus Christ, as Head of the Church is "in the midst." Matt. 18:20.

Read these Scriptures:

"Know ye not that ye are the Temple of God, and that the Spirit of God dwelleth in you?" I Cor. 3:16, 17.

"What? Know ye not that your body is the Temple of the Holy Ghost which is in you?" I Cor. 6:19.

"In whom all the building fitly framed together groweth unto an Holy Temple in the Lord: in whom ye also are builded together for an Habitation of God through the Spirit." Eph. 2:21-22. Refer also: II Cor. 6:16.

Thus it is seen, both in typical persons and creations, that God established a pattern and revelation where THE NAME OF GOD was recorded and placed. All of these things were but types and shadows, prophetic of and pointing to Christ and His Church.

If God was concerned about the Place for His Name, and caused His Name to dwell therein in Tabernacle or Temple, how much more is He concerned about His Name in the New Testament dwelling Place?

These things were material and typical structures, and they pointed to the spiritual and antitypical Habitation of God. They pointed to the TRUE Tabernacle, the TRUE Temple, the TRUE dwelling place of God by the Spirit, even to Christ and His Church.

If Christ and His Church now constitute THE Tabernacle and THE Temple of God, then we must and do find that "THE NAME" is placed, set, put, and indeed recorded therein! The members of that Church must bear that Name!

The Doctrine of the Name of God is not founded upon types, but the types illustrate the Doctrine. The Tabernacle and Temple were types, but God actually dwelt there by His Name. His Name is Himself!

CHAPTER III

THE REVELATION OF THE NAME TO MOSES

As noted in a previous section, "The Question of the Saints," we found that the only person who received some specific revelation about the Name of God was Moses. Moses was a Prophet, Priest, Judge and King.

In this section we consider and develop the thoughts involved in this revelation and the answer of God to the question of Moses.

Read the Scripture section as found in Exodus 3:1-17.

Moses was keeping the flock of Jethro his father-in-law. As he led the flock out to the backside of the desert to Mt. Horeb, the Angel of the Lord appeared to him in a flame of fire out of the midst of a bush.

The bush burned with fire yet was not consumed.

As Moses turned aside to see the great sight, a Voice called to him out of the midst of the bush. The Voice called him by name and told him to put off his shoes as he was standing upon "holy ground," made holy by the Glory and Presence of God in the midst of that bush of fire.

The Angel of the Lord said to Moses:

"I am the GOD of Abraham,
         the GOD of Isaac,
         the GOD of Jacob." Exodus 3:6.

The word for "GOD" here is the Hebrew word "Elohim," a word denoting plurality of Divine Persons. It is a uni-plural word. It is significant of the Eternal Godhead, the Creator, even the Father, the Son and the Holy Sprit.

As the Angel of the Lord continued to speak to Moses, He gives him a charge which is to be laid upon him, a Divine commission <u>to deliver the Children of Israel out of the bondage and oppression of Egypt upon the basis of the Covenant made with the three fathers, Abraham, Isaac and Jacob</u>.

The Scripture tells us "Moses said unto God (Elohim), Behold, when I come unto the Children of Israel and shall say unto them, the GOD of your fathers hath sent me unto you, and they shall say to me, <u>WHAT IS HIS NAME</u>? what shall I say unto them?" Exodus 3:13.

This can also be rendered correctly, "WHO IS HE?"

In fuller and richer meaning, Moses is not inquiring about the actual Name but about what it means. The concept "to know a name" in Hebrew does not simply mean acquaintance, but implies experiential knowledge.

Moses is actually wanting to know His Name in experiential power. The Name always meant the Nature, the Character and Power of the Person, as it pertains to God.

This is why God could say that Israel would "know that I AM THE LORD (YAHWEH) your God." Exodus 6:7; 14:4; 16:12.

It meant that Israel would come to know the Name, Yahweh, their Covenant God, through experience. This is why Pharoah was raised up. That the power of that Name in redemptive activity would be known in all the earth. Exodus 9:16.

The occasion here of God giving a charge to Moses to lead His people out of the bondage of Egypt is significant for the revelation of His Name.

The theology of the Egyptian priests retained a magical notion very vital to the Egyptian's religion, namely that the knowledge of a god's name gave power over him.

However, YAHWEH (The LORD or JEHOVAH) has no need to conceal His Name, because man, His creation, has no power over Him, whether he knows His Name or not.

Indeed it is this very concept that Yahweh will play with and finally confound and ultimately contradict. The Egyptian theology concerning the "mystery" of the name of the gods is playfully toyed with by God. Their gods had their names.

This is why He said that He would bring plagues upon Egypt to execute judgment upon all the gods of Egypt. Exodus 12:12. Egypt and the surrounding nations worshipped all sorts of gods. They deified and idolized created things. Hence, in contrast to Egyptian theology, the very revelation of the Name of God gives promise of God's power over sinful men through REDEMPTIVE deliverance.

As already noted, "God" is not a Name. It was not enough for Moses to go down to Egypt and say "GOD hath sent me." Nor was it sufficient for Moses merely to distinguish this "God" by saying "The GOD of your fathers, Abraham, Isaac and Jacob, hath appeared to me and sent me." No! This GOD must have a Name. Moses must have and know THE NAME OF GOD, THE NAME OF ELOHIM."

It must be A NAME which expresses WHO God is, A NAME which distinguishes Him from all Egyptian and other heathenish nations and their strange gods with their special powers.

When God said to Manoah, " Why askest thou thus after My Name, seeing it is secret?", the word "secret" in Hebrew means "a mystery or that which brings wonder or awe."

Hence the revelation of THE NAME to Moses and the manifestation of its power would bring wonder and awe both to the Israelites and to the Egyptians.

In Exodus 3:14, 15 is given the Divine and sublime answer to Moses' question.

"And GOD (Elohim) said unto Moses: I AM THAT I AM, and He said, thus shalt thou say unto the Children of Israel, I AM hath sent me unto you. And God said moreover unto Moses, Thus shalt thou say unto the Children of Israel, the LORD GOD of your fathers, the GOD of Abraham, the GOD of Isaac, and the GOD of Jacob, hath sent me unto you: THIS IS MY NAME FOREVER, and this is My memorial unto all generations."

Here God expresses or declares Himself in His own essential Nature and Being. He expresses WHO or WHAT HE IS in Himself.

"I AM THAT (WHO) I AM."
"I AM hath sent me unto you."

His Name identifies Himself, even as any person is to be identified by his proper name.

"I AM" is the self-declaration of God's own Being. This was the Name of God revealed to Moses at the burning bush.

It is worthy to note that God does not tell Moses to go and repeat these exact words to Pharoah or the Egyptians. Moses does not use this primary and original declaration of God's Name because it is God Himself who alone can say or declare this. It is God expressing Himself WHO HE IS. God only can truly say "I AM WHO I AM." Moses cannot say it. No man can say it because of what this Name expresses.

He says, "THIS IS MY NAME FOREVER AND MY MEMORIAL UNTO ALL GENERATIONS."

The God of Abraham, of Isaac and of Jacob is thus self-declared and self-Named eternally as "I AM WHO I AM," or "I AM," or "YAHWEH." Our English translation is "JEHOVAH."

The Name "I AM WHO I AM" expresses several most important truths concerning the very Nature and Being of God and these relative to His Eternal Attributes. There are three distinct theories of the meaning of the Name of God, YAHWEH, each of them having a measure of truth and a consideration of these will be appropriate here.

The Meaning of "YAHWEH" or "I AM WHO I AM" or "JEHOVAH"

1. The Ontological Meaning:

   That is, that meaning which pertains to the very Nature and Essence of the Being of God.

   The word "Ontology" comes from the Greek words "on ontos," BEING, and "logos" DISCOURSE. Hence it is the doctrine of being. It involves the very attributes which constitute the Being of God. It pertains to the Nature, Essence, Attributes and Qualities of the very Being of God.

   These are seen in the following paragraphs.

   (a) "YAHWEH" or "I AM" expresses Eternity of Being.

      This Name of God expresses Eternity of Being. Without Beginning, without End. No Angel, no Man, no Created being could say this. Man enters by birth, leaves by death and the place thereof knoweth him no more.

      Man is finite, a creature of time, having age and decay around and within. God alone can truly say "I AM." That is, The Eternally Present One.

      "I AM" comprehends One Eternally Present God.

      "I AM" comprehends Time Past, Time Present, Time Future. In other words, Timelessness, Eternity of Being.

This is implied in Revelation 1:4, 8, where it speaks of God and the Son. "From Him which _is_, and which _was_, and which _is_ _to_ _come_."

There never was a time when God did not exist. There never will be a time when He does not exist. He is YAHWEH, The Eternal, The I AM WHO I AM.

(b) "YAHWEH" or "I AM" expresses Self-existence.

This Name of God also expresses that which pertains to Self-existence.

"I AM" expresses He who exists in and of and by Himself. The Self-existent One.

All creation and all creatures owe their very existence to Him. All depend upon Him for their existence. None are independant. God alone as the "I AM" is the only independant One. He is the very Life-source the Origin and the Sustainer of all life.

Self-existence declares the fact that He is the Life-source of all creatures. He has life in Himself. He is the Self-existent God. John 1:1-4. Acts 17:28.

(c) "YAHWEH" or "I AM" expresses Omnipotence, Omnipresence, and Omniscience.

"I AM" expresses the essential attributes of God. That is, those attributes or qualities belonging to God which make God alone the One true God.

"I AM" expresses Omnipotence. He is All-powerful.

"I AM" expresses Omnipresence. He is All-present, everywhere present at the same time.

"I AM" expresses Omniscience. He is All-knowing, All-seeing, He sees and knows all things at the same time.

He could not be All-powerful, All-seeing and knowing and All-present at all times if He were not "I AM." He is "I AM" by Name and Nature.

There is a richness, a height, depth, length and breadth which no words of finite man can adequately express in the Name of God, "I AM."

It expresses all that God is in His own essential Nature and Being. To summarize; it expresses Eternity of Being, Self-existence, Unsearchableness, Omnipotence, Omnipresence, Omniscience, Infiniteness, Independance, Beginning and Ending, Alpha and Omega, the One who is the Uncreated God. He is the Source and Sustainer of all things.

2. The Activistic Meaning:

The second view of the Name of God is the Activistic one. This view declares the activity of God, rather than His essence or being as in the Ontological view. It portrays the great personal intensity and exalted character of that Name.

As a Hebrew verb the Tetragrammaton (as YAHWEH is spoken of by the Hebrews) must be parsed as third person singular, Qal, Imperfect.

The name of God, Yahweh, is a verbal substantive from the Hebrew word hyh, meaning "to be." (Raymen Abba, "The Divine Name Yahweh," Journal of Biblical Literature, 80:324, p. 324, December, 1961).

This is why the Activistic View insists upon the translation of ehyeh asher ehyeh of Exodus 3:14 as the future tense. The translation would have to be "I will be what I will be." The imperfect tense of the Hebrew is the regular tense for the future tense significance. Thus the Name of God also has in its usage throughout the futuristic implication in the imperfect tense. A balanced approach sees the truth in both Ontological and Activistic Views.

The following extracts are taken from "The Companion Bible" commenting on Exodus 3:14, 15.

> "It is God Himself, ELOHIM, the Triune God who thus speaks and says, 'I AM THAT I AM' or 'I AM'."

> This expression occurs only twice, and that is here in these verses in Exodus.

> The Hebrew is 'EHYEH ASHER EHYEH'; "I will be what I will be (or become)."

> God always says such when He speaks of Himself, but when He will be spoken of by others (by Moses), it is the LORD (Jehovah).

> He is the I AM, The ETERNAL.

> Revelation 1:4 in the New Testament is the equivalent and the expression of "I AM."

> > "HIM which is (continuance of time present),
> >   which was (continuance of time past),
> >   which is to come (continuance of time future)."
> > (Emphasis mine)

The Name "I AM WHO I AM" is never specifically translated as such in the Authorized Version (although its equivalent "I will be" is used several places, i.e., Exodus 3:12; Joshua 1:5, 9; Judges 6:16) in the Old Testament until we come to the New Testament where the Lord Jesus Christ Himself uses it. The Jews recognized it as the Name of God, the Name of Deity and thus took up stones to stone Jesus when He expressed it or uttered it. Compare John 8:52-59 with Leviticus 24:16.

"Ehyeh asher ehyeh" is not the Tetragrammaton but an explanation in expanded form of the Tetragrammaton.

The futuristic implication tells us "I will be all that is necessary as the occasion will arise." Isaiah 7:14; Psalm 23:1; Exodus 3:12.

"I will be with thee" is the equivalent of "I AM with thee." Joshua 1:5,9.

This effective presence in the Name pointed to the ultimate fulfilment in Christ Jesus. When He came He brought forth the emphasis of the present tense, "I AM." He identifies Himself as the "I AM."

Refer to Appendix on the "I AM's of Jesus."

The emphasis in this view reveals a God who is active in the behalf of His people, and a God who will be all that He is to His own. His existence is not abstract but active.

He is not merely a God having all the essential attributes which make Him God. He is a God who favours His people and is and will be active in His presence with them.

3. The Covenantal Meaning:

The previous views are undoubtedly true, however they do not constitute the full truth expressed in this Name of God. The predominent truth in this Name of God revealed to Moses is the Covenantal meaning.

This is based on the connotative significance from the contextual usage of this Name with redemptive purpose and revelation on the basis of God's promise to Abraham in the Covenant made with him.

"And God heard their groaning, and God remembered His Covenant with Abraham, with Isaac and with Jacob." Exodus 2:24.

It was upon the basis of the Abrahamic Covenant, a Covenant of Grace, an unconditional Covenant, that God appeared to Moses and sent him to bring deliverance to His people Israel.

Thus His existence as implied in the Name is not only just self-existence in the abstract, but existence to meet His people's need and REDEEM them. It was the Covenant of REDEMPTION that was involved here. This is why God calls Himself "the God of Abraham, the God of Isaac and the God of Jacob."

"YAHWEH" or "I AM WHO I AM" or "JEHOVAH" is the REDEMPTIVE NAME of God: This is the dominant factor in the revelation of the Name to Moses.

The Redemptive Name "Yahweh" reveals that He is existent to redeem them and meet their needs.

He is the great "I AM," existent and active to redeem them.
He is the great "I will be," existent to always meet their needs.
He is YAHWEH ELOHIM, the Redeemer Creator. It is generally translated, LORD GOD.

The general term, Elohim, occurs frequently in Scripture (2,555 times) along with the Name, Yahweh. Yet the usage of these two terms is carefully distinguished.

ELOHIM describes God as the CREATOR of the world and its universal governor. This is especially noted in the Chapter on Creation, Genesis Chapter One, where ELOHIM is dominant.

YAHWEH describes God as the REDEEMER, as having entered into a historical relationship with mankind, and in particular here with the nation of Israel. This is especially noted in the Genesis Chapters 2 to 4, after the entrance of sin into the world. Here the revelation is of YAHWEH in redemptive activity. Although the significance of that Name was not revealed to Eve, yet the Name is predominant in this section because sin having entered the world through Adam's disobedience demands YAHWEH'S redeeming grace being manifested.

It is distinctly the REDEMPTIVE NAME OF GOD. This is the full significance of that which is revealed to Moses. The futuristic connotation pointed to the Redeemer to come.

What About Exodus 6:3?

A word as to the text found here would be appropriate. The verse is quoted in full here for our consideration.

> "And God (Elohim) spake unto Moses, and said unto him,
> I am the LORD, and I appeared unto Abraham, unto Isaac,
> and unto Jacob by THE NAME OF GOD ALMIGHTY (El Shaddai),
> but by MY NAME YAHWEH (Jehovah) was not known to them."

There are two theories on this question. One is the Mosaic view, which states that the Redemptive Name was not revealed or known to the Fathers, Abraham, Isaac and Jacob.

The other is the Pre-Mosaic view which holds that this Name was known but not understood in all its implications.

The Bible does not say unmistakably that the Name Yahweh is a new Name to Moses and the Israelites. The difficulty arises from the numerous appearances of the Name Yahweh in the Genesis account.

The compound Redemptive Name JEHOVAH JIREH (Genesis 22:14) is given to Abraham at the typical offering up of his Only Begotten Son, Isaac (Heb. 11:17). Also there are 162 occurrences of the Name Yahweh in Genesis, written by Moses. Again there are 34 occurrences of the Name Yahweh in the mouth of the speakers of Genesis. One cannot say that Moses put these occurrences into the mouths of the Patriarchs.

Therefore, although the Patriarchs must have known the Name, they obviously had no understanding of it, especially in its fullest meaning, the COVENANTAL aspect of REDEMPTION for His people.

It is this which awaited Moses to whom it is indicated that he will first have an understanding of the meaning of the Name, unknown to the Patriarchs and unknown in Pre-Mosaic times. It was needful that God demonstrate His Name with REDEMPTION that the connotation of the Name with redemption be understood in that respect.

Thus the meaning of Exodus 6:3 would be, "And I showed Myself to Abraham, to Isaac, and to Jacob in the character of El Shaddai, but in the character expressed by My Name YAHWEH I did not make Myself known to them." The sense "in the character of or capacity of" means that God did not reveal to the Patriarchs those qualities of His Being which are signified by YAHWEH.

The predominant revelation and Name of God known to Abraham, Isaac and Jacob is that Name "El Shaddai," or "God Almighty." Genesis 17:1; Exodus 6:3.

The meaning of Exodus 6:2, 3 is simply this. "By My Name YAHWEH (Jehovah) was I not known, (that is, I was not understood) to them"

It is this Name that is to be made known in all the earth. God speaks through Moses to Pharoah saying, "And in very deed for this cause have I raised thee up, for to shew in thee My power; and that MY NAME may be declared throughout all the earth." Exodus 9:16; Romans 9:17.

This is seen in the historical manifestation of the character and power of that Name in REDEMPTION and COVENANTAL DELIVERANCE as in the plagues upon Egypt and the final Exodus of Israel out of the House of Bondage.

YAHWEH as a Proper Name

YAHWEH is always a proper Name. It is not a title but a PERSONAL NAME that assured God's Covenantal dealings with His people, Israel. It is never prefixed by the article nor suffixed by a possessive pronoun in the Hebrew. It is never followed by a word in the genitive nor does it ever occur in the genitive. Constructions like "the Yahweh" or "our Yahweh" or "Yahweh of Israel" are not possible. According to the Semites, a proper Name was determined in itself and could not be according to Obermann, "made subject to determination by any external means. (Obermann, Julian. "The Divine Name YHWH in the Light of Recent Discoveries," Journal of Biblical Literature, 68:305, December, 1949)."

The Holy Tetragrammaton

The Hebrew writing of the Name of God, the Name of Jehovah, was expressed by four letters and these were known as "The Holy Four Letters," that is, YHWH (Yahweh).

This was called "The Holy Tetragram" or "Nomen Tetragrammaton." To the Jews it became the "Incommunicable Name," "The Ineffable Name," or "The Unutterable Name." The Tetragrammaton was the name par excellence "God's own Name," the separated, special Name peculiar to God. It was His proper Name as distinct from designations, the Name which is generally kept secret and uttered only on special occasions. There happened to the Name of Yahweh precisely what the Old Testament said should not happen. Yahweh became a God with a secret Name like any other god. Knowledge of this Name became an instrument of power and magic, because of the explanation of "uttering the Name" given by the Rabbis in Leviticus 24:11, 16. They said, "If any one utters the Name let him die the death."

"Smith's Dictionary of the Bible," Page 374, states:

> "The true pronunciation of this Name, by which God was known
> to the Hebrews, has been entirely lost, the Jews themselves
> scrupulously avoiding every mention of it, and substituting
> in its stead one or others of the words with whose vowel
> points it may happen to be written. This custom which had
> its origin in reverence, and has almost degenerated into a
> superstition, was founded upon an erroneous (?) rendering

of Leviticus 24:16 (in the Septuagint Version) from which it was inferred that a mere utterance of the Name constituted a capital offence" - hence the term, "the ineffable Name" (or unutterable).

Modern scholars have acquired the pronunciation YAHWEH from the use in compounded names.

There must have been some recognition of its meaning in Messiah's times as seen in the reaction of the Jews against Jesus when He said, "Before Abraham was, I AM." John 8:56-59 with Leviticus 24:11-16, 23. This is why they sought to stone Him.

Many times in the Synagogues, the Name YAHWEH was never read or uttered by the leaders or the people but they substituted the Name ADONAI while others simply would pronounce the Hebrew "HA SHEM" which means "THE NAME" rather than say the incommunicable Name, the ineffable, the unutterable Name of the Lord, or YAHWEH, or JEHOVAH.

The listeners knew WHO was meant!

> "The Name" in Hebrew is "ha Shem."
> "The Name" in Greek is "to Onoma."

An Ancient Jewish saying concerning His Name says, "Among the creatures they and their names are two different things; but respecting the blessed God, Himself (I AM) is His Name, and His Name (I AM) is Himself."

"The Companion Bible," Appendix 4, and 32, gives a list of 134 passages where "out of extreme (but mistaken) reverence for the 'ineffable Name,' YAHWEH (JEHOVAH), the Ancient custodians of the Sacred Text substituted ADONAI." These in the A.V., and R.V., are all written, "LORD."

Hence we have the following:

I AM WHO I AM --- Original form spoken by God Himself.

YAHWEH (YHWH) --- Hebrew form, or the Holy Tetragrammaton.

ADONAI or ADON --- Hebrew form and used at least 134 times as a substitute for Yahweh.

JEHOVAH or LORD --- English translation for the above Hebrew.

KURIOS or LORD --- Greek form and inadequate equivalent.

Thousands of Jews would rather die than call or acknowledge Caezar to be "LORD" for they knew and understood clearly that this was the Name of God, the Name of Diety. It was not a mere title but a proper, indeed THE proper Name of God. The tragedy today is that the Name of God as revealed in "LORD" has become such a lifeless word and the full glory of its meaning lost over the years. The Church has been robbed of its full truth and significance. There needs to be a fresh understanding, quickening, insight and illumination concerning this glorious Name of God.

Clearly, undoubtedly, the Name of God under the Old Covenant was revealed as "YAHWEH" or "LORD" or "JEHOVAH."

This Name occurs in its regular form 5,321 times in the Old Testament, as the Proper Name of God. When you include the compounded and contracted usages of that Name, then there are 6,823 occurrences of some form of that Name.

What is His Name? His Name is "I AM," "YAHWEH," or "The LORD."
How long is this Name to be? The answer is, Forever!
To how many generations? The answer is, to ALL generations.

This is the Name given to Moses as his Divine credentials. Not to Jacob, not to Manoah is the revelation given. Even Agur undoubtedly does not receive the full implication in that Name. It is given to Moses.

In closing off this section, one adds a further quotation from "Vos, Geerhardus, Biblical Theology, Grand Rapids, Michigan, Wm. B. Eerdman's Publishing Company, 1959, page 129."

> "With this feature of the sovereignty shown in redemption is connected the specifically Mosaic name of God, Jehovah. This form is a pronunciation in which the vowels of Adonai were given to the consonants of the name in question. The writing of these vowels sprang originally from the Jewish scrupulousness refraining from the utterance of this sacred name altogether. Because Adonai was always read in place of it, therefore, when vowels were added for convenience' sake the vowels required for the reading of Adonai were simply attached. It was, of course, never contemplated at that time that the consonants standing in the text, and which it would have been the height of impiety to remove, should have in pronunciation joined to them these alien vowels. This was first done in Christian reading, when the old Jewish scrupulosity was no longer felt, and thus the hybrid form Jehovah arose. It has been in use since the sixteenth century."

In the light of all this, when the English translation is used throughout these notes, it is with this understanding of the Name. Listed below are a few of the numerous Scriptures which tell us His Name.

1. "This (I AM, or the LORD) is My Name forever, and My memorial unto all generations." Exodus 3:15.

2. "The LORD is His Name." Exodus 15:3.

3. "I am the LORD, that is My Name." Isaiah 42:8.

4. "The LORD is His Name." Jeremiah 33:2.

5. "The LORD is His Name." Amos 5:8

6. "They shall know that My Name is the LORD." Jeremiah 16:21.

7. "That men may know that Thou whose <u>Name</u> alone is <u>JEHOVAH</u>." Psalm 83:18.

8. "The <u>LORD</u> <u>JEHOVAH</u> is my strength and my song." Isaiah 12:2.

9. "I am the <u>LORD</u>, I change not." Malachi 3:6 with James 1:17.

God has never revoked this Name. It is His Redemptive Name and all the compound Redemptive Names of God are built upon this foundation.

(Refer to Compound Redemptive Names of Jehovah - Appendix.)

MINISTRY IN 'THE NAME' IN THE OLD TESTAMENT

In the Book of Exodus the power of 'The Name' is revealed.

It is under the Ministry of Moses that the power of THE NAME OF GOD is first manifested.

All the plagues upon Egypt and the Egyptians were the result of the power of that Name as revealed to Moses at the burning bush. Exodus 3:14-17.

The separation of Israel and Egypt and the Divine protection in the midst of these plagues was all on account of the power of that Name, the I AM, the LORD God.

The deliverance from Egypt through the Blood of the Passover Lamb was through the manifested power of that Name. Exodus Chapters 4-12.

The Crossing of the Red Sea and the defeat of the hosts of Pharoah was done in the majesty and might of that Redemptive Name. Exodus Chapters 13 and 14.

As soon as Israel crossed the Red Sea, Moses sang this song: "The LORD is His NAME." Exodus 15:3.

Thus the power of 'The Name' is seen in the Book of Exodus.

In the Book of Judges, the signs and wonders and miracles performed by the ministry of the Judges was by virtue of that Name also. Judges 6:24.

In the Book of Numbers we find God commanding Moses to speak to Aaron and his sons in blessing the children of Israel, to "put (call upon or invoke) MY NAME upon the children of Israel, and I will bless them." Numbers 6:22-27.

One of the oldest acts in Patriarchal times was "to call upon THE NAME of the Lord." Genesis 4:26.

"Abraham built an altar and called upon THE NAME of the Lord." Genesis 12:8.

Joel the Prophet stated, "Whosoever shall call upon THE NAME of the Lord shall be delivered." Joel 2:32 with Acts 2:21.

Patriarchs, Saints, Prophets and Priests and Kings were to call on 'The Name,' that is, on the Person of the Lord, the Redeemer. To call upon 'The Name' was to invoke 'The Name' or have that Name invoked upon them. The 'calling upon The Name' meant that they acknowledged the LORD as their God and Redeemer.

"If My people which are called by MY NAME shall humble themselves and pray ... then will I hear from heaven and heal their land." II Chronicles 7:14.

The Prophets always ministered in THE NAME of the Lord and by THE WORD of the Lord. II Chronicles 28:9; Jeremiah 15:16.

They had power to curse or bless in THE NAME. II Kings 2:24.
They had to speak the Word of the Lord in THE NAME. Deut. 18:18-22.
Judgment was visited upon false Prophets who dared to presume to prophecy in THE NAME of the Lord. Jer. 11:21; 23:25-27.

<u>The Priests</u> were chosen to minister in the Sanctuary in THE NAME of the Lord.

"I will sing praise unto Thy Name." II Samuel 22:50.
"Make mention that His Name is exalted." Isaiah 12:4.
"O LORD, our LORD, how excellent is Thy Name in all the earth." Psalm 8:1.
"I will lift up my hands in Thy Name." Psalm 63:4.
"Unite my heart to fear Thy Name." Psalm 86:11-12.
"Holy and reverend is His Name." Psalm 111:9.
"Thou hast exalted Thy Word even above all Thy Name." Psalm 138:2.

The Congregation was to worship, glory and bless the Name of the Lord. I Chron. 16:2-10. Israel, as a Nation, was warned in the Ten Commandments concerning His Name.

"Thou shalt not take the Name of the LORD thy God in vain." Exodus 20:7.
"Thou shalt not profane My Name." Leviticus 19:12.

Everything centered around THE NAME of the LORD in the Old Testament. Read also the following Scriptures. Deut. 18:5-7; 21:5; Isa. 61:6; Mal. 1:6; I Chron. 23:13. Deut. 12:1-14. Duet. 16:2, 6, 11, 15.

The student may take a Concordance and check 'The Name' as pertaining to the Lord in the Old Testament and find numerous references.

All true and proper Ministry in the Old Testament by Patriarchs, Prophets, Priests, Kings and Judges was fulfilled in and by and through the power of "The Name" of the LORD as in the Name of the LORD GOD.

It is this Name of God which is used thousands of times, and it is only of this Name that He expressly declares, "This is MY NAME ... FOREVER, and My memorial to all generations."

SECTION II

THE GODHEAD NAME or THE TRIUNE NAME

CHAPTER IV

THE GODHEAD NAME

OR

THE TRIUNE NAME

THE NEW TESTAMENT NAME OF GOD - THE TRIUNE NAME

Having considered the revelation of the PERSON OF GOD as given in the Old Testament and New Testament Scriptures, in this section THE NAME OF GOD comes under consideration, particularly in that which is consummated in the New Testament. As in all truth, the New Testament is the fulness of the fragmentary truth given in the Old Testament. The Old Testament pointed to and made way for the New Testament.

It is impossible to read the New Testament without coming to a recognition of the fact that THE NAME which is stamped upon its pages is THE NAME of the LORD - JESUS - CHRIST.

This TRIUNE NAME, either in part or the whole is used hundreds of times in the New Testament. Whereas the Name which was impressed upon the Old Testament was "The LORD GOD," the Name which is impressed upon the New Testament is "The LORD JESUS CHRIST."

A cursory glance over the Gospels, the Acts, and the Epistles shows that the Name of the "Lord," "Lord Jesus," "Jesus Christ," "Christ Jesus," or "Lord Jesus Christ" is dominant throughout.

It is the Writer's firm conviction that when THE TRIUNE NAME of the LORD JESUS CHRIST is interpreted, THE PERSON (or, The Persons) involved in that Name is (are) revealed. The Name is a revelation of The Nature.

In this section the glories of this Triune Name will be explored, and by using the Law of Interpretation of Names it will be discovered that this Name involves the Eternal Godhead, as Father, Son and Holy Spirit. More than that, it should be seen that the Triune Name of the Lord Jesus Christ is the Triune Name of the Triune God. It is the Godhead Name. Of all the Jehovahistic Compound Redemptive Names ever to be revealed, the Triune Name of the Lord Jesus Christ is the greatest, both in this world and in the world to come. Ephesians 1:21.

Our premise therefore is as follows. The New Testament Triune Name of the Lord Jesus Christ, when properly understood by interpretation, is the Name of the Eternal Godhead, as Father, Son and Holy Spirit, and it is also the Name of the GODHEAD BODILY!

With those of Malachi's time (Malachi 3:16), let us continue to THINK upon His Name!

SIGNIFICANCE OF "THE NAME"

There is a significance pertaining to Names and the Interpretation of Names found in Bible times, both Pagan and Hebrew history confirming this.

1. **In Hebrew History.**

    The Israelites had an awareness of the significance of the Name and the potential therein. Naming an object, person, or place meant more than just the utterance of a name over them. It established a dominion and possession over that subject.

    Following are illustrations of these conclusions:

    > Adam named all the creatures which God brought to him. Genesis 2:19-20. Thus he exercises dominion over creation and relates all to his sphere of rule. The creatures were named according to their natures.

    > The Lord called Israel _by Name_ and claims the nation as His own. Isaiah 43:1.

    > The Name of the Lord is also _named_ upon Israel and thus they become His people. Isaiah 43:1; 63:19, II Chronicles 7:14.

    > The Name of Yahweh is _named_ over the Temple. Jeremiah 7:10.

    > The Name of Yahweh is _called_ upon the Ark of the Covenant. II Samuel 6:2.

    > The City of Jerusalem is the City where the Name of God is _named_ also. Jeremiah 25:29; Daniel 9:18. Thus the City is His City.

    > God knew Moses _by name_. Exodus 33:12,17. Jeremiah is known _by name_. Jeremiah 15:16.

    > Names of progenitors are carried on in the descendants, for the children are to keep alive the _name_ of their fathers. Genesis 21:12; 48:16. II Samuel 18:18.

    > If a man dies without children, his relative is to carry on his _name_ by marriage to the wife of the deceased. Deuteronomy 25:5-10 with Numbers 27:1-11.

    > The _name_ of the wicked can be blotted out. Joshua 7:9; Isaiah 14:22; with Exodus 17:14.

    > The _name_ of the righteous are written in the Book of Life. Exodus 32:32; Psalm 69:28; with Isaiah 4:3 and Ezekiel 13:9.

2. **Patriarchal Times** show the significance of Names and their Interpretation.

    > Jacob called the place of Angelic visitation, "Beth-EL," "House of God." Genesis 28:17,19.

    > Adam called his wife's Name, "Eve," "Mother of the living." Genesis 3:20.

Noah's name means "Rest." Genesis 5:29.

The Tower of Babel was interpreted as "Gate of Confusion." Genesis 11:9.

Isaac was named "Laughter" in connection with the laughter of Abraham and Sarah. Genesis 17:17; 18:12; 21:6.

Jacob and Esau had prophetic names given to them. Genesis 25:25-30. Hosea 12:4.

Jacob's twelve sons also were named with prophetic significances. Genesis 29:31 -- 30:24.

3. Gentile Kingdoms knew the significance of Interpreted Names also.

Joseph is given a name, "Zaphnath-paaneah," "Saviour of the world." Genesis 41:45. He lived according to this name, bringing the bread of life to all who came.

Daniel and his companions had their names changed. Daniel 1:7. The new Babylonish names expressed their change of position to exalted dignity in the Kingdom, and the changing of their Hebrew names showed their dependant state. The purpose was to cause them to forget the name of the True God and become identified with the Babylonian gods. Interpret the names and the truth is discovered.

4. Period of the Prophets attest also to this symbolic use of names.

Isaiah and his children were given symbolic names. Their names indicated that judgment is coming to Israel, yet a remnant would be saved. Isaiah 7:3; 8:3. Isaiah and his children were for "signs and wonders." Isaiah 8:18.

Hosea and his children were also given symbolic names suitable to the spiritual condition of Israel and God's dealings with the nation. Hosea 1:6,9.

In the name "Immanu-EL" there was a prophecy of salvation in a name. Isaiah 7:14; 9:5 with Jeremiah 23:6; Zechariah 6:12.

5. New Names for the Saints confirm this significance.

God changed Abram and Sarai's names to Abraham and Sarah. That is, to "High Father, a Father of many nations," and his wife from "Contentious" to "Princess." Genesis 17:5,15.

God changed Jacob's name to Israel, "Prince having power with God and with men and prevailing." Genesis 32:28,29.

The Lord promises a new name for Jerusalem in due time. Isaiah 62:2; Zechariah 8:3.

The righteous are promised a new name also. Isaiah 65:15.

The new name meant not only blessing for the bearer but for others too. Genesis 12:2 and 48:20.

The Son of God gave three of His disciples new names, these were a promise of what their character and nature would become in due time. Mark 3:16,17; John 1:42.

The Good Shepherd knows His sheep by name (i.e., by nature).   John 10:3.

The overcomer will receive a new name in a white stone that only he himself can appreciate. Revelation 2:17.

The names of the twelve Apostles and the names of the twelve Tribes of Israel are to be found in the Eternal City of God. Revelation 21:14, with Luke 10:20, Revelation 3:8, 13:8, 17:8, Phil. 4:3, Hebrews 12:23.

The Name denotes the person, his identity, his nature and character.

6. Pagan History gives evidence of the corruption of the truth relative to Names and their Interpretation.

The belief was universal that the name of an object, person or angelic being was more than a mere label. The name expressed the personality.

Various customs and rites were used to find a suitable name for a child and when that name was invoked upon the child it set in motion the virtues and power contained in that name.

This was also believed relative to the name of the gods. Only as men knew the name of their god could they call upon him and experience his power.   This was claimed to be so by the invocation of the name. When the name was invoked or pronounced, it set the god working in the behalf of the one invoking.   Hence the reluctance of the gods to let men into the secret of their names because of the magical power connected with the name.

Thus the Romans and Greeks called on the name of their numerous gods, invoking their powers, essence and virtues in behalf of those invoking.   They sought to know the nature and essence of their gods by their names. They believed by uttering the name the god would be brought under the power of the speaker as by a spell. Whatever a person desired of a god, he had but to speak "the name" and it would be fulfilled.

The Magicians of Egyptian, Persian, Syrian and Babylonian history, worked in this way. They claimed revelation of the name of the gods. They would ask "What is his name" and thus purport to have received an answer by which they could conjure up answers for the people subject to their magical powers. As the Magician invoked the magical name, "the name" would work of itself. The name meant the god himself.

Even the "Holy Four Letters" of the True Name of God "YAHWEH" took on, in the minds of the Hebrews a magical belief for the one who could pronounce it.

All of this enlightens us how Names and their Interpretations degenerated into superstitious rites in the magical use of the name of the gods. Behind every heresy there was originally some precious truth which became corrupted over the centuries.

7. <u>Interpret the Name</u>.

Paul, using the Law of Interpretation of Names, revealed who Melchisedek was. This is seen in Hebrews 7:1,2. "Melchisedek ... first by <u>interpretation</u> King of Righteousness and after that also King of Salem, which is, King of Peace."

Jesus Himself also used this Law, as seen in John 1:42. "Thou art Simon, the son of Jona: thou shalt be called Cephas which is <u>by inperpretation</u>, a stone."

And again, "We have found the Messias, which is, <u>being interpreted</u>, the Christ." John 1:41.

God changed the Names of Abram and Sarai to Abraham and Sarah. Genesis 17:5, 15.

God changed Jacob's Name to Israel. Genesis 32:28.

God named children even before their birth. Isaac is an example of this. Genesis 17:19.

The Israelites often incorporated parts of the Elohistic or Jehovahistic Compound Names into the Names of their children. This has already been noted. Examples which show this are Names like "Dani-EL," "Jo-EL," "Eli-Jah," revealing a part of the Name of God therein. There are hundreds of examples of this truth. Any Bible Dictionary of "Interpretation of Names" will confirm this.

"The Name" in Bible times was always significant of "The Nature" or "The Person" behind or at the back of that Name, and this is consistent throughout the whole of the Word of God, both Old and New Testaments. A New Name spoke of the New Nature, the New Character.

To interpret "The Name" was to interpret "The Nature" of the Person or Persons behind that Name. A case in point is Nabal. He was true to his Name.

" ... for <u>as his name is</u>, <u>so is he</u>; Nabal ("Fool") is his name, and folly is with him ... " I Samuel 25:25.

If this is true of mere creatures, how much more is it true of God Himself. When we interpret the Names of God we interpret the Nature, Attributes and Character of God. The Person behind that Name is interpreted.

All of this brings us now to **THE NAME** which is impressed upon the pages of the New Testament.

"THE NAME IN THE FOUR GOSPELS"

As we study the Gospels, The Acts and The Epistles, we see how everything pertaining to the Church, or to the believers, was to be done "In The Name." (Greek "to onoma," "the Name")

Just as The Son of God did nothing in His own Name, but ministered and worked in His Father's Name, so He tells us to do everything in His Name and not in our own Name.

Let us take as our text for this chapter, the verse in Colossians 3:17.

"And whatsoever ye do in WORD OR DEED do all 'In The Name' of the Lord Jesus."

As everything was done "In The Name of the LORD GOD" in the Old Testament, by Prophet, Priest, King and Saints, now everything is to be done "In The Name of the LORD JESUS" by Ministers and Saints.

It proves that the Two Divine Persons involved in "The Name" are co-equal in all things, and it proves the absolute Deity of the Son of God.

Let us consider in this chapter the "word and deed" done "In The Name" of the Lord Jesus, as recorded for us in the Acts, the Gospels and the Epistles, for this verse covers all "doing and saying."

Each Gospel brings out some different aspect of "doing and saying" in His Name that is not brought out in the other Gospels.

1. The Name in Matthew's Gospel

The first verse concerning "The Name" is found in Matthew 1:21-25. "Thou shalt call HIS NAME 'JESUS,' for He shall save His people from their sins." Here it is the Saviour's own personal Name. The Name in which alone is salvation from sin. The Name which speaks of His redemptive ministry and sacrifice, on Calvary. It is The Name of His sinless humanity.

Matthew 1:23. "Call HIS NAME 'IMMANU-EL' which being interpreted is 'GOD with us." This wonderful Name shows that JESUS is not only a MAN, but that He is GOD, that He is God with us! God, The Son! God Incarnate! He is the God-Man!

In Matthew 6:9, Jesus taught His disciples to pray and the first thing in this prayer is, "Our Father, which are in heaven, HALLOWED BE THY NAME ..." Jesus taught His disciples to Hallow His Father's Name, even as He did.

Again in Matthew 7:22, Jesus warns of false prophets, likened to wolves in sheeps clothing and trees without fruit, and He foretold that on the Judgment Day, many would say to Him, "Have we not prophecied IN THY NAME, LORD, LORD! And IN THY NAME have cast out devils? And IN THY NAME done many wonderful works?" But He replies that He never knew them, commanding them to depart from Him because they were workers of iniquity! This is typical of the false prophets in the Old Testament who dared to presume to "prophecy In The Name of the Lord," yet were workers of iniquity. And many today under The Name of "Christ" or "Christ-ianity" dare to use His Name but are workers of iniquity. These will be recognized only by their fruits.

In Matthew 10:22, Jesus foretold the fact that His disciples would be "Hated of all man FOR HIS NAME'S SAKE." How true this was, is seen in the Early Church, as well as today! The Name of Jesus Christ is hated by religious hypocrites, by false religions, and cults of the devil; by wicked godless men. Many millions have been martyred for The Name of Jesus, because they were "Christ-ians."

Matthew 12:41. Here we have a prophecy concerning the Gentiles coming into the blessing of Salvation, through the Lord Jesus Christ, which we see fulfilled in the Book of Acts. "IN HIS NAME shall the Gentiles trust." As Israel, the Chosen Nation, had trusted "In The Name" of The LORD GOD under the Old Covenant, so under the New Covenant of Grace, the Gentile Nations would come to trust "In The Name" of the LORD JESUS, for salvation. To trust in His Name would be to trust in Him and His atoning work on Calvary.

Matthew 18:5 pronounces a blessing upon children, being received. "He that receiveth a little child IN MY NAME receiveth Me." The Son of God became a little child in incarnation and all have to become as little children in order to enter the Kingdom of God, for of such is the Kingdom. Here His blessing rests upon children and those that minister to the children "In His Name."

In Matthew 18:20 we have the marvellous declaration of the Lord's Presence everywhere with His saints at all times, as they gather for worship. "Where two or three are gathered together IN MY NAME (or INTO MY NAME. Amp. N. T.) there I AM in the midst." The believer gathers together "in or into His Name," and this constitutes His Church, and guarantees the Presence of the Risen Head in the Midst. As God was "in the midst" of the Burning Bush, and His Name was declared as "I AM" from there, and signs and wonders were done in that Name, so the Church is now to be the Burning Bush, with the LORD, The I AM, in the midst, and His voice is heard in the presence of His people, amidst signs and wonders in His Name. People, like Moses, will become conscious that they are upon Holy Ground.

Matthew 19:29 tells us that those who "Forsake all FOR HIS NAME'S SAKE" will receive their reward both here and in the world to come. He forsook all, to come to earth to pay the price of atonement, and was rewarded of His Father, so will those who forsake all to follow Him and glorify His Name.

Matthew 21:9 tells us Jesus rode into Jerusalem, as foretold in Zechariah 9:9, on the ass, and the multitudes cried out in praise, "Blessed is He that cometh IN THE NAME of The LORD." That is, "Blessed is He (The Son) that cometh in The Name of The Lord (The Father's Name!)." Jesus repeats this same verse in Matthew 23:39 concerning His Second Coming, for as a whole the Jewish Nation rejected His First Coming "In His Father's Name" (In The Name of The LORD), and thus desolation, rejection and blindness fell upon Jewry until the end of this Church Age. Prior to Christ's Second Coming, the eyes of Jewry will be opened and it is then they will truly say, "Blessed is He that cometh (the second time) in The Name of the Lord." It is then that they will look on Him whom they pierced and rejected, because He ministered in His Father's Name, but with eyes opened, they will rely on Him, and realize the glorious truth that He did come the first time "in His Father's Name," and that The Son is partaker of His Father's Name, in His exaltation. That The Father made His Son "Lord" so that every knee should bow and every tongue should confess to the Glory of God. He comes "in and with His Father's Name" as King of Kings and LORD of Lords!

Once more in <u>Matthew 24:4-5</u> Jesus warns that many deceivers would arise in the last days, "and many shall come <u>IN MY NAME</u>, saying <u>I AM</u> (Christ), and shall deceive many."

It shows that in the last days the glorious truth of The Name "I AM" will be seen by many, and that Satan will seek to counterfeit this Name through false deceivers, antichrists and false prophets, etc., who will try to appropriate this Name of the Burning Bush to themselves, and many will follow them and be deceived by Satan and his ministers clothed as ministers of light. But, as before mentioned, no created being can use The Name I AM truly because of all it comprehends. Only by a true understanding of the truth of "I AM" will believers be able to recognize the false claims of these imposters.

It is worthy to note that the Name "I AM that I AM" or "I AM" as declared by God in Exodus 3:14, is changed in verse 15 to the "LORD God," and never again used in the Old Testament until JESUS, The SON OF GOD comes to earth in the form of man! Ever after it is The LORD God ...."

The same is true in the New Testament. JESUS, The SON OF GOD, declares The Name "I AM" by right of His own Deity, as One of the Persons in Elohim, but ever after in the Gospels, it is always The LORD Jesus!

The Old Testament: I AM that I AM.   The LORD God.
The New Testament: I AM.   The LORD Jesus.

Thus The Name "I AM" can only be applied to GOD in Three Persons, never to man!

In verse nine of the same chapter in Matthew 24, Jesus repeats the fact that His disciples will be "Hated for <u>MY NAME'S SAKE</u>," in contrast to the false who use His Name to deceive in verse five.

Some will suffer for "<u>His Name's sake</u>." It is vividly portrayed in the Old Testament by the true and false prophets. The false prophets used His Name to deceive the people. The true prophets suffered for The Name, as they ministered faithfully to the people. But God shall let the false proceed so far and no further. He let Jambres and Jannes go so far with their false signs and counterfeit miracles, before Pharoah and Moses and Aaron, as these ministered "In The Name of the LORD" (I AM), and thus their folly was manifest to all. II Timothy 3:8-9.

So, for Elijah and the Prophets of Baal, God, the True God, answered by fire. He is against the false prophets and religions that dare to presume to use His Name, and they shall be cut off. Deuteronomy 18:20-22. (Isaiah 4:1).

Matthew's Gospel closes with the last mention of "<u>The Name</u>" in <u>Matthew 28:19</u>.

"Baptizing them <u>IN THE NAME</u> of The Father, and of The Son, and of The Holy Spirit." This verse is the crowning glory and truth of all the Scriptures concerning "The Name" in Matthew's Gospel.

We have noted that "The Father's Name" is to be hallowed. Matthew 6:9. And that believers would gather together "In My Name," that is, "The Son's Name."

In The Son's Name children would be blessed, the Gentiles would trust, false deceivers would presume to use His Name etc., and now the close of this Gospel brings "THE NAME" into view in relationship to THREE DIVINE PERSONS; even The Father, The Son, and The Holy Spirit.

"The Name" then in Matthew's Gospel concerns Three Persons, even The Eternal Godhead, revealed as, The Father, The Son, and The Holy Spirit.

2. The Name in Mark's Gospel

Mark's Gospel has about ten references to "The Name."

It begins in Mark 6:14, "HIS NAME was spread abroad." This is after the sending forth of the twelve Apostles, and the effective ministry that was manifested in healing the sick, and casting out devils, that "His Name was spread abroad."

His Name was "JESUS," The Saviour. Saving from sin, sickness, and from Satan! His Name was manifested in saving ministry. Everyone wanted to know how and where the Apostles received power to do these things. The answer was "In The Name of JESUS." Thus "HIS Name was spread abroad."

Mark 9:37 repeats the same blessing upon the receiving of children "IN HIS NAME," as in Matthew's Gospel. Verse 41 tells us that even a cup of water given to drink "IN MY NAME" shall be rewarded.

In Mark 9:38-39 we have an interesting episode not given in Matthew's Gospel, concerning sectarianism, and the matter of ministries. The disciples, especially John the beloved, saw "one casting out devils IN THY NAME and he followed not US, so we forbad him."

Here the disciples manifest a sectarian spirit, and attitude to another who ministered in The Name of Jesus, yet because he didn't belong to their group, they endeavored to forbid to minister in The Name of Jesus. But the Lord Jesus rebuked them saying, "Forbid him not, for there is no man which shall do a miracle IN MY NAME, that can speak lightly of Me, for he that is not against US, is on our part."

What a strike at the denominational spirit and sectarian attitude of the believers today! It seems apparent that this one was ministering freely, not belonging to any group. He was casting out devils, which was no mean ministry, as none had such a ministry in the Old Testament. Even the seventy others returned rejoicing that "even the devils were subject to them IN THY NAME." And this one was casting out devils In The Name of Jesus; which shows that somewhere the Lord Jesus had met him and commissioned him to do such in His Name. Yet the disciples manifested a sectarian spirit in spite of the blessing upon the ministry of this one.

Thus Christ's attitude should be ours today! All that minister truly "In His Name" whether inside or outside of denominational walls, and who follow not "us," should not be forbidden to do so.

Mark 11:9-10 repeats what Matthew's Gospel tells us concerning The Son of God coming "IN THE NAME of the LORD."

Mark 13:5-6 also repeats Matthew's warning concerning those who deceive people through the use of The Name "I AM" in the last days. And verse 13 tells again of the true believers being "Hated for MY NAME'S SAKE."

The last reference we have of "The Name" is in Mark 16:15-18. Jesus commands His Disciples to preach the Gospel to every creature, in all the world, and to baptize those that believe. Then in verse 17 He promises, "And these signs shall follow them that believe;

> IN MY NAME: They shall cast out devils, they shall speak with new tongues, They shall take up serpents, and if they shall drink any deadly thing it shall not hurt them; they shall lay hands on the sick and they shall recover."

Though these verses are attacked by many unbelievers today, as not being in some of the earliest Manuscripts, it is interesting to note that every one of these signs, (except one) are manifested in the Book of Acts, under the ministry of the Early Church, as will be seen.

"Preaching the Gospel to every creature, Healing the Sick, Casting out Devils, Speaking with New Tongues, etc.," all is to be done IN HIS NAME.

Mark's Gospel gives us these additional things concerning "The Name" which are not recorded for us in Matthew's Gospel.

It is interesting to note that the emphasis in Mark's Gospel is more on THE SON'S NAME, than any other Name! And particularly in The Signs that follow in the preaching of the Gospel.

3. The Name in Luke's Gospel

Luke's Gospel gives about twelve references to "The Name," which are the same almost as in Matthew and Mark.

Luke 1:31; 2:21. Thou shalt call HIS NAME "JESUS." The saving Name.
Luke 9:48. Receive a little child IN MY NAME. The Name of blessing.
Luke 9:49-50. One casting out devils IN THY NAME. The all-powerful Name.
In Luke 10:17, the seventy disciples return with joy, saying, "LORD, even the devils are subject unto us IN THY NAME."

In verses 18-19, Jesus said, "I beheld Satan fall as lightning from heaven, and behold, I give you power over all the power of the enemy, to tread upon serpents and scorpions, and nothing shall by any means hurt you." This is the same language as Mark 16:16, concerning "taking up serpents in HIS NAME and not being hurt of them."

In verse 20 He tells them not just to rejoice that devils are subject to them, IN HIS NAME, but rather rejoice that THEIR NAMES are written in the heavens.

What a warfare in the spiritual realm had been let loose, through the operation of the power of The Name of Jesus. For several thousand years, Satan and his demon powers held sway over the nations, and over the bodies, souls and minds of men. Now ONE appears in the form of Man and attacks his Kingdom of

Darkness, of Sin and Sickness and Death and Demons. Never before in Old Testament days had anyone the ministry of casting out of demons, and now THE SON OF GOD appears to conquer Satan of his power over the lives of mankind. The twelve are sent forth by Him. The seventy are sent forth. Great victory is manifested. The demons who enslaved people in sin, sickness, disease, oppression, and bondage, now leave the bodies and minds of their captives as the disciples utter the power of THE NAME OF JESUS!

They knew who "this Jesus was!" They knew Him in His pre-existant state, as THE WORD, the Eternal Son of God. They know Him now, veiled in human form. They know He has power over them. They know that they have no ground in Him to work upon. They know Him as the Sinless, Spotless Son of God. They know He has authority over them, and that He has power to torment them, and send them to the Abyss. They know their time is coming for eternal judgment. And thus when Jesus sends these disciples forth, and the power of THE NAME is manifested, they obey and depart. They cannot resist The Name of Jesus. The demons recognized the power of The Name of Jesus then, and do today, but seek to blind God's people, and the Church, to the power and the use of that Name in casting them out from their strongholds.

Blind religious leaders opposed Christ, saying He cast out devils by the prince of devils; yet they professed to "trust in The Name of Jehovah" and their whole ministry was powerless, and ineffective to help and release men and women in bondage to Satan. Yet when The Son of God came and worked "in His Father's Name," they jealously accused Him as being of the devil!

The following verses are repeated as in Matthew and Mark's Gospel. Luke 11:2. 13:35. 19:38. 21:8, 12, 17.

Luke 24:47 is the last reference to "The Name" in this Gospel. Again it is in the last Commission of Jesus to His disciples. "That repentance and remission of sins should be preached IN HIS NAME among all nations, beginning at Jerusalem."

Repentance and remission of sins had been preached by the Prophets under the Old Testament "in The Name of the Lord," and now under the New Testament Dispensation, repentance and remission of sins was to be preached to all nations, "in The Name of the Lord," that is; THE NAME OF THE LORD JESUS! Because it is only through Him, through His Blood, through His atoning work on Calvary, through His Name which involves this whole work, that remission of sins is possible! Jesus Christ is God's Way of repentance and remission of sins among all nations, and there is no other way, no other Name given among men whereby we must be saved.

The Gospel of Luke thus gives another particular truth concerning "The Name" which is not given in Matthew and Mark's Gospel.

4. The Name in John's Gospel

John's Gospel brings forth further light on "The Name" not found in any of the other Gospels. Let us note the truths brought out in these verses on "The Name" as in John.

John 1:12. "But as many as received Him, to them gave He the power (authority, privilege) to become the sons of God, even to them that BELIEVE ON HIS NAME."

68

To "believe on His Name" means to "adhere to, trust in and rely upon Him." It is not mere mental assent to various facts concerning Him, but it means a full complete surrender of oneself over to His keeping, trusting Him wholly for salvation and eternal life. For salvation from sin. His Name is "JESUS," which interpreted means, "He shall save His people from their sins." And to "believe on His Name" is to trust Him to be saved from all sin.

John 2:23. "Many believed in His Name, when they saw the miracles which He did." His miracles were the proof of His Name! They were a revealing of that Name, and the ministry and power of that Name. Saving His people from sin, from sickness, disease and death, and Satan, as The Saviour. His Name meant "Saviour" and the miracles were glorious proof of His Name. Here it is recorded that they believed IN His Name, while in the previous verse quoted, they believed ON His Name! To believe ON His Name is in salvation from sin, as a sinner. It is casting oneself wholly ON Christ! As Saviour. To believe IN His Name is in the believer's life as a child of God, in prayer to God The Father, using "The Name" of Jesus in prayer and petition.

John 3:18 tells us that "he that believeth not is condemned already because he hath not believed IN THE NAME of the Only Begotton Son of God." This is The Name in which is either salvation or condemnation. It is either life or death according to every man's attitude to it. To accept "The Name" is to rely on, and believe in and on that Name for salvation, now and eternally. To reject "The Name" is to be damned, to be under condemnation, now and eternally. This is "The Name" which God has given for all mankind, by which they might be saved. And there is salvation in no other Name. This is the one and only Name given, under heaven, by which men must be saved. Acts 4:12.

John 5:43, and John 10:25. Jesus declares that "I am come IN MY FATHER'S NAME," and "The works I do, I do IN MY FATHER'S NAME." This is The Name He told His disciples to "hallow" in Matthew 6:9. Luke 11:2. As all Old Testament Prophets ministered "in The Name of The Lord," so it was in order that the Son of God, THE Prophet, should minister and work "in The Name of The LORD," which was His Father's Name. Dueteronomy 18:15-18.

That is why the people declare in John 12:13, "Blessed is He that cometh IN THE NAME OF THE LORD." Because The Son came in His Father's Name, He ministered in His Father's Name, and this is The Name He hallowed in His life, and which we are to hallow in our prayer.

John 12:28 gives us the prayer of Jesus, after the visit of the Greeks "to see Jesus." He foretold His coming death as "the grain of wheat falling into the ground to die to bring forth fruit," and then prayed, "FATHER, GLORIFY THY NAME." And what was the response to this prayer? "There came a Voice from heaven, saying, 'I have glorified it, and will glorify it again'." The people thought that it thundered, others thought an angel spoke to Jesus from heaven, but it was the same voice as declared in Jordon's waters, "This is My Beloved Son, in whom I am well pleased." It was The Father's Voice, declaring He had glorified HIS NAME, and would again glorify HIS NAME, and this was, and would be, glorified, in and through THE SON!

The Father glorified HIS NAME again, when He placed HIS NAME UPON THE SON in exaltation, making Him "LORD."

It is The Father's Name that Jesus spoke so much about in His High Priestly prayer in John 17.

Note: vs 11 FATHER ... keep through THINE OWN NAME those Thou has given Me.
      vs 6 Father ... I have manifested THY NAME unto the men Thou gavest Me.
      vs 12 Even as I have kept them IN THY NAME ...
      vs 26 I have declared unto them THY NAME, and will declare it.

This is The Name He taught His disciples to hallow. This is The Name He came in and ministered in. This is The Name He manifested and declared to the disciples. This is The Name He asked His Father to glorify, even His Father's Name. And this is The Name He commanded His disciples to baptize converts in in Matthew 28:19, in union with The Son and The Holy Spirit.

John 14:13-14, 15:16, 16:23-24, 26 give some wonderful verses concerning "The Name," for in these verses Jesus gives His disciples the legal right to use His Name in prayer to the Father, God.

Note these glorious Scriptures:

"Whatsoever ye shall ask IN MY NAME, that will I do, that The Father may be glorified in The Son."

"That whatsoever ye shall ask The Father IN MY NAME, He may give it you."

"IN THAT DAY (when The Holy Spirit is come), ye shall ask Me nothing. Verily, I say unto you, that whatsoever ye shall ask The Father IN MY NAME, He will give it you. Hitherto (up to this time) have ye asked nothing IN MY NAME. AT THAT DAY ye shall ask IN MY NAME."

No one had a right to use His Name unless He gave them authority to do so. Here in these verses Jesus gives them the authority, the privilege and right to use His Name!

Up to this time no one had ever asked The Father "in Jesus' Name." All Old Testament Saints had to go to God, through Aaron the High Priest, and he bore their Names upon the Breastplate of Judgment, and the Onyx Stones, "before the LORD." Israel presented Aaron with their incense and he offered them to the LORD as the prayers of the people, upon The Golden Altar of Incense. Now Jesus Christ, The Son of God, stands as God's Anointed High Priest, and tells His disciples that they may now approach God The Father, THROUGH HIM, through His Blood and Sacrifice, and IN HIS NAME!

What does The Father think of His Only Begotten Son? Is He not The Son of His Love? What does He think of THE NAME of His Only Begotten Son? The Father has given His Son the highest Name both in this world and that world to come. All The Father's delight is in His Son, and the perfect work of Atonement that He accomplished at Calvary. The Son is The Father's ordained, anointed Priest. The Mediator between God and Man. Thus when the believer comes to The Father asking some need, and he says, "I ask this IN THE NAME of JESUS ..." The Father sees the believer, not coming in his own virtue or righteousness, or of himself, but actually coming in the virtue and righteousness of Jesus and in all that The Son is! And Jesus said, He will do it: The Father will do it, so that The Father will be glorified in the Son, and in the use of THE SON'S NAME!

The Son glorified His Father's Name; The Father glorified The Son's Name!

That is why <u>John 20:31</u> declares, "These things are written that ye might be-lieve and that believing ye might have <u>LIFE THROUGH HIS NAME</u>," or as the Amp. N. T. puts it, "that believing ye might have <u>LIFE THROUGH WHAT HE IS</u>."

His Name is what He is! Himself is His Name, and His Name is Himself!

<u>ALL THAT HE IS</u>, we present to The Father, when we ask <u>IN HIS NAME</u>!

The Amp. N. T. again declares these verses as "Whatsoever ye ask The Father in My Name -- that is; <u>presenting ALL I AM</u>, The Father will do it."

So we present "what He is" to The father, when we ask "in His Name." His Name on earth in the Church takes the place of His physical presence. The Holy Spirit is in that Name, manifesting the power of the Risen Lord in the Church, by "The Presence."

"Where two or three gather together IN or INTO MY NAME, there I AM (The Pres-ence) in the midst." Matthew 18:20.

How wonderful are these Scriptures on "The Name" in John's Gospel. Thus this Gospel brings out truth concerning "The Name" not recorded in the previous gospels.

SUMMARY OF "THE NAME" as in the GOSPELS

Note that each of the four Gospels bring out some particular aspect and use of "The Name."

1. Matthew's Gospel speaks particularly of "The Father's Name" and "The Son's Name" and then closes with the command of "The Name of The Father, and of The Son, and of The Holy Spirit" in Water Baptismal Formula. This is the only Gospel of the four which refer to a Triadic form, or Triune Name to be used in the ordinance of Baptism. Matthew 28:19. Matthew 18:20. This is the only Gospel which decalres "The Name" in which believers gather into.

Matthew 1:21	Thou shalt call His Name JESUS. Verse 23.	
1:23	Call His Name IMMANU-EL, which is, GOD with us.	
6:9	Our Father, which are in Heaven Hallowed by Thy Name.	
7:22	In that day, many shall say, 'Have we not prophecied in Thy Name, and in Thy Name cast out devils, in Thy Name done many wonderful works.'	
10:22	Ye shall be hated of all men for My Name's sake.	
12:21	And in His Name shall the Gentiles trust.	
18:5	Receive such a little child in My Name.	
18:20	Where two or three are gathered together in My Name, there AM I (I AM) in the midst.	
19:29	For My Name's sake.	
21:9	Blessed is He that cometh in The Name of the LORD.	
23:39	Blessed is He that cometh in The Name of the LORD.	
24:5	Many shall come in My Name, saying I AM.	
24:9	Shall be hated of all nations, for My Name's sake.	
28:19	Teach all nations, baptizing them in The Name of The Father and of The Son, and of The Holy Spirit.	

2. Mark's Gospel emphasizes "The Son's Name" and what is to be done in that Name. This is the only Gospel which particularly closes with the Signs which follow the preaching of the Gospel "in His Name." Mark 16:16-17.

Mark 6:14	His Name was spread abroad.	
9:37	Receive one of such children in My Name.	
9:38	Saw one casting out devils in Thy Name.	
9:39	No man can do a miracle in My Name and speak lightly of Me.	
9:41	Give a cup of water to drink in My Name.	
11:9-10	Blessed is He that cometh in The Name of the LORD.	
13:6	Many shall come in My Name, saying I AM.	
13:13	Shall be hated of all men for My Name's sake.	
16:17	These signs shall follow them that believe: In My Name, they shall cast out devils, they shall speak with new tongues, they shall lay hands on the sick, they shall take up serpents, and if they drink any deadly things, it shall not hurt them.	

3. Luke's Gospel speaks of "The Father's Name, and The Son's Name," repeating all that Matthew and Mark do concerning such. This Gospel is the only Gospel that closes with the command that the Gospel of repentance and remission of sin must be preached "in His Name." Luke 24:47.

Luke	1:31	Shall bring forth a Son ... call <u>His Name</u> JESUS. Luke 2:21.
	1:49	He that is mighty ... Holy is <u>His Name</u>.
	9:48	Receive such as this child in <u>My Name</u>.
	9:49	Saw one casting out devils in <u>Thy Name</u>.
	10:17	Devils are subject unto us through <u>Thy Name</u>.
	11:2	Our <u>Father</u>, which art in Heaven, Hallowed be <u>Thy Name</u>.
	13:35	Blessed is He that cometh in <u>The Name</u> of the LORD.
	19:38	Blessed be The King, that cometh in <u>The Name</u> of the LORD.
	21:8	Many shall come in <u>My Name</u>, saying I AM.
	21:12	Taken before Kings and Rulers for <u>My Name's</u> sake.
	21:17	Be hated of all men for <u>My Name's</u> sake.
	24:47	That repentance be preached in <u>His Name</u> amongst all nations.

4. John's Gospel brings out the truth of "The Father's Name" and "The Son's Name" in a way that none of the previous Gospels do. The emphasis is on "Life in The Name" of the Only Begotten Son of God. This Gospel is the only Gospel which declares the right, legally, of believers to use "The Name" in prayer to The Father God. This Gospel records the majority of the "I Am's" of Jesus. (Refer to Appendix.)

John	1:12	To them that believe <u>on His Name</u>.
	2:23	Many believed <u>in His Name</u>.
	3:18	Believed in <u>The Name of the Only Begotten Son of God</u>.
	5:43	I am come in <u>My Father's Name</u> ... another shall come in his <u>own Name</u>.
	10:25	The works that I do in <u>My Father's Name</u>.
	12:13	Blessed is He that cometh in <u>The Name</u> of the LORD.
	12:28	<u>Father</u>, glorify <u>Thy Name</u>.
	14:13	Whatsoever ye shall ask in <u>My Name</u>.
	14:14	If ye ask anything in <u>My Name</u>.
	14:26	The Comforter, whom The Father will send in <u>My Name</u>.
	15:16	Ask The Father in <u>My Name</u>.
	15:21	For <u>My Name's</u> sake.
	16:23	Whatsoever ye shall ask The Father In <u>My Name</u>.
	16:24	Hitherto have ye asked nothing in <u>My Name</u>.
	16:26	In that day ye shall ask in <u>My Name</u>.
	17:6	<u>Father</u>...I have manifested <u>Thy Name</u> unto the men Thou gavest Me.
	17:11	Keep through <u>Thine own Name</u>, those Thou has't given Me.
	17:12	I have kept them in <u>Thy Name</u>.
	17:26	I have declared unto them <u>Thy Name</u>, and will declare it.
	20:31	That believing ye might have life through <u>His Name</u>.

"THE NAME" IN THE BOOK OF ACTS

The Book of Acts is the Early Church demonstration of all the truth of "The Name" as recorded or commanded in the four Gospels.

The Book of Acts could rightly be called "The Acts of The Holy Spirit," in the Church, the Body of Christ.

As we study the short history recorded in Acts, covering about thirty to forty years, and consider the Acts of the Early Church, one cannot help but notice that the whole of the activity centered around "The Name" and the power and operation of that Name.

"The Name" was one of The Keys of The Kingdom given to the Church, and they used it in the preaching of the gospel, with signs following. All "doing and saying" was done "in The Name of the Lord Jesus Christ."

"The Name" meant "The Person" in the Acts of the Apostles. All that Jesus Himself had been to them in Person, His Name became the same to them. Actually His Name took His place in the Early Church. It was not just a theory, a matter of words or names. It was not conjured up as a magical invocation of a name of some god. "The Name" represented all that Jesus Christ was, all that He had done, and all that He was able to do and be in the Church. What the Name of the LORD GOD had meant in the Old Testament so the Name of the LORD JESUS meant in the New Testament.

Let us briefly trace the exciting story of the use of "The Name" in the Book of Acts, the Acts of the Holy Spirit.

For it will be seen, that as The Son of God, The Head of the Church, did all His "saying and doing In His Father's Name" (words and deeds), so The Church, His Spiritual Body, did all it's words and works "in The Name of the Lord Jesus." The Son represented and declared The Father to the world. The Church represents and declares The Son of God to the world as The Saviour.

In Acts three the first miracle of healing is performed in The Name of Jesus Christ. Jesus had given His Disciples the right to use His Name "in that day," when the Holy Spirit would come to them. John 14:13-15; 15:16.

He had also promised in Mark 16:17 that these signs would follow them that believe "in His Name," one of which was the healing of the sick.

In Acts 3:6, Peter said to the lame man at the Gate Beautiful, "Silver and gold have I none, but such as I have give I thee; IN THE NAME of Jesus Christ of Nazareth, rise up and walk. And he took him by the right hand and lifted him up, and immediately his feet and ankle bones received strength." The man went into the Temple, walking and leaping and praising God, as the wondering crowd gathered around him and Peter and John.

Peter asked the people, "Why look so earnestly upon us? As though by our own power or our holiness we had made this man to walk!" To the man in need, Peter said "Look on us!" To the wondering crowd, Peter said, "Why look on us?" It was not the power or holiness of Peter or John, but the power and holiness of the Risen Christ, which had made this man whole. And in verse 16 Peter says, "And HIS NAME, through faith IN HIS NAME, hath made this man whole.

Peter and John had faith in The Name for the healing of the lame man. It is not recorded that the lame man had the faith to be healed, for apparently he didn't expect to be healed, but was expecting alms! But the Apostles had faith in The Name, for The Name meant the Person. They demanded in His Name that the lame be made whole, and the man recovered both instantly and miraculously! So the Apostles testified to the people that it was done through the power of A NAME!

In Acts four we have the record of the Apostles being taken before the Council and the very High Priests who brought about the Crucifixion of Jesus Christ of Nazareth, even Annas and Caiaphas.

Acts 4:7 says, "And when they had set them in the midst, they asked, 'By what power, or BY WHAT NAME have ye done this'?" What a question! What a challenge! What an opportunity! And Peter, as spokesman again, centers all his message to the Council on the power of THE NAME OF JESUS!

In verses 10-12 he declares, "Be it known unto you all that BY THE NAME OF JESUS CHRIST of Nazareth, whom ye crucified, whom God raised from the dead, even by Him doth this man stand before you whole. This is The Stone which was set at nought of you builders, and is become the Head of the Corner, neither is there salvation IN ANY OTHER, for there is NO OTHER NAME under heaven, given among men, whereby we must be saved."

Peter, filled with the Holy Spirit, declares these glorious truths concerning "The Name." Verse 8.

What was the result? In verse 17-18, after admitting that it was a notable miracle which could not be denied, "they called them and commanded them not to speak at all or teach in THE NAME OF JESUS, or "in or about this Name." Amp. N. T.

Notice that these are religious men, the religious leaders of the day, the very High Priests of God; yet in their folly and blindness after crucifying Jesus of Nazareth, contrary to the Laws of Moses, yet unconsciously fulfilling these same Laws, they now command and threaten the disciples not to teach or preach "in The Name of Jesus." Or, as the Amp. N. T. puts it, "not to converse in any way or teach at all in or about The Name of Jesus." These religious leaders could not rejoice or praise God for the miracle standing right before their eyes, because of spiritual blindness, envy and jealousy, which testified of their own powerlessness to meet the needs of the people. They realized, too late, that God had by-passed them, and that "a New Thing" was springing up in the earth under the Outpouring of the Holy Spirit, and that "the Ecclesia - The New Covenant Church" was beginning to be manifest, of which Jesus of Nazareth was the Head!

The glorious truth of the healing before them was the fact that the very Man they had crucified WAS ALIVE! They knew that these disciples could not have healed the man of themselves, or by their own Name and power! They knew it had been done by the power of A Name. And when the Apostles declared it was through the power of The Name of Jesus, they were filled with rage against the use of His Name!

Though He was not here on earth, though His Body had disappeared from the tomb and the Priests had paid the soldiers out of the Temple funds to keep the matter of the earthquake and the resurrection of Jesus quiet, He had left HIS NAME here for the disciples to use.

His Name actually took His place on earth! And the use of His Name produced the same results as He did here in Person. To use The Name, or to teach and preach in The Name of Jesus, meant to teach and preach The Person of Jesus! It meant that He was indeed resurrected, proving that they had crucified the very Son of God. His Name in operation was proof that He was indeed alive. A dead man's name would have been powerless, and no one could use a dead man's name to do a notable miracle like this. If Jesus of Nazareth was dead, His Name would be useless and powerless. But His Name in operation proved He was risen, and that He was ascended to The Father's Right Hand, and that He was backing up the use of His Name on earth. Mark 16:19-20.

He told them in John "that whatsoever they ask The Father IN HIS NAME, He would do it." And He did it! He confirmed His Word with signs following. He worked with them from Heaven in the use of His Name. They could not separate His Name from Him. His Name is Himself. He now has all power in heaven and in earth. What boldness Peter manifests as He declares that "this Name" is THE ONLY NAME in which salvation could be found. What a challenge! The religious leaders knew that under the Old Testament, "Whosoever called on The Name of the LORD shall be delivered." Joel 2:32. Acts 2:21.

And now Peter says that God has given His Only Son "THE NAME" in which alone is salvation. This is The Name The Father God has given among men whereby they must be saved. If man desires to come to God for salvation, then there was only ONE NAME through which they could approach God, and that was His Way, through the Person of the LORD JESUS CHRIST!

Perhaps the Sanhedrin at first thought that the disciples were using the Name of a false god and suspected idolatry in the healing of the lame man. However they were to find out that this was done by the Name of Jesus of Nazareth. By the power of that Name. ·

Why did these religious leaders fear "The Name" of Jesus? What was there to be concerned about in the preaching and teaching of "The Name?" Because The Name meant The Person, and The Name in operation was proof that The Person was alive! No wonder they commanded them not to teach at all in The Name of Jesus!

After the Apostles were set free, they returned to their own company, and together lift up their voices in prayer, praying that they might have "boldness to preach THE WORD, and that signs and wonders may be done in THE NAME of Thy Holy Child Jesus." And in response to this PRAYER, the place is shaken and all are filled afresh with THE HOLY SPIRIT and preach The Word with boldness.

These are the Keys of the Kingdom given in Matthew 16:18-20, to the Church, and these are the Keys to the Book of Acts used by the Early Church.

The Word reveals His Name, and God has exalted His Word above His Name. He has also placed His Name upon The Word, and it is The Holy Spirit who gives power to use The Name effectively, according to The Word.

In Acts five, after great power is manifested in healing the sick, and casting out of devils "in His Name," the disciples are brought before the Sanhedrin again. What spiritual blindness was upon the religious leaders, who were the recognized Anointed of the Lord, and whose responsibility and ministry it was to reveal the True God to the people through the Temple Ministry and the Sacred Scriptures, yet they fail to recognize God's Christ!

In spite of the fact that people were healed and delivered from the power of Satan, and evil spirits, and diseases, they challenge the Apostles again in Acts 5:27-28, "Did we not straitly command you that ye should not TEACH IN THIS NAME, and behold ye have filled Jerusalem with your doctrine, and intend to bring this Man's blood upon us!"

It is quite evident that "The Name" was not just a theory in the Early Church. It was not just a mere side-issue, or a mere doctrine, or a theological argument; it was A POWER, and it always meant THE PERSON whose NAME IT WAS! They dreaded and feared THE NAME - in operation! And though the charge was that they filled Jerusalem with "their doctrine," they knew WHO was meant in the doctrine! Had they not cried in blind rage and fury at Pilate's Judgment Hall, "His Blood be on us and our children!" Matthew 27:25. Yet here they seek to evade the charge and self-invoked curse of Innocent Blood on their heads! After further threatening them, and beating them, in verse 40, "they commanded them that they should not SPEAK IN THE NAME OF JESUS!"

However, verse 41 tells us, that "they departed from the presence of the Council, rejoicing that they were worthy to SUFFER SHAME FOR THIS NAME!"

Here we have the beginning of the fulfillment of Jesus' words in Mark 13:9-13, and Luke 21:12-17. Jesus told His disciples that the time would come when they would be taken before Councils, and Rulers FOR HIS NAME'S SAKE. He said that they would be HATED FOR HIS NAME'S SAKE, and they would be beaten. But they were not to take any thought of what they would answer, for The Holy Spirit would speak through them, in that same hour, giving them what to say, "that it would be A TESTIMONY unto them." The Testimony of The Name of Jesus!

And so they have a foretaste of the opposition to "The Name" of Jesus, and being "hated for His Name's sake," and "suffering for The Name." Stephen laid down His life because of The Name and Testimony of Jesus before the Council in Acts 7:58-60. cp. Psalm 44:20-22. Romans 8:36. III John 7. Matthew 10:22.

The next mention we have of "The Name" is in Acts eight, under Philip's Ministry, as the Evangelist.

Philip went down to Samaria (verse 5) and preached Christ unto them. The Lord confirmed His Word with signs following, as promised in Mark's Gospel, and "in His Name" miracles were wrought, and unclean spirits were cast out and there was great joy in that city. In verse twelve we read, "But when they believed Philip preaching the things concerning THE KINGDOM OF GOD AND THE NAME OF JESUS CHRIST, they were baptized, both men and women."

John the Baptist, Jesus, and the Apostles preached The Gospel of the Kingdom of God, and Philip also preached it. His message included "Repent for The Kingdom of Heaven is at hand," but Philip linked with The Kingdom of God THE NAME OF JESUS CHRIST! The reason is clear, for the only way into The Kingdom of God is through The Lord Jesus Christ Himself. He is The Door to The Kingdom, He is the Gateway, through the New Birth. One has to be born into The Kingdom of God, and that is through the New Birth. The New Birth takes palce in those who received Him, Jesus Christ, and believe in and on His Name!

Philip not only preached "The Name," he demonstrated the Power of "The Name." Thus "The Name" was the center of Philip's preaching in Samaria.

Acts nine brings us to the conversion of Saul, who later became Paul, the Apostle. The whole of his conversion centers around the revelation of what was in "The Name" of Jesus!

Saul, the destroyer, the Pharisee, breathed out threatenings and slaughter against the disciples of the LORD! That is, The LORD JESUS! He went and received authority from the Chief Priests "to bind all THAT CALL ON THE NAME." Verse 14. It was alright for the Saints "to call on The Name of the LORD GOD" as the faithful had done for centuries in Israel; but "to call on The Name of the LORD JESUS," that was blasphemy, in the eyes of Saul, as well as the religious leaders.

It was the association of The NAME "LORD" - The Name of Deity - with The Name of "JESUS" that incurred the wrath and hatred against the Early Church, of religious men, and Judaism, as a whole. To ascribe and make JESUS "LORD" was to accept His claims to Deity, and recognize Him as Deity - equal with GOD, The LORD, in bearing THE NAME OF DEITY!

Thus Saul, jealous of The Law, and the Traditions of the fathers, zealous of God The ONE LORD in Israel (Duet. 6:4), persecuted those who "Called on The Name of the LORD JESUS."

But what happens as he journeys on the Damascus Road? Suddenly a light, above the brightness of the noonday sun shines about him and he falls to the ground. He hears a voice from heaven saying, "Saul, Saul, why persecutest thou ME ...? Verse 3-4.

Saul, religious zealot, blameless as touching the righteousness of the Law, a Pharisee, brought up at the feet of Gamaliel, recognizes that it is a Divine visitation. Just as God arrested Moses at the burning bush; and others of the Prophets and Patriarchs by Divine visitation, and voice from heaven; Saul recognizes that GOD is visiting him here on the Damascus Road. So great is the glory and the light, above the noonday sun!

What does Saul reply? "And he said, 'Who art THOU LORD?'' Verse 5. Saul knew it was God, DEITY, speaking from heaven to him, and he called GOD "LORD."

The name of Deity, as revealed to Moses at the Burning Bush!

But imagine his amazement when "the voice" answers, "I am JESUS Whom thou persecutest ... it is hard for thee to kick against the pricks."

So this "voice," this ONE whom Saul called "Lord," supposing it to be "the LORD GOD," was none other than "THE LORD JESUS!"

What did it all mean? It meant that JESUS OF NAZARETH was all He claimed to be; that He was indeed THE INCARNATE SON OF GOD, that He was DEITY made flesh; and that He had been crucified, buried, resurrected, and was indeed ascended to the Father's Right Hand and had poured out the Promised Holy Spirit upon those who believed on HIS NAME!

All these facts would begin to dawn on Saul's bewildered and amazed mind, as he listened to the voice tell him what he should do in obedience to the heavenly vision.

The voice that spoke to Moses long ago out of the Burning Bush, declaring His Name as "I AM WHO I AM" even as "The LORD GOD ... this is MY NAME - FOREVER;" now speaks again - THROUGH THE SON OF GOD, exalted, as "The LORD JESUS....."

No wonder Paul's epistles all center around "The Name," and no wonder that he sums all doing and saying in Col. 3:17, by exhorting the believers, "And whatsoever ye do in WORD or DEED - DO ALL IN "THE NAME" of the LORD JESUS ...."

And later on, in Acts 26:9, when Paul stands before Kings and Rulers, for "His Name's sake," he gladly testified, "I verily thought that I ought to do many things contrary to "The Name" of Jesus of Nazareth, which things I also did in Jerusalem, and many of the saints did I shut up in prison, having received authority from the Chief Priests; and when they were put to death, I gave my voice against them. And I punished them oft in every Synagogue, and compelled them to blaspheme; and being exceedingly mad against them, I persecuted them even unto strange cities."

Paul, or rather, Saul, helped do the very things Jesus foretold in Mark 13:9-13, John 16:1-4 and Luke 21:12-19.

This is "The Name" which Saul fought against. This is "The Name" he accepts under Divine Visitation. This is "The Name" he lived and died for. This is "The Name" he was hated for, even The Name of the LORD JESUS CHRIST!

In fact it was for "The Name" that Paul was apprehended of The Lord Jesus, according to Acts 9:14-17, and the word to Ananias.

Ananias fears to go to Saul because of his persecution of the Saints "who called on Thy Name" until the Lord Jesus reassures him with these words, "Go thy way, for he is a chosen vessel unto Me - TO BEAR MY NAME before the Gentiles, and Kings, and the Children of Israel." "And I will show him how great things he must SUFFER FOR MY NAME'S SAKE."

Thus Saul is chosen to "bear The Name" and to "suffer for The Name." This is "The Name" in which the Gentiles would trust. Matthew 12:17-21, and this is "The Name" for which men would hate the believer, and for which the believer would suffer.

Acts 9:17 closes with a touching scene as Ananias enters the house, and "putting his hand on Saul, says, "Brother Saul, The LORD ... even JESUS ... that appeared unto thee in the way hath sent me unto thee ...." The very same language as on the Damascus Road ... "The LORD ... JESUS ...." What joy and confirmation to Saul's heart. No wonder the scales fell from his eyes as the glory of the Risen Christ flooded his soul.

Acts 22:16 tells us that Saul arose "calling on The Name of The LORD." That is, The LORD Jesus!

After his conversion, he immediately preaches "CHRIST." Acts 9:20. While in verse 21 his hearers are amazed, saying, "Is this not he that destroyed them which called on THIS NAME?" Verse 29. Saul spoke boldly in The Name of the LORD JESUS!

In Acts ten to eleven we have the record of the Gospel being taken to the Gentiles. As before noted, Matthew 12:21 foretold that "In His Name shall the Gentiles trust." But how could they trust in His Name, if they had never heard of that Name? Thus the Holy Spirit commands Peter, after the vision, to arise and go with the three men, nothing doubting. Peter journeys to the house of Cornelius, a Gentile, and gave them words whereby they could be saved.

In verse 42, Peter testifies, "To Him - Jesus of Nazareth - give all the Prophets witness, that THROUGH HIS NAME whosoever believeth in Him should re--ceive remission of sin."

And as Peter declares the Death, Burial and Resurrection of Jesus, the Holy Spirit falls upon the Gentiles, and "they trust in His Name," even The Saving Name of the Lord Jesus Christ!

Later on in Acts 15, after a number of Gentile Churches had been established through the Apostolic Ministry of Paul certain Jews seek to bring the Gentiles into the bondage of The Law and Circumcision, mixing Law and Grace.

The Ministry and The Elders of the Church at Jerusalem gather together to discuss the matter, and James declares in his testimony, in verse 14, "that God at the first did visit the Gentiles, to take out of them, a people FOR HIS NAME," and in verse 17 says, "the Gentiles upon WHOM MY NAME IS CALLED, saith the LORD."

The means of Jew and Gentile being made one is in and through THE NAME of The Lord Jesus Christ, called upon them both, uniting each in Him. The Name is called on them, and they call on the Name. All are one in His Name. Jews and Gentiles, which for thousands of years had been ir-reconcilable, are made "one new man" through the Cross and The Name of Jesus Christ. God thus visits the Gentiles for the purpose of "taking out a people FOR HIS NAME!"

Paul is the one chosen to "bear that Name" and declares that Name to them. Peter also declared The Name of salvation unto them, for there is no other Name given under heaven, among men, Jew or Gentile, by which they must be saved.

Acts 15:26 says that these "men have hazarded their lives FOR THE NAME OF THE LORD JESUS CHRIST." The full glory of that Triune Name.

The power of The Name is manifested in Paul's ministry in Acts 16:16-18, as a certain damsel possessed with a spirit of python (divination) followed Paul many days, declaring that these men are servants of the Most High God who show unto men the way of salvation. Paul was grieved in his spirit, realizing that it was an evil spirit testifying, and "turned and said to the spirit, I command thee in THE NAME OF JESUS CHRIST to come out of her; and he came out that same hour."

Thus the power of The Name, "My Name" according to Mark 16:16 is manifested in casting out devils. The demons knew the power of The Name. They knew they had to submit to that Name. They knew they had to obey that Name, spoken in The Spirit and declared in faith through the Apostle Paul.

Without doubt the effect of the power of "The Name" spread abroad through the cities, for we read in Acts 19:11-20, where God wrought special miracles by the hands of Paul, so that from his body, aprons were taken to those who were sick, and their diseases and evil spirits departed from them. Then we read, "that certain of the vagabond Jews, exorcists, took upon them "to call over them which had evil spirits THE NAME of the LORD JESUS, saying, 'We adjure you by JESUS whom Paul preaches.'"

But what was the result? The man in whom the evil spirit was answered and said to these Jews, "Jesus I know, and Paul I know, but who are you?" The man leapt upon them, overcame them, so that they fled out of the house naked and wounded. This became known to all the Jews and the Greeks dwelling at that place, "and fear fell on them all, AND THE NAME OF THE LORD JESUS WAS MAGNIFIED."

Exorcism was not just a magic formula to the Apostle Paul. "In the Name of Jesus Christ" was not meant to be interpreted as such, nor is it to be interpreted that it works simply at the whim or fancy of any person. It is Jesus Himself who heals. It is the presence of the Lord that makes whole and causes evil spirits to leave the oppressed and possessed. The one who uses "The Name" must be in right relationship with Him whose Name it is. These sons of Sceva use the right formula but the Name is powerless on their lips. The Jewish exorcists who Name the Name of Jesus find this Name does not work for them like a magic formula.

Thus in the light of Matthew 7:21, 22 and Mark 9:38, the Name of Jesus shows its power only where a man is joined to Jesus in faith and obedience and does the will of God. One cannot use the Name of Jesus for selfish and independant ends. The power of the Name is not conjured up by some magical compulsion.

The Lord Jesus gave only His disciples the right to use "His Name." These vagabond Jews were not His Disciples, and had no right to the use of "His Name." And the evil spirits knew it. They knew and confessed that JESUS had authority over them and that they would have to obey Him. They also knew that PAUL had power and authority over them "In The Name of Jesus" and they knew Paul could effectively use The Name to cast them out. But they also knew that these Jews did not have the power of "The Name," and because of their hatred "For The Name of Jesus," attacked those who dare presume to use that Name against them.

Truly, as Luke 10:17-20 writes, "Even the devils are subject unto us THROUGH THY NAME." So Paul's Name was published abroad in the heavenly places, where principalities and powers and wicked spirits held sway. No wonder "The Name" was magnified! For none dare use it unless they belonged to Him. None had power or the right to use His Name if they were not of Him.

Thus the whole of the Book of Acts centers around the power and demonstration of A NAME - even THE NAME of the LORD JESUS CHRIST! Jesus Christ is back of that Name, because it is His Name. All the fulness of the Godhead is in that Name. All authority in heaven and in earth is His, and is manifested in that Name. It is the greatest Name, and when we remember and consider all that was done "In the Name of the LORD GOD" in the Old Testament, and then compare all that was done "In The Name of the LORD JESUS CHRIST" in the New Testament, in the Book of Acts, it proves conclusively that "The NAME of the LORD JESUS CHRIST" is The Name of God, revealed as Father, Son and Holy Spirit, and that the fulness of The Divine Name - THE NAME - is in the SON OF GOD! Father, Son, and Holy Spirit, co-equal in all things, and partakers and sharers together in the Divine Name and all it involves.

The Name IN OPERATION was proof of the RISEN CHRIST. His Name would certainly have no power if He were dead. And as Moses and Aaron did signs and wonders by the Rod of God in The Name of the great "I AM" (The LORD GOD), so did the

Early Church use "THE NAME OF JESUS" (The "I AM" - The LORD JESUS CHRIST) as THE ROD OF GOD, to do signs and wonders.

If Judaism could have stopped the apostles ministry and speaking and teaching in the Name of Jesus, they would have stripped the Church of its power.

God's desire is that the Church today cease from magnifying the sectarian and denominational names which divide the Body of Christ, and declare the glory of THE NAME which unites, even THE NAME of The LORD JESUS CHRIST. This Name has lost none of its power or authority. It is the same yesterday, today and forever, because the ONE WHOSE NAME IT IS is THE SAME, YESTERDAY, TODAY, and FOREVER! Heb. 13:8 and Mal. 3:6. It is The Name which unites the True Church and this True Church will be recognized by the use, operation and demonstration of the power of this Name. All things are subject to His Name, and that Name has been given to the Church to use for His Glory, "that The Father may be glorified in The Son," and in the use of HIS NAME! "IN HIS NAME" means "in His place, as His representatives, in His stead." He is in Heaven, The Church is on earth, "in His Name."

SUMMARY OF "THE NAME" IN ACTS

Acts 2:21	Call on the Name of the Lord shall be saved.
2:38	Repent, be baptized, in the Name of Jesus Christ, receive the Spirit. Note here the Spirit and the Name together.
3:6	In the Name of Jesus Christ rise and walk.
3:16	His Name, through faith in His Name. Not our power or holiness.
4:7	By what power or Name have ye done this?
4:10	Be it known unto you that by the Name of Jesus Christ of Nazareth.
4:12	No other Name under heaven given to men whereby we can be saved.
4:17	Do not speak or teach in this Name any more.
4:18	Teach and preach in the Name of Jesus.
4:30	Signs and wonders, by the Name of Thy Holy Child Jesus.
5:28	That ye should not teach in this Name.
5:40	Beat, commanded them that they should not speak in the Name of Jesus.
5:41	Rejoiced that they were worthy to suffer for His Name.
8:12	Philip ... preached the Kingdom of God and the Name of Jesus Christ.
8:16	Baptized them in the Name of the Lord.
9:14	Bind all that call upon Thy Name.
9:15,16	Chosen vessel to bear My Name before Gentiles ... suffer for My Name.
9:21	Preached boldly in the Name of the Lord Jesus. (See also verses 27 and 29.)
10:43	That through His Name, whoso believeth receives remission of sins.
10:48	Baptized in the Name of the Lord.
15:14	Take out of the Gentiles a people for His Name.
15:17	The Gentiles, upon whom My Name is called.
15:26	Hazarded their lives for the Name of the Lord Jesus Christ.
16:18	I command thee in the Name of the Lord Jesus Christ.
18:15	If it be a matter of words or Names.
19:5	Baptized in the Name of the Lord Jesus.
19:13	Took upon them to call over the spirit possessed the Name of Lord Jesus. They fled, naked. No power to use the Name.

```
Acts 19:17   The Name of the Lord Jesus was magnified.
     21:13   I am willing to die for the Name of the Lord Jesus.
     22:16   Arise, be baptized ... call on the Name of the Lord.
     26:9    I do many things contrary to the Name of Jesus of Nazareth.
```

Everything was done in the Name of the Lord Jesus Christ in the Book of Acts. One of the Keys of the Kingdom of God. Note in the above Scriptures that there is salvation, healing, signs, wonders, faith, water baptism, Holy Spirit baptism, preaching, teaching, etc., all to be done in this Name!

"THE NAME" IN THE EPISTLES

The revelation and use of "The Name" (Greek, "to onoma") as in the Epistles can only be considered in brief. There we find that the activity and life of the Church is centered about "The Name," that is, THE PERSON of Jesus Christ.

The Name in Romans

Romans 1:5. Paul desired, "Concerning Jesus Christ our Lord ... obedience to the faith among all Nations, THROUGH HIS NAME, among who ye are also the called of Jesus Christ."

Romans 2:24. Paul charges the Jew with the fact "that THE NAME OF GOD is blasphemed amongst the Gentiles" by the way they lived contrary to The Laws of God. The Nation had been chosen under Moses to "bear The Name of the Lord" upon them. Numbers 6:27. They had received the Commandments concerning "taking the Name of the Lord" in vain. Exodus 20:7. Yet they had departed from the Living God, and thus HIS NAME was blasphemed amongst the Gentiles. Ezekiel 36:21-23.

Romans 9:17. Paul quotes Exodus 9:16 concerning "God raised up Pharoah for the very purpose THAT HIS NAME might be DECLARED throughout all the earth!" And we know all that was wrought in and through the power of that Name in Israel's deliverance. So God desires that His Name be declared throughout all the earth.

Romans 10:13 is a quotation of Joel 2:32, even as Peter quoted the same in Acts 2:21. "Whosoever shall call on THE NAME of The Lord shall be saved." Paul had called on The Name of the LORD - JESUS - and was saved, even as all the saints called on The Name of the LORD - GOD!

Romans 15:9 is a quotation of Psalm 18:49 in a prophecy of Jesus Christ "Singing unto THY Name," that is; THE FATHER'S NAME! Compare also Hebrews 2:12.

The Name in Corinthians

I Corinthians 1:2. "Unto the Church ... with all that in every place CALL UPON THE NAME of Jesus Christ, our Lord, both theirs and ours." This "Calling on The Name" was the invocation of "The Name" and constituted His Church. Matthew 18:20. Where two or three gather IN MY NAME: I AM in the midst. Old Testament and New Testament Saints "Called on The Name," as well as "The Name being called on them."

I Corinthians 1:10. Paul says, "I beseech you BY THE NAME of The LORD JESUS CHRIST, that ye all speak the same thing, and that there be no divisions among you, but that ye be perfectly joined together in the same mind and in the same judgment."

Paul's appeal to Unity in the Church was by the UNITY of the TRIUNE NAME! The Corinthians were sectarian, carnal man-worshippers, "I of Paul, I of Apollos, I of Peter, I of Christ," after various names, but Paul appeals to them by The Name of the Person who was crucified for them.

How typical of sectarian names, and denominational names, of founders names, which divide the church today! Neither Paul, Apollos, Peter or any of the founders of denominations today, died for the Church! The Lord Jesus Christ was crucified for the Church, and His Name should be the ground of, and source of unity, amongst the believers who "call on that Name, everywhere, in all places."

I Corinthians 5:4-5 commands Church Discipline. "In THE NAME of our LORD JESUS CHRIST when ye are gathered together, and my spirit with the Power of our LORD JESUS CHRIST, to deliver such an one over to Satan for the destruction of the flesh, but that the spirit may be saved in the Day of the Lord Jesus."

Thus The Name was to be invoked in the administration of discipline. What a solemn thing this was. The Name meant life or death. It had the power to loose or bind, and The Lord Jesus in heaven worked with His Church on earth in the use of this Name in discipline.

I Corinthians 6:11. It is in this Name "that ye are washed, but ye are sanctified, but ye are justified, in The NAME of the LORD JESUS and by The Spirit of God." The Name washes, The Name sanctifies, The Name justifies us unto God.

The Name in Ephesians

Ephesians 1:21. Paul tells us that The Lord Jesus Christ has been "set far above all principalities, powers, and might, and dominion, AND EVERY NAME THAT IS NAMED; not only in this world, but also in that which is to come!"

Of course we understand that this does not mean above The Father's Name; for the Father's Name is the greatest Name that is Named; but it means here that The Father has given His Name to the Son, making Him The LORD JESUS CHRIST, in His exaltation according to Acts 2:34-36, to the Glory of God, The Father. According then to this Scripture there is no greater Name in this world, or the world to come ever to be revealed, than The Name of The LORD JESUS CHRIST! This is the greatest, and highest and most glorious of all The Names of God, because it expresses and involves the greatest and the highest and the most glorious, even GOD as FATHER: SON: HOLY SPIRIT; The Fulness of the Godhead BODILY revealed in The Son!

Not only so, but Ephesians 3:14-15 tells us that this Triune Name is The Family Name. "For this cause I bow my knees unto THE FATHER OF OUR LORD JESUS CHRIST, of Whom the whole family in heaven and earth IS NAMED ...." Thus this Name, the greatest Name, is the family Name, the One Name of which every member of the Household of Faith partakes of.

As every member of the earthly family partakes of the Family Name, so do the members of the heavenly family partake of the NAME OF GOD! They "call on that Name, and The Name is called on them," even as in the family. The Son of God partakes of His Father's Name, making Him the LORD Jesus and we partake of The Son's Name, by being made CHRIST-ians. Acts 11:26.

Ephesians 5:20 exhorts us "to give thanks always for all things unto God The Father IN THE NAME of our Lord Jesus Christ." Approaching God The Father, through the Son, in and through His Name: The Name that The Father has given us to approach Him in.

The Name in Philippians

Philippians 2:9-10, Paul tells us again of the glorious exaltation of Jesus in "The Name." "Wherefore (because The Son humbled Himself in obedience to the death of the Cross) GOD has highly exalted Him (Christ Jesus) and given Him A NAME WHICH IS ABOVE EVERY NAME (except The Father's Name), that AT THE NAME OF JESUS ... every knee should bow, and every tongue should confess that JESUS CHRIST IS 'LORD' ... TO THE GLORY OF GOD THE FATHER!"

For "LORD" is THE FATHER'S NAME, and THE FATHER'S NAME UPON THE SON! This corresponds with Ephesians 1:21, concerning Jesus Christ being exalted above every Name in this world and the world to come.

The Name in Colossians

It is no wonder then that Paul says in Colossians 3:17, "And whatsoever ye do in WORD AND DEED, DO ALL "IN THE NAME" of THE LORD JESUS." It covers all "saying and doing" of the Church.

The Name in Thessalonians

II Thessalonians 1:12. Paul prays "That THE NAME of our LORD JESUS CHRIST may be glorified in you, and ye in Him, according to the Grace of our God and The LORD JESUS CHRIST."

How can this Triune Name be glorified in us?   He can only be glorified as "LORD" when He is truly "LORD" of all in our lives, over everything we have, and ever hope to be.   The Name of "JESUS" can only be glorified in us as we know Him according to that which that Name means, "Saving His people from sin." The Name "CHRIST" can only be glorified in us by letting The Holy Spirit abide in Anointing power and ministry, as a True Anointed One, a Christ-ian indeed!   Or as Paul says in Romans 13:14, "Put ye on The LORD JESUS CHRIST."

II Thessalonians 3:6.   Further Church Discipline is "Commanded in THE NAME of the LORD JESUS CHRIST ... that ye withdraw from every brother that walketh disorderly...." Thus every believer should walk according as He walked, walking according to The Name and all it means in being invoked upon the believer.

The Name in Hebrews

Hebrews 1:4 confirms Ephesians 1:21 and Philippians 2:9-10, concerning this greatest Name. "THE SON ... hath by inheritance obtained A MORE EXCELLENT NAME than Angels."   And Psalms 8:1, 9 tells us what "this more excellent Name" is. "O LORD, our LORD, how EXCELLENT IS THY NAME in all the earth!" Psalms 110:1 and Acts 2:34-36 tell us that The Father God made JESUS "LORD" when He sat at the Right Hand of the Majesty on High.   The Angels were created by God, and given their Names; but The ETERNAL SON of God, Uncreated, but Begotten, inherited His Father's Name!

In Hebrews 2:12 (Psalms 22:22) Jesus Christ, The Son of God, says, "I will declare THY NAME (that is; The Father's Name!) unto My brethren, and in the midst of the Church will I sing praise unto Thee!" Cp. Psalms 18:49. This is The Father's Name He manifested and declared to the Disciples as in John 17:6, 11-12, 26.

In Hebrews 6:10 the believers manifested "the love towards His Name."

Hebrews 13:15. "By Him (Jesus) therefore, let us offer unto God the sacrifice of praise, giving thanks to HIS NAME."

The Name in Timothy

I Timothy 6:1. Paul exhorts that the believer walks "that THE NAME OF GOD and HIS DOCTRINE be not blasphemed," while in verse 3, he speaks of "the wholesome words of our LORD JESUS CHRIST and the doctrine which is according to godliness."

Thus the Name of God is expressed fully in The Name of the Lord Jesus Christ even as The Doctrine of God is expressed fully in the Doctrine of The Lord Jesus Christ. This is The Doctrine of The Father and The Son. II John 9. John 7:16-17.

As the Jews caused The Name of God to be blasphemed by the way they lived, contrary to that Holy Name invoked upon them, so does the believer - the Christ-ian - cause The Name of Christ to be blasphemed if they live contrary to that Holy Name. For this reason Paul says again in II Timothy 2:19, "Let every one that NAMETH THE NAME OF CHRIST depart from iniquity." Which reminds us of the words of Jesus in Matthew seven, concerning those who had done various things "In His Name," yet He tells them to depart because they were workers of iniquity! Either we depart from iniquity because of His Name upon us, or else He will tell us to depart from Him for using His Name while being workers of iniquity.

The Name in James

James 2:7 speaks of those who "blaspheme that worthy (precious) NAME by the which ye are called." Or "The Name which was bestowed or invoked upon you."

James 5:10. The Prophets who have spoken IN THE NAME OF THE LORD, are an example of suffering affliction and patience. As all prophets who truly spoke in The Name of Jehovah, suffered, so will the believer who truly lives according to that Name.

James 5:14. James closes his epistle with the sick calling for the elders of the Church, "to pray over them, anointing them with oil IN THE NAME OF THE LORD, and the prayer of faith shall save the sick, and the Lord shall raise them up." Thus Prayer for the Sick, Anointing them with Oil, the Symbol of the Holy Spirit, is to be all done "in The Name of the LORD, even The LORD JESUS CHRIST." For He has been revealed as "The LORD that healeth thee ...." Exodus 15:26.

The Name in Peter

I Peter 4:14. "If ye be reproached for THE NAME OF CHRIST, happy (blessed) are ye." This is linked with "suffering for The Name" as foretold by Jesus in Mark 13:13, but in it Christ is glorified, for He suffered for His Father's Name, and we will follow in His steps and suffer for "His Name."

The Name in John

John the Beloved repeats in his Epistles the same truths as in the Gospel concerning "The Name."

I John 2:12. "Your sins are forgiven you, FOR HIS NAME'S SAKE." That is, because they received and believed on and in His Name for salvation, as declared in John 1:12. Acts 4:12.

I John 3:23. "This is His Commandment that we should BELIEVE ON THE NAME OF HIS SON JESUS CHRIST, and love one another." I John 5:13 also.

III John 7. "They went forth FOR HIS NAME'S SAKE." It is clear that "His Name" here is The Name of the Lord Jesus Christ.

Thus "The Name" is stamped upon the Epistles to the Churches. This is The Name The Early Church met and called upon. It was The Name which was called upon them. This was The Name in which all preaching and teaching, all signs and wonders, praying for the sick, casting out of devils, church discipline, prayer, praise and worship, all "word and deed" were done in "The Name of the Lord Jesus!"

DO ALL IN THE NAME OF THE LORD JESUS

"And whatsoever ye do in word or deed, do all in THE NAME of the Lord Jesus." Colossians 3:17.

As everything was done in "The Name" of the Lord God in the Old Testament, so we find that everything is done in "The Name" of the Lord Jesus in the New Testament.

The following gives a Table of Scriptures on the things that were done in His Name as seen in the Gospels, the Acts and the Epistles. All show the importance and the place that the Name of the Lord had in the Early Church. It was not just a doctrine. The Name meant the Person.

It will be most profitable for the Student to read all these Scriptures and allow the light of the Word of God to shine upon the power and glory of "The Name."

SUMMARY OF SCRIPTURES

1. Repentance in His Name. Luke 24:47. Acts 2:38.

2. Signs and Wonders in His Name. Mark 16:17. Acts 4:30.

3. Casting out devils in His Name. Mark 16:17. Luke 10:17-19. Acts 19:11-12.

4. Healing the sick in His Name. James 5:14. Acts 3:6,16. 4:30.

5. Speak with New Tongues in His Name. Mark 16:17. Acts 2:4. John 14:26.

6. Taking up serpents in His Name. Mark 16:17. Acts 28:1-6.

7. Drinking any deadly thing in His Name. Mark 16:17.

8. Preaching and Teaching in His Name. Acts 4:7, 17-18. 5:28, 40. 8:12.

9. Salvation in His Name. Acts 2:21. 4:12. Romans 10:13. Matthew 1:21-23.
   Acts 16:31.

10. Praise, Praise, and Worship in His Name. Romans 15:9. Hebrews 13:15.
    Ephesians 5:20.

11. Remission of sins in His Name. Luke 24:47. I John 2:12. Acts 10:43.

12. Church Discipline - in His Name. I Corinthians 5:4. II Thessalonians 3:6.

13. Washing, Sanctification, Justification in His Name. I Corinthians 6:11.
    II Timothy 2:19.

14. Unity of believers in His Name. I Corinthians 1:10. Ephesians 3:14-15.
    Matthew 12:21. Acts 15:14-17.

15. Reproach and Suffering for His Name. I Peter 4:14. Acts 5:41. 9:15-16.
    15:26. 21:13. 26:15. Mark 13:13. Luke 21:17. Matthew 10:22. Hebrews
    13:13-15.

16. Calling upon The Name. Acts 9:14. 22:16. I Corinthians 1:2. James 2:7.
    Joel 2:32. Acts 2:21.

17. Believing in and on His Name. John 1:12. I John 3:23. 5:13. Acts 10:43.

18. Life in His Name. John 20:31. 2:23.

19. Church gathers in His Name. Matthew 18:20.

20. All Prayer to God The Father in His Name. John 14:13-15. 16:24. 15:16.

21. Ministries bear The Name in witness. Acts 8:12. 9:13-16.

22. All believers are to glorify His Name. John 12:28. cp. II Thessalonians
    1:12. II Timothy 2:19.

23. Children received and blessed in His Name. Luke 9:48. Matthew 18:5.

24. Word and Deed all to be done in His Name. Colossians 3:17.

25. <u>Hold Fast His Name</u>. Revelation 2:13. 3:8.

26. <u>The Name is called upon the believer</u>. James 2:7. Acts 11:26. 26:28. Revelation 3:12. 14:1. 22:4, with Isaiah 56:5. 62:2. 65:15.

27. <u>For His Name's sake</u>, i.e., for Him. Whatever is done to or for His Name is done to or for Him. His Name is His representation in earth. Matthew 19:29. 24:9. I John 2:12. III John 7.

SECTION III

WHAT ABOUT "THE NAME" IN WATER BAPTISM

CHAPTER V

WHAT ABOUT "THE NAME" IN BAPTISM

THE PROBLEM STATED

There remains one area concerning "The Name" which was purposely not dealt with in the previous chapters. This is that which pertains to "The Name" in water baptism.

Generally speaking, there is no great problem in the Church or in Church History relative to the Name of the Lord Jesus Christ and its place in the function of the Church.

No real controversy exists over the use of "The Name" for repentance, salvation, healing the sick, excorcism, prayer, worship and praise. None seem to contest the fact that this Name is actually called upon or invoked individually by the believer and corporately in the Church.

It is recognized that there is power in the Name of the Lord, that it is not a magic formula or a meaningless rite.

"The Name" represents the Person. All He is in Himself, all that He in power, all that He has done in redemptive work for His people.

When all of the above is done in "The Name" it speaks of the truth that all proceeds to and from the Father through the Son, the one and only Mediator between God and Man.

However, when it comes to "The Name" to be used in regard to water baptism, great controversy arises.

The problems basically center around the interpretation of baptism as an ordinance, as to form or mode and also as to the words of a formula (if any) to be used in the administration of this rite.

The questions fall into three areas for discussion: Form, Formula and Interpretation.

1. What is the FORM or MODE of baptism. Sprinkling or immersion? Is baptism really necessary?

2. What is the FORMULA or particular words to be used in baptism. Should the Triadic Formula be quoted as found in Matthew 28:19?

   Should the Name of the Lord, or Jesus Christ, or Lord Jesus Christ, as in the Book of Acts, be called upon?

   Should it be both Matthew 28:19 and the Triune Name of the Lord Jesus Christ? Or, is the real essential the act of obedience by the individual and not any words of any particular Formula? Is the condition of the heart being right with God that alone is acceptable regardless of Mode or Formula?

   Again, is a Formula required at all? Can any set Formula be found in the New Testament or Church History at all? Do words really matter at all?

3. What is the real INTERPRETATION or spiritual significance of baptism? How is baptism to be interpreted as set forth in the New Testament?

Endless strife and divisions have resulted in the Church over the centuries in an endeavour to solve these problem-questions. Undoubtedly, for many, the problem cannot and never will be dissolved.

In the Section under consideration, the writer presents what he believes is an explanation and interpretation of those Scriptures pertaining to "The Name" in water baptism.

It is not proper exegesis to build any doctrine on one Scripture only. If one is to arrive at the whole and complete truth on any given subject, then every Scripture reference pertaining to that subject must be considered. Then each Scripture must be interpreted as part of and in the light of the whole set of Scriptures.

Hence, in the following chapters, every reference to water baptism and "The Name" used in reference or association with baptism will come under consideration.

By doing this it will be found that the Name of the Lord, or Lord Jesus, or Jesus Christ is associated in water baptism. How is this to be reconciled with the Triadic Formula of Matthew's Gospel for baptism to be in the Name of the Father, Son and Holy Spirit?

By interpreting "The Name" of the LORD - JESUS - CHRIST it will be discovered that this all-glorious Triune Name involves the Godhead as Father, Son and Holy Spirit. It will also be discovered that this Name is expressed in Him who is the Fulness of the Godhead Bodily. Colossians 1:19; 2:9.

No real problem exists over the use of "The Name" in everything else done in the Church. Why then should there exist great controversy over the use of "The Name of the Godhead" in water baptism?

It seems as if there is almost something Satanic in the hatred of the truth as pertaining to baptism. This is evidenced in the endless divisions, strife and bitterness in Church History. "The Name" may be used for everything else, but let it be associated with water baptism, then immediate conflict is manifested.

May the following pages be a reconcilable answer to these questions.

THE NEW TESTAMENT NAME OF GOD ASSOCIATED WITH THREE DIVINE PERSONS

The New Testament Name of God is associated with Three Divine Persons: the Father, the Son and the Holy Spirit.

When we look at the Four Gospels in reference to "The Name," it should be seen that this Name involves the Eternal Godhead.

Jesus said to His disciples that they were to make disciples of all Nations, "Baptizing them in THE NAME of the Father, and of the Son, and of the Holy Spirit." Matthew 28:19.

Thus THE NAME of the Father, and of the Son, and of the Holy Spirit is involved in Water Baptism. It is the Name of the Godhead.

Let us consider several references from the Scriptures relative to "The Name" of God.

1. The Father's Name:

    "Our FATHER, which art in Heaven, hallowed be THY NAME," Matthew 6:9.
    Jesus said, "I am come in MY FATHER'S NAME." John 5:43.
    Jesus prayed, "FATHER, glorify THY NAME." John 12:28.
    He also declared that He had revealed His Father's Name to His disciples. John 17:6, 11, 12, 26.
    The Great Commission involves making disciples of all Nations, "Baptizing them in THE NAME of THE FATHER..." Matthew 28:19.

    Hence it is clear from just these several Scriptures that THE FATHER God has A NAME, a Name which is to be hallowed and glorified, a Name into which disciples are to be baptized.

    What is "THE NAME of THE FATHER?" "What is HIS NAME...if thou cans't tell?" Proverbs 30:4.

2. The Son's Name:

    The following Scriptures will suffice as pertaining to the Son's Name.

    Jesus Himself said that the disciples would be "taken before Kings for MY NAME'S sake." Luke 21:12.
    He also said, "Ye shall be hated of all men for MY NAME'S sake." Luke 21:17.
    For the gathering together of His people, He promised: "Where two or three are gathered together in MY NAME, there AM I (I AM) in the midst." Matthew 18:20.
    In the Commission, he promised, "In MY NAME they shall cast out devils..." Mark 16:17.

    In the Great Commission, as recorded in Matthew's Gospel, He said to His disciples to go and preach to all nations, discipling them and "...baptizing them in THE NAME of THE FATHER and of THE SON..." Matthew 28:19.

    Again, it is clear that these passages show that worship is to be centered around His Name, signs and wonders would follow in His Name in the preachin of the Gospel, and His disciples would suffer for His Name's sake.

And again, Baptism was not only to be in "The Name of the Father," but also, "of The Son."

What is "THE NAME of THE SON?"   "What is His SON'S NAME, if thou cans't tell?" Proverbs 30:4.

3. The Holy Spirit's Name:

Possibly the one and only specific reference showing that the Holy Spirit is associated with "The Name" is found in Matthew 28:19, where Jesus commands the Disciples to "Baptize in THE NAME...   of The FATHER,
                                                 and of The SON,
                                                 and of The HOLY SPIRIT."

This verse and command quoted from Matthew's Gospel is remarkably connected with the Prophetic Question of Agur in Proverbs 30:4. Let us compare the verses.

Proverbs 30:4	Matthew 28:19
"What is His Name (The Father's Name), And what is His Son's Name (The Son), if thou canst tell?"	"Baptizing in The Name of the Father, And of the Son, And of the Holy Spirit."

It is worthy to note that Agur makes reference to THE NAME of TWO DIVINE PERSONS of the Godhead, even the Father and the Son.   He makes no reference to The Name of the Holy Spirit.

However, when Jesus gives the Command, He commands Baptism to be administered in The Name of the Father, and of the Son, and of the Holy Spirit. This Command is that which involves the Eternal Godhead, Three Persons, even the Father, Son and Holy Spirit.   He brings in the Third Person, the Blessed Holy Spirit.

The reason why Agur does mention the Name of the Holy Spirit could be because it is the New Testament, more than the Old Testament, which brings into operation and manifestion the full experiential knowledge of the Holy Spirit in the saints.

It is the ministry of the Holy Spirit to bring the full and clear revelation of the Godhead Name.

In other words, THE NAME OF GOD in the New Testament is linked with Three Persons in the Godhead.   And, be it noted, that wherever this expression is used both in Old or New Testament, it is always used in the singular form and never in the plural form. That is, "In THE NAME," not "Names."

It is Baptism into THE NAME (singular) of THE FATHER,
                                                 and of THE SON,
                                                 and of THE HOLY SPIRIT, or, Baptism into the
                                                 Name of the Godhead.

The thoughts brought to mind here pertain to singularity of "The Name," yet plurality of "The Persons."

The Name:

The Greek "eis to onoma" ("into the name") implies only one Name for Three Persons. Matthew 28:19.

However, this should be considered along with the Old Testament prophecies of Agur and Zechariah and other Scriptures which speak of the Father's Name and the Son's Name.

Agur asks, "What is HIS (The Father's) Name AND what is HIS SON'S Name, if thou cans't tell?" Proverbs 30:4.

Zechariah in his prophecy pointed to a compound or collective Name.

"And the LORD (Jehovah) shall be King over all the earth, and in that day there shall be ONE LORD and His NAME ONE." Zechariah 14:9.

It will be remembered that the word for "one" is the Hebrew word "echad" which contains the concept of a collective unity into a oneness, a being united into one. It implies a compound unit, as in Deuteronomy 6:4.

Zechariah is prophesying of the fact that there would come a time when the LORD would reveal a NAME that would be ONE NAME or a UNITED NAME. The Name is One Name yet a Compound Name. In other words, a Three-in-one Name and a one-in-three Name. A TRIUNE NAME for the TRIUNE GOD!

The Persons:

"Baptizing into the Name of the Father, and of the Son and of the Holy Spirit..." Matthew 28:19.

The Greek article "tou" ("the") repeated each time is absolute proof for the Godhead, or the Three distinct Persons in the Godhead, Father, Son and Holy Spirit. Matthew 28:19.

Plurality of Divine Persons is seen here. The Three Persons of the Godhead are Triune in Nature and Essence.

Thus when Jesus commanded Baptism to be "In THE NAME," the singular usage of "The Name" spoke of the UNITY of this Name, and when He continued by saying it must be in the Name "of the Father, and of the Son, and of the Holy Spirit." this spoke of the PLURALITY of the Persons involved in this One Name.

The Name of God is a compound Name, a Three-in-one Name or a One-in-three Name. It is a Triune Name involving the Eternal Godhead, as Father, Son and Holy Spirit. As God is One in Three, or Triune, so He has revealed His Name to be a One in Three or Triune Name. This is the Name of the Godhead.

The BEING of God is revealed as One in Three, or Triune.
The NAME of God is also revealed as One in Three, a Compound or Triune Name.

The Command of Jesus joins Three Divine Persons in "The Name."

John Peter Lange in "The Gospel according to Matthew" (Translated from the Third German Edition, with additions by Philip Schaff.   New York; Charles Scribner's Sons, 1899) p. 558, comments on this verse of Matthew 28:19 in the following way:

> "The Name refers to each of the Persons of the Godhead. The plural form ta onomata, would have pointed to Thritheism; while the singular, in its distributive application to Father, Son, and Spirit, brings out in the one name the equality as well as the personality, of the three Divine Names in one name."

He further makes a footnote in which he quotes from Meyer (p. 619, 5th edition of 1864) who wrote:

> "...since the singular signifies the definite name of each one of the three, so that eis to onoma must be supplied before tou huiou and before tou hagiou pneumatos, compare Apoc. XIV.I: to onoma autou kai to onoma ou patres autou."

In other words, the Greek not only shows the use of the ONE NAME for the TRIUNE GODHEAD but also that there is ONE NAME of the Father, and ONE NAME of the Son and ONE NAME of the Holy Spirit. In Revelation 14:1 the text supplied "The Name" twice by saying, "Having His Name (The Son's Name) and His Father's Name..."

The grammatical construction may allow the verse to reveal both aspects of "The Name."

```
                          of the Father              )
"Baptizing into THE NAME and of the Son              )   ONE NAME
                          and of the Holy Spirit." )
```

```
               THE NAME of the Father and     )
"Baptizing into THE NAME of the Son and       )   THREE-FOLD NAME
               THE NAME of the Holy Spirit."  )
```

> The Greek construction has the possibility of there being not only One Name for the Triune God but also a Three-fold Name for the Triune God. In other words, Three Divine Names revealed in One Name which is spoken of as "THE NAME."

> Thus, when comparing Proverbs 30:4 with Zechariah 14:9 and Matthew 28:19 relative to the subject of "The Name," we find that the Hebrew and Greek languages allow "The Name" to be One Name yet Three Names, or a TRIUNE NAME.   This Name is the compound Name of Yahweh or Jehovah. It finds its richest, fullest and most comprehensive revelation in the Triune Name of the LORD JESUS CHRIST.

Having considered the truth that the GOD of the Bible is revealed in THREE PERSONS yet ONE GOD, then it should be evident that THE NAME of the God of the Bible will be THREE-IN-ONE NAME!   The New Testament Name of the LORD JESUS CHRIST is a united Name, a Compound Name. It is a uni-plural Name.

A proper interpretation of this Name shows how the whole Godhead is involved in it.

One God and One Name speaks of Unity.
Three distinct Persons and Three distinct Names speak of Compound Unity.
A Triune God is revealed in the Bible and a Triune Name is revealed in the Bible.

This brings to remembrance the question of the Old Testament saints.

1. Jacob asks the Angel, "What is Thy Name?" Genesis 32:29.

2. Moses asks the Angel, "What is Thy Name?" Exodus 3:14.

3. Manoah asks the Angel, "What is Thy Name?" Judges 13:17, 18.

4. Agur asks the question, "What is His Name and what is His Son's Name?" Proverbs 30:4.

Moses and Agur both receive revelation. In Proverbs 30:9 Agur speaks of taking the Name of the Lord in vain. However, as already dealt with, it is Moses who receives distinctive revelation of that Name.   The reason why the others did not receive the answer to their question is that the set time for the Son of God to be manifested in human form had not yet come. The reason why Moses especially received it was because of the Redemptive and Covenantal power which was to be manifested in the exodus of Israel out of Egypt.

And well may we ask, "What is THE NAME of the Father, and of the Son and of the Holy Spirit?"

In the New Testament is found an answer. Here the Name of God is a Triune Name of God is a Triune Name which comprehends the Godhead, and this Name is the greatest Name to be revealed, both in this world and that world to come, because it comprehends the greatest, even the Father, the Son and the Holy Spirit. Ephesians 1:21.

"The Name" in the New Testament is manifestly seen to involve Three Persons in the Godhead.

1. <u>The Father has a Name</u>.
    Proverbs 30:4; John 10:25; Romans 2:24; Revelation 14:1; 3:12.

2. <u>The Son has a Name</u>.
    Proverbs 30:4; John 14:13, 14; 15:16; 16:23; Isaiah 7:14; 9:6; I John 5:13.

3. <u>The Spirit has a Name</u>.
    Matthew 28:19 is the only distinct reference to this.

    Baptism is administered in "The Name" of the Father, and of the Son and of the Holy Spirit.   The Name of a Person is a mark of what He Himself is, the Name expreses the character.

FATHER, SON AND HOLY SPIRIT - TITLES OR NAMES

A study of the Scriptures will show that "Father, Son and Holy Spirit" are not used in the sense of being <u>proper Names</u> of God, but rather to express that eternal relationship existing in or between the Three Persons in the Godhead. This is also used expressly for the purpose of redemptive revelation to man.

The following Scriptures speak for themselves that "Father, Son and Holy Spirit" do not constitute THE NAME of God.

1. <u>"FATHER" is not The Father's Name.</u>

   Natural and Scriptural reasons confirm this to be so.

   (a) <u>Natural reasons.</u>

   Ask any child of reasonable age, "What is your Father's Name?" and no intelligent child would reply by saying "Father."

   To answer any question concerning "What is your Father's Name" on Legal or Government Documents with the answer "Father" would certainly not be acceptable.

   Nor would such an answer be of any use or value in a Bank Draft, or any other Official Form.

   No man is rightly a father until the birth of a child, and there are millions of "fathers," earthly fathers, in the world. Yet every father has his own Name.

   How meaningless it would be to call all fathers, "Father." For "Father" is not, and cannot be a proper Name.

   It simply declares a parental relationship and is used strictly for each family involved.

   Thus, from a family, a natural or a legal standpoint, "Father" is not a proper name, nor can it be used as such. It is a family title declaring relationship, but every father has his own specific Name.

   (b) <u>Scriptural reasons.</u>

   But seeing that we speak of GOD the FATHER, our Heavenly Father, let us turn to the Word of God and let it answer that "Father" is not the proper Name of God.

Consider the following verses:

"What is His Name (The Father's Name), . . . if thou canst tell?" Proverbs 30:4.
"Baptizing them in the <u>Name</u> of the <u>Father</u>..." Matthew 28:19.
"Our <u>Father</u> which art in heaven, hallowed by Thy <u>Name</u>." Matthew 6:9.
"I am come in My <u>Father's Name</u>." John 5:43.
"The works I do, I do in My <u>Father's Name</u>." John 10:25.
"<u>Holy Father</u>...I have manifested <u>Thy Name</u> unto them..." John 17:6.
"Having His <u>Father's Name</u> in their foreheads." Revelation 14:1.
"<u>Father</u>, glorify <u>Thy Name</u>." John 12:28.

If "Father" was a proper Name for God, then these Scriptures would be meaningless. Each declares that the Father has a Name, not that "Father" is a Name. The Gospel of John is called "The Gospel of the Father and the Son," because here, more than in any other Gospel, that Father and Son relationship is fully expressed. However, Father and Son are not used as proper Names.

(Note: The one and only Scripture where "Father" is used as a Name is found in Isaiah 9:6. "Unto us a child is born, unto us a Son is given and His Name shall be called, Wonderful, Counsellor, the Mighty God, the Everlasting Father, the Prince of Peace."

This Scripture is a prophecy of the Son of God, not of the Father. This Scripture does not state that the Son is the Father, for, the Son is eternally the Son, the Father is eternally the Father, and the Holy Spirit is eternally the Spirit.

The prophecy shows that the Son is given a five-fold Ministry as expressed in each meaning of these designations.)

Thus not one verse in the Bible, from Genesis to Revelation, ever declares that "FATHER is My Name." "Father" is not the Father's Name.

Undoubtedly when it speaks of "Baptizing them in The Name of <u>THE</u> Father..." it means <u>THE</u> Heavenly Father, as distinguished from all earthly fathers as the Greek article shows. But baptism is to be in the Name OF the Father. Therefore, what is THE FATHER'S NAME?

2. "SON" is not <u>The Son's Name</u>.

For the same reasons as above, neither can "Son" be a proper Name but simply an expression of family relationship.

Natural and Scriptural reasons again forbid "Son" being a Name. No where in natural or Biblical history is "Son" used as a child's proper Name.

No one just names their son, "Son."

Consistency of Scriptural interpretation demands that all created things, all creatures, animals, birds, trees and all mankind, have their own appointed Names.

Adam named all the animals which God created and brought to him to name. Genesis 2:19-20.

Birds and animals have their names, for "bird" or "animal" are not proper names.

And this is so for all creation. In mankind, fathers, mothers, brothers, sisters, and sons and daughters all have their proper names. These designations only express family relationship.

How much more shall the Father God name His Only Begotten Son?

Jesus is called "The SON of David," expressing Kingship. Matthew 9:27.
He is called "The SON of Man," speaking of His humanity. Matthew 16:13.
He is called "The SON of Abraham," fulfilling the Covenant Seed. Matthew 1:1.
He is also called "The SON of God," expressing His absolute Deity as the Only begotten of the Father. Matthew 16:16.

None of the above are proper Names. Abraham, Isaac and Jacob had their sons, but never named them "Son." Each son had a proper name.

If earthly fathers give to their sons proper names, shall not the Heavenly Father give to HIS SON a proper Name? John 3:16; Matthew 3:17.

"Unto us a child is born, unto us A SON is given..." Isaiah 9:6-9.
"A virgin shall conceive and bear A SON and shall call His Name IMMANU-EL ..." Isaiah 7:14.

For this reason Agur asks "What is His Son's Name...if thou canst tell?" Proverbs 30:4.

Not one verse, from Genesis to Revelation, ever declares that "SON is His Name." The Scripture does expressly state what the Name of the Son is. Therefore, what is THE SON'S NAME?

3. "HOLY SPIRIT" is not the Holy Spirit's Name.

"Holy Spirit' is not a proper Name, but expressly refers to the Third Person in the Eternal Godhead.

The Holy Spirit is co-equal and co-eternal with the Father and the Son. He is designated as the HOLY Spirit to distinguish Him from all other created spirits, good or evil.

Angels are created and are ministering spirits. Hebrews 1:14.
Man is essentially a spirit being, housed in a mortal body.
I Thessalonians 5:23.
Demons or devils are created, but fallen, spirits.
Satan himself is a created being and a fallen spirit being.
God is the Father of all spirits. Hebrews 12:9.

All spirits are created of God. The HOLY SPIRIT is uncreated; He is part of the very essence and being of God. He is designated to distinguish Him from all created spirits, whether good or evil, angelic, human or demonic. All spirits have names.

Never does it state that "The Holy Spirit is His Name."

The Holy Spirit has many Titles. The Holy Spirit is known and understood through many symbols.

> He is called "The Spirit of Grace." Hebrews 10:29.
> He is called "The Spirit of Holiness." Romans 1:4.
> He is called "The Spirit of Truth." John 14:26; 15:26.
> He is called "The Spirit of Judgment and the Spirit of Burning."
> Isaiah 4:3-4.

And He is called by many other Titles, all of which set forth some attribute, or some characteristic phase of His ministry in the redemptive plan.

He is known also under the symbols of a Dove, Oil, Rivers of Living Water, Dew, and others. Each symbol sets forth some typical function of His ministrations in the Church.

None of these are proper Names. He is THE Holy Spirit, the Third in the Eternal Godhead, indwelling the multitude of believers. He shares in the compound Name of the Godhead.

"Holy Spirit" is not a Name, but a Person, expressing relationship in the Godhead.

What then is THE SPIRIT'S NAME?

The Scriptures never declare that "Father, Son and Holy Spirit" is THE NAME of God but simply declares this to express the Eternal relationship existing in the Godhead.

If Baptism is to be "In THE NAME OF the Father, and OF the Son, and OF the Holy Spirit" and "Father, Son and Holy Spirit" are not proper Names, then WHAT is THE NAME OF THE FATHER, AND OF THE SON, AND OF THE HOLY SPIRIT?

This brings us to the answer to this question in the following sections.

THE NAME OF THE FATHER

What then is THE FATHER'S NAME?

The dictionary defines "Name" as "a word, or phrase by which a person, thing or class is known, a title."

It defines the word "Title" as "the Name of a poem, book, picture, etc." The truth we are searching for here is that which pertains to the PROPER NAME of God; not any Name or any Title.

God has unmistakably revealed what His proper Name is. This Name is not a mere title.

Therefore, what is THE NAME of THE FATHER? Let the Scriptures speak for themselves; both Old and New Testaments.

THE OLD TESTAMENT

The great outstanding Person and Presence in the Old Testament Age is that of God the Father. The Son of God is seen in Theophanic revelation. The Spirit of God is spoken of also. But the Old Testament is pre-eminently the ministry and revelation of God the Father.

It is there that the Father's Name is first revealed. This Name was declared to Moses at the burning bush. Exodus 3:1-15. In reality, the Name given to Moses here is actually the Name of Elohim, which is the uni-plural word for the Triune God. It is actually the Name of the Godhead, Father, Son and Holy Spirit. Thus God spoke to Israel saying, "YAHWEH our ELOHIM is one YAHWEH." Deuteronomy 6:4. That is, Jehavah God is a compound Jehovah God. The Triune God was revealed in Israel's National Tenet of Faith. However, in the Covenantal and Redemptive revelation of God to His people, THE FATHER GOD is the First Person in the order of Self-revelation. Let the Student refresh his mind again on this Section as covered earlier in these notes.

Moses asks: "What is His Name?" God answers: "I AM THAT I AM: Thus shall ye say I AM hath sent me unto you." verse 14.

And then in verse 15, God continues to speak saying, "Thus shall ye say, the LORD God of your fathers hath sent me unto you. This is MY NAME, forever; and this is My memorial unto all generations."

There can be no mistake in the declaration of the Father's Name.

> "This is my Name forever, and My memorial unto all generation."
> Exodus 3:15.
> "The LORD is His Name." Exodus 15:3.
> "I am the LORD, that is My Name." Isaiah 42:8.
> "The LORD is His Name." Jeremiah 33:2.
> "The LORD is His Name." Amos 5:8.
> "They shall know that My Name is the LORD." Jeremiah 16:21.
> "That men may know that Thou whose Name alone is JEHOVAH." Psalms 83:18.

Nothing could be plainer than that set forth in these Scriptures. Never does it state that "FATHER" is His Name, but continually does it declare that "The LORD is His Name."

This Name is used thousands of times in the Old Testament. Of no other Name or Title is God so emphatic. This is the Name of His Self-revelation.

"Whosoever shall call on the Name of the Lord shall be delivered." Joel 2:32.

THE NEW TESTAMENT

The New Testament confirms that Name which is declared in the Old Testament. It is not just a mere Title, but the proper Name of God, the Father's Name.

> "Whosoever shall call on the Name of the LORD shall be saved." Acts 2:21.
> "The Lord said unto my LORD." Acts 2:34. The Father speaking to the Son calls Him "LORD." The Father is Lord, and the Son is Lord. Refer also to Mark 12:29-36.
> "Seasons of refreshing shall come from the Presence of the Lord." Acts 3:19.
> "The LORD your God shall raise up a prophet like unto Moses." Acts 3:22.
> "Blessed is He (The Son) who cometh in the Name of the LORD (The Father's Name)." John 12:13.
> "I am come in My Father's Name." John 5:43. i.e., The Name of the LORD.
> "I thank Thee Father, LORD of heaven and earth." Luke 10:21. cf. Matthew 11:25-26.
> "LORD God Almighty..." Revelation 16:7.

It will be remembered that the Hebrew word is <u>YAHWEH</u>, or, I AM WHO I AM,
the English translate it <u>JEHOVAH</u>, or LORD,
the Greek word is <u>KURIOS</u>.

No Greek word was found to adequately express the glory of that Name of God as in the Hebrew language. Even though the Greek writers quoted Old Testament passages where "LORD" was used, they could only use the equivalent, yet inadequate word, "KURIOS," or "LORD."

Some contend that the Name "LORD" is a mere Name, or Title, and simply means "Master." This robs the Lord God of the full glory that He expresses in this proper Name. How meaningless it would be if every verse was translated "MASTER God" instead of "LORD GOD." The richness of the redemptive Name is lost if this is all that this glorious Name means.

This thought will be amplified further when the application of this Name "LORD" is seen in the Name of the "<u>LORD</u> Jesus Christ."

In the appropriate section it will be shown how the Father, Son and Holy Spirit share in the Name "LORD" as revealed in the burning bush. For our present consideration, this is firstly the Name of the Father. The Father is First Person in the order of redemptive purpose, then the Son, and then the Holy Spirit. Hence, the Father bears the Name "LORD" first.

THE FATHER'S NAME IS "LORD."

This is "The Name" that Jesus taught us to hallow.
"Our <u>Father</u>, which art in heaven, hallowed by <u>Thy Name</u>." Matthew 6:9.

This is the Name which He said He had revealed, declared and manifested to His Disciples.
"<u>Father</u>...I have manifested <u>Thy Name</u> unto them." John 17:6, 11-12, 26.

This is the Name He ministered in.
"I am come in <u>My Father's Name.</u>" John 5:43.

This is the Name that He commanded His disciples to baptize in, saying, "Baptizing them in <u>THE NAME of THE FATHER</u>..." Matthew 28:19.

The Name of the Father is "<u>LORD</u>." Read also Revelation 3:12 and 14:1.

AND OF THE SON

Agur's prophetic question asked, "What is His Name, and what is HIS SON'S NAME, if thou canst tell?" Proverbs 30:4.

The first part of this verse also asks, "Who hath ascended up into heaven, and who hath descended?"

The answer is given for us in the New Testament Scriptures that it was THE SON of God who ascended after He first descended into the lower parts of the earth.

Compare these Scriptures: John 3:13; 6:62; Ephesians 4:8-10; Acts 2:34; Romans 10:6.

Each of these verses tell that it was the Son of God who ascended back to the Father after accomplishing the work of redemption at Calvary. Now He is seated at the Father's Right Hand as the exalted Son.

Hence, it is this verse which asks the questions concerning the Father's Name and the Son's Name.

Jesus commanded His disciples to "Baptize in THE NAME OF the Father, AND OF the Son..." Matthew 28:19.

The Father's Name has unmistakably been declared as "LORD." And there should be no doubt in any believer's mind about THE SON'S NAME. Every true believer counts this Name as the sweetest Name on mortal tongue. Untold millions of Hymns and Songs have been written about the glory, the preciousness, the virtue and power of THE SON'S NAME.

Never does the Scripture say that "SON" is His Name. The Son's Name is not "Son" for "Son" is not a proper Name as has already been noted.

Let the Scriptures speak for themselves once more concerning the Son's Name.

The Angel Gabriel said to the Virgin Mary, "Thou shalt bring forth A SON...and thou shalt call HIS NAME "JESUS." Luke 1:26-32.

The Angel spoke to Joseph in a dream concerning his espoused wife, Mary, saying, "She shall bring forth A SON...and thou shalt call HIS NAME 'JESUS.' And she brought forth her firstborn Son and called His Name 'JESUS.'" Matthew 1:21 through 25.

To Mary and to Joseph the Son's Name was given before His birth. There is no chance of a mistake here.

It is worthy to see the fulfillment of the Rite of Circumcision here, for, even though the Name was given before birth, it was not actually declared or invoked upon the Holy Child until the eighth day, which was the day of the Rite of Circumcision when all children born in Israel were named according to the "Covenant of Circumcision." Compare Genesis 17 with Acts 7:8.

The Name was given or provided by God, but it was invoked by the Priest in the Temple at circumcision.

> "And when eight days were accomplished for the circumcising of the Child, HIS NAME was called 'JESUS' which was so Named of the Angel..." Luke 2:21.

It is the privilege of all fathers to Name their sons. Thus God the Father Named His Only Begotten Son. The Father God publicly acknowledged that Jesus was His Son. Matthew 3:17; 17:5. No controversy exists over the Son's Name.

It is <u>not</u> the Father's Name.
It is <u>not</u> the Spirit's Name. It never was, nor ever can be. It is eternally the Son's Name. This Name can never be applied to any other Person in the Godhead. It is the central Person's Name, the Name of the Son. It was this Name that was nailed to the Cross. Matthew 27:37. It is this Name which is the answer to the questions of Jacob, of Manoah, and of Agur. It is this Name which was the "Wonderful Secret" which could not be revealed until the Son was manifested in the flesh in His incarnation and Virgin Birth. It is the Name of the Eternal Word, THE WORD made FLESH. John 1:1-3, 14, 18. It is the Name of His sinless Humanity.

Though the Son of God has <u>many Names and Titles</u>, only this Name is His distinct, unique and peerless personal Name.

<u>"What is His Son's Name</u>, if though canst tell?" Proverbs 30:4, compare with Isaiah 7:14; 9:6.

<u>The Son's Name is "JESUS."</u>

Thus we are to Baptize in "THE NAME of the Father, and of the Son..." Matthew 28:19. That is, "THE NAME of the LORD...JESUS..."

AND OF THE HOLY SPIRIT

Continuing to use the Law of Interpretation of Names, we come to the third part of the Triune Name.

Having established from the Scriptures the Name of the Father as "LORD" and the Name of the Son as "JESUS," let us approach the Name in which the Holy Spirit's work and ministry is to be known and understood.

The Prophetic question of Agur in Proverbs 30:4 was two-fold, enquiring after the Name of the Father and the Name of the Son. No question is asked there concerning the Name of the Holy Spirit.

The questions concerning the Father's Name and the Son's Name have been answered. But what of the Name of the Holy Spirit? Does the Holy Spirit have a Name? What is the Name that the Holy Spirit is to be recognized in?

It is worth pointing out in this part of our study that the Holy Spirit, the third Person in the Godhead, does not speak of Himself. He ever points to the Father and to the Son; and though He is the Inspirer of the Word of God, He only speaks that which is given Him to speak. He does not glorify Himself, but always speaks and represents another. John 14:13-15.

There seems to be but one reference to "The Name...of the Holy Spirit." Matthew 28:19. This is in union with the Father and the Son.

This self-effacing ministry of the Holy Spirit, especially relative to His Name, is typified for us in Genesis 24. There Abraham (the Father) sends for his Servant (Unnamed in the chapter, but Named in Genesis 15:1-3), to seek a Bride for his Only Begotten Son, Isaac.

The Servant does not speak of himself, but points the Bride to the Father Abraham and to the Only Son, Isaac. He does not mention his Name once in this chapter.

All of this typifies the ministrations of the Godhead. The Father God, typified in Abraham, sends His Holy Spirit, as typified in the Unnamed Servant, to seek a Bride, which is the type of the Church, for His Only Begotten Son, Jesus Christ.

The Holy Spirit does not speak of Himself or His own Name but ever points to the Father and the Son.

Therefore, in no specific Scripture does the Holy Spirit state, "This...is My Name."

This is not to say, however, that the Holy Spirit is not recognized in some Name, for He is. There is some Name in which the Spirit is to be known and understood.

This is seen by the very command of Jesus, as in Matthew 28:19, for the Ordinance of Baptism is to be "in THE NAME OF the Father, and OF the Son, AND OF THE HOLY SPIRIT."

This is implied in Zechariah 14:9, "In that day there shall be one Lord and His Name one." That is, a compound Name.

It is <u>one Name</u> according to Matthew's Gospel. It is a <u>compound Name</u> or a united Name according to Zechariah. Matthew 28:19.

The Name of the Lord Jesus Christ is a compound Name, and it is a Name in which the Father, Son and Holy Spirit share.

According to the command of Jesus, there must be a Name in which the Father, Son and Holy Spirit share a co-equal part and it is this Name which is to be invoked in baptism. It is a three-in-one Name and a one-in-three Name, or simply, a Triune Name.

The one and only Triune or compound redemptive Name revealed in tri-unity in the whole Bible from Genesis to Revelation is THE NAME of the LORD - JESUS - CHRIST.

1. THE FATHER'S NAME is translated as LORD, as seen in the first part of the Triune Name.

2. THE SON'S NAME is translated as JESUS, as seen in the central part of the Triune Name.

3. THE HOLY SPIRIT'S NAME is interpreted and revealed in ministry in the third part of the Triune Name, in the Name CHRIST or, more correctly, in the CHRISMA.

The only remaining part of the Triune Name is the third part, and as we interpret the meaning of this Name, it will be found that the Holy Spirit is revealed in and through this part of the Triune Name.

If the Holy Spirit is not recognized in this part of the Triune Name, even as the Father and the Son are recognized in the first and central parts, then where is He to be recognized? For He is a partaker and sharer of "THE NAME," the TRI-UNE NAME.

Let us turn to the Scriptures and amplify these statements. As the significance of the Name "CHRIST" is considered, the truth hidden therein may be discovered.

Generally speaking, there is no problem or misunderstanding concerning the Name of the Father, or the Name of the Son, but difficulty and misunderstanding arises over the Name in which the Holy Spirit is recognized. For this reason this portion of our study is developed more fully in order to help us appreciate and understand that which is implied in the Name "CHRIST."

A distinct and manifest reference to the Holy Spirit is found in the Epistle of John, I John 2:20, 27. We quote the portions of verses under consideration.

1. "Ye have an UNCTION (ANOINTING) from the Holy One." I John 2:20.
2. "The ANOINTING teacheth you of all things." I John 2:27.
3. "The ANOINTING which ye have received of Him abideth in you." I John 2:27.

Here are found three explicit references to the Holy Spirit as THE ANOINTING.

A Prophecy confirming this is found in Isaiah 10:27.

"The yoke shall be destroyed because of THE ANOINTING." i.e., Because of the Holy Spirit.

The Greek word for "ANOINTING" is "CHRISMA," which is the Greek NAME for "OIL."

The Holy Spirit is the Anointing, the Oil, the Divine Unction, the Chrisma. This is HIS NAME. This is "the Name as ointment (anointing) poured forth." Song of Solomon 1:3. The Name is significant of the Nature or the Ministry of the Spirit. What then is THE NAME of the HOLY SPIRIT? His Name is expressed in "CHRISMA," the Anointing Oil, the Holy Oil. As oil is one of the most prominent symbols of the Holy Spirit in the Scripture, it is most fitting that this noun or name be used of the Spirit because it is significant of His ministry and work.

The very Name "CHRIST" actually involves the Godhead as Father, Son and Holy Spirit, in Divine operation. This may be seen in the Greek words involved in that which pertains to the Anointing.

1. CHRIO (Greek. (Verb)

    The Anointer - The Father is the One who anoints. He who is the Anointer. Luke 4:18; Acts 4:27; II Corinthians 1:21; Hebrews 1:9. "God anointed (Chrio) Jesus of Nazareth with the Holy Ghost and power." Acts 10:38.

2. CHRISTOS (Greek. (Noun)

    The Anointed - The Son is the One who is anointed. He who is Anointed. John 1:41. "We have found the Messiah, which being interpreted is, the Christ." Matthew 14:16; 26:63; John 6:69; 11:27; 20:31. Used about 360 times in the New Testament.

3. CHRISMA (Greek. (Noun)

    The Anointing - The Holy Spirit is the One who is the anointing. He who is the Anointing. I John 2:20, 27, 29. "The Anointing which abides...teaches you." The Hebrew word for "Anointing" is "Mishchah." Exodus 29:7, 21; 30:25, 31; Leviticus 8:10; 12, 30. The Hebrew word for "Anointing" in Isaiah 10:27 is "Shemen," or "Oil."

Iranaeus, one of the Early Church Fathers, wrote concerning Baptism in the Name of "Christ" on this wise.

"By Baptism in the Name of CHRIST, is to be understood;
He who anointed,
He who was anointed,
And the anointing itself by which He was anointed;
In other words, FATHER, SON and HOLY SPIRIT."
    (Jones, Catholic Doctrine of the Trinity, Page 57, 83, Vol. II.
        Iranaeus 50.3., 100.20.)

The source of the Name "CHRIST" and the Name "CHRISMA" is found in the verb "CHRIO," thus the Godhead is involved in the interpretation of this Name.

Who is the Divine Unction? Who is the Divine Chrisma? Who is the ANOINTING OIL?

The HOLY SPIRIT is and only may be expressed as the "Chrisma," or "The Anointing."

It was the CHRISMA that made Jesus of Nazareth the CHRISTOS.
It was the ANOINTING that made Him the ANOINTED.

For 30 years the Son of God was known as Jesus of Nazareth, but when He was anointed by the Father God in the River Jordan with the Holy Spirit, the Anointing Oil, from then on He was known as JESUS CHRISTOS or Jesus ANOINTED! It was only after the Holy Spirit came upon the Son of God that He was publicly and officially recognized in Jewry as the Christ, the Messiah, the Anointed.

Though He was born "A Saviour which is Christ the Lord" (Luke 2:11), He did not receive the fulness of that which is in these Names until the appointed times. This will be seen in the subsequent chapter.

Who or what made Him the Anointed? Who or what made Him the Christ? It was the Anointing, the Oil, the Holy Spirit. The Anointing constituted Him The Anointed! The Chrisma made Him the Christos!

Thus wherever and whenever the New Testament uses this Name "Christ," it is done with the understanding of the interpretation of that Name. It always involves the Holy Spirit as the Anointing Oil.

The early believers were first called "CHRISTIANS" at Antioch. Acts 11:26. I Peter 4:16. Why? Because they belonged to Christ, and because of the Anointing upon them.

A CHRISTian is an Anointed one, one who has received the Holy Spirit in Anointing, even as Jesus became the Christ by reason of the Holy Spirit in anointing upon Him.

This does not make us the Christ of God, but it is significant of the fact that the anointing which was upon the HEAD does flow down upon the BODY, even the Church. Psalms 133; II Corinthians 1:21.

This is the reason why the Name "Christ" is used more explicitly in the Epistles. It is never used promiscuously.

Hence the Church is called "The Body of CHRIST." I Corinthians 12:27.
Paul speaks of the Mystery of "CHRIST in you, the Hope of Glory."
Colossians 1:27.
Again, when speaking of the history of Israel, he reminds the Corinthians, that "The Rock that followed them (Israel) was CHRIST." I Corinthians 10: 4. That is, the Rock was Anointed. It was the Anointed Rock, anointed with oil.

This Name is a Name used for the Head of the Church and His Body.

"As the Body is one, and hath many members, and all the members of that one Body, being many, are one Body, so also is <u>CHRIST</u>." I Corinthians 12: 12.

The reason the BODY is called "CHRIST" is because of the Person and Presence of the Holy Spirit as Anointing Oil upon both Head and Body.

Any Scripture read in the light of these things will always show the Presence of the Holy Spirit either upon Jesus, the Head of the Church, or upon the members of the Church which is His Body.

The Name "CHRISMA" interpreted is that part of the Triune Name used to designate the Holy Spirit is His Anointing ministry, upon the Son of God, or upon the believers. It is used to designate the nature and characteristic function of the Holy Spirit; that is, the Anointing manifested.

(Note: Sometimes the question is raised concerning Scriptures which speak of "The Blood of CHRIST." Hebrews 9:14. It means "The Blood of the ANOINTED." Jesus was that Anointed One. It was His Blood. But who or what made Him the Anointed? It was the Anointing, the Holy Spirit upon Him. And it was by the Eternal Spirit He was able to offer Himself without spot to God.

The truth here is that it was the <u>CHRISMA</u> (Anointing) which made Him the CHRIST (Anointed). If this fact is kept in mind, then any Scripture read in the light of these statements will be clearly understood. The Name "Christ" always involves the Person and Presence of the HOLY SPIRIT upon the Son of God. The Name "Christian" always involves the Person and Presence of the Holy Spirit in Anointing on the believers, the Church.)

Thus whether the Scriptures use "Christ," or "Christ Jesus," or "Jesus Christ," or the "Lord Jesus Christ," it is that third part of the Triune Name interpreted which involves the Person and Presence and Unction of the Holy Spirit as Oil, the Anointing manifested.

<u>In the Old Testament:</u>

1. The <u>Priests</u> were anointed at 30 years of age. Psalms 133; Exodus 29:7; 30:30; 28:41; Leviticus 4:3.
2. The <u>Prophets</u> were anointed. I Kings 19:16-19; cp Isaiah 61:1.
3. The <u>Kings</u> were anointed. I Samuel 10:1; 16:13; 9:16; I Kings 1:34, 39, 45; Psalms 89:20.
4. The <u>Tabernacle</u> was anointed, with all the vessels to be used in ministry before Jehovah. Exodus 40:10, 11; 30:26; Leviticus 8:10; Numbers 7:1, 10, 84, 88.
5. The <u>leper's</u> cleansing involved anointing with oil. Leviticus 14:4-18.
6. The <u>Rock</u> "Bethel" was anointed by Jacob, the third person of that trinity of men, Abraham, Isaac and Jacob. Genesis 28:18; I Corinthians 10:4; Genesis 31:13.
7. All these Offices and things were prophetic types of the Son of God. These Offices of Prophet, Priest and King were called "<u>JEHOVAH'S A-NOINTED</u>."

Read these Scriptures.   Psalms 105:15;   I Samuel 2:10, 35; 12:3-5; 16:6;
Psalms 2:2; 45:7; 20:6; 84:9; Zechariah 4:14; Isaiah 45:1.

We ask, What made these persons "The Anointed" or "Messiahs?" The answer is
evident.   It was when the Holy Anointing Oil was poured upon them. Exodus 30:
22-33.

It was THE ANOINTING (Chrisma) which made them THE ANOINTED (Christos, Messiahs).

They could not be "The Anointed" without "The Anointing."

The Hebrew word for "Anointed" is "Mishchah." Daniel 9:24; John 1:41.
The Greek word for "Anointed" is "Christos." John 1:41; 4:25.

All of these things pointed to Jesus of Nazareth, who would be THE Messiah,
THE Christ, THE Lord's ANOINTED (Psalms 2:2).

He is Prophet, Priest, King, Tabernacle, Bethel-Rock, and He was anointed in
Jordan by the Father with the Holy Spirit.

Most Bible Students agree that the Anointing Oil is one of the most prominant
and distinct symbols of the Holy Spirit, His function and characteristic mini-
stration.

The Holy Spirit Himself is "The Holy Divine Oil." He Himself is "The Anointing
Oil."

This symbol is wonderful in its illustration of the Person, Work and Ministry
of the Spirit.   It is the Father's own appointed symbol of the Holy Spirit,
both in Old and New Testaments.   It sets forth typically the nature and function of the Holy Spirit.   Joshua and Zerubbabel are called "The Two Anointed
Ones," or "The Sons of Oil" by reason of this anointing upon them for the work
of restoration. Zechariah 4:14, with Marginal reference.

In David's anointing by Samuel, we see the Holy Spirit working in connection
with the symbol of His own Being.   When the oil was poured upon him, then the
Spirit (the Divine OIL) came upon him.   This constituted "The Anointing."
I Samuel 16:13.   .

Hence it is befitting that God should use this most prominant symbol to help
us understand the NAME of the Spirit, particularly as it is used in the Triune
Name.

In the Name "Christ" is hidden the symbol of the Holy Spirit, that is, "Oil."

This Holy Oil was commanded and ordained of God as to its ingredients. It was
given by revelation of God and made by the wisdon of God. It was "Most Holy,"
and not to be substituted, imitated or poured on flesh. It was for service to
God alone (Exodus 30:22-33).

All of this shadowed forth the Person and Operations of the Blessed Spirit of
God, the Divine Chrisma. "CHRISTOS" represents the work of the Holy Spirit.

There are many types and shadows of the Son of God, the Sacrificed One, set forth in the Old Testament. And it has pleased God to shadow forth the Holy Spirit in all these persons, places and things that were anointed with the Holy Anointing all.

An interesting area is that set out in Webster's and Collin's English Dictionaries concerning the "Chrisma." Following are a number of related words which show how A NAME was so often involved in the "Chrisma."

1. Chrism - Noun, Holy oil. Oil which was used in the administration of baptism, ordination and extreme unction.
2. Chrisma - An unguent, from Chriein, to rub, anoint.
3. Chrismation - The act of applying the chrism, or consecrated oil.
4. Chrismal - A vessel to hold the holy oil.
5. Chrismon - A monogram formed of the first two letters in the Greek Name of Christ.
6. Christen - To give a Name in baptism; to christen a child.
   To baptize (a person) as a religious rite. To baptize in the Name of Christ.
   To Name; to denominate; applied to things.
7. Christening - The act of conferring baptism, especially when accompanied by the Naming of the baptized.

Kittel's Theological Dictionary of the New Testament (p. 493-580) gives an exhaustive section on the history and development of the Hebrew and Greek words for "Anointed."

The anointing meant the oiling of the body or parts of it. It was also used in healing ministry. This was to be distinguished from that anointing as understood in a legal action. The Old Testament anointing involved oil being poured upon the head of the one anointed. The aim of this was to give to the anointed one power, strength and dignity. Sometimes this was done by pouring out oil out a horn (I Samuel 16:13; I Kings 1:39), or a vessel (I Samuel 10:1; II Kings 9:3, 6). It was generally done at Yahweh's command, and was significant of the Spirit and charge coming upon that individual.

The Messianic ideas took time to develop in Israel. This is seen in the Historical Books, the Kingly Psalms as well as through the writings of the Prophets. Psalms 2:6; 110:1, 3; 89:19; 132:11.

The New Testament brings the Messianic expectations to their full clarity as in the person and ministry of Jesus Christ.

In various forms the Title or Name "Christ" occurs about 529 times altogether in the New Testament, 379 of these being Pauline usage, and the rest distributed among the other writers. The emphasis is upon the Messiahship of Jesus of Nazareth. The Epistles of Paul make particular emphasis on this Name "Christ." It is not used promiscuously.

In the non-Christian world, where the word CHRISTOS was not understood, it became a nickname or an assumed name attached to the Name of Jesus or to the disciples of Jesus. It was practically unintelligible except in tne world of Judaism.

Though at first recognized as a Title, it is at Antioch that CHRISTOS was taken to be a proper Name outside of the believing community, probably being the name of a god in the understanding of the heathen. As time developed it became a second Name attached to the personal Name of Jesus.

The Johannine writings and some of the early fathers show that awareness of the questions posed by CHRISTOS as being very much alive.

"The Companion Bible" comments on Acts 11:26 saying, "Though the Name (Christian) may have been given first by the Gentiles in mockery, the usage of the word by the Holy Spirit indicates its real origin was Divine. The Jews could not have given the Name. "Christos" was to them a sacred word."

On "CHRISMA" Kittel writes:

> When the community is assaulted by antichrists it can resist only in the power of the Spirit, the chrisma, 2:20, 27. The use of this term, which means "anointing oil" implies that the community is anointed with the Spirit, this being the basis of the fact that it belongs to Christ. Chrisma imparts to the community its comprehensive knowledge..which confers on it the clarity of faith and judgment and the assurance in life and decision that comes from its relationship to God. This statement about the chrisma of the community is directly connected with what Christ says about the paraklates in John 14:8-10, 13. The community has received the chrisma as a power which remains in it and gives it comprehensive and reliable instructions, 2:27...chrisma which is itself the teacher.... This shows how strongly in John the understanding of the Messiah is determined by the anointing of the Spirit and how the relation between the Son and the sons, which is based on reception of the Spirit, finds an echo in the connection between the anointed One and tne anointed."

Kittel's Theological Dictionary of New Testament words, p. 572.

In a footnote under the same subject of the anointing, p. 580, Kittel notes:

> The symbolism and sacrament of anointing, as well as many Christian and Gnostic speculations, rest on this. God the Father anointed Christ with the Spirit. Luke 4:18. Christ anoints the world and the Church. This stress on anointing retains the true content of the title or name Christ in the sense of active or passive unction. (Emphasis mine)

The Son of God, Jesus of Nazareth, is indeed the Christ of God but it was the Divine CHRISMA, the Holy Spirit as that Holy Oil which constituted Him in that ministry and office. It is in this significance that the Holy Spirit is known and understood in the third part of the Triune Name.

In summary we gather together the main facts of this section of our study.

1. The Baptismal Command demands the invocation of the Name of the Father, and of the Son, and of the Holy Spirit, or a Triune Name. Matthew 28:19.

2. The only Triune Name in the whole revelation of God is the Triune Name of the LORD - JESUS - CHRIST.

3. The Scripture in Matthew's Gospel is the one and only specific Scripture which speaks of the Father, Son and Holy Spirit in association with "THE NAME." It shows that Father, Son and Holy Spirit are sharers and partakers together of A NAME, spoken of as "THE NAME," and that this Name is the Name of the Godhead. Therefore it must be a Triune Name in which Father, Son, and Holy Spirit share a co-equal part. One Name, yet a Compound Name!

4. By the Law of Interpretation and Significance of Names, as well as by the Scriptures themselves, these conclusions present themselves:

     The Father's Name is "LORD."
     The Son's Name is "JESUS."
     The Holy Spirit's Name is "CHRISMA."

5. This command recognizes Father, Son and Holy Spirit as Three Divine Persons, co-equal in glory, majesty, honour, and power, sharers and partakers together in the same Divine Name, the Triune Name of the Eternal Godhead, which is THE NAME of the LORD - JESUS - CHRIST.

     It is this Sacred Name of God which is to be invoked in Water Baptism, bringing the believer into full Covenant relationship with the Godhead.

6. It is in this way that the Holy Spirit is partaker of the Triune Name and is to be understood in THE NAME of the Father, and of the Son, and of the Holy Spirit in obeying the Baptismal Command.

                              (Of the Father,
Thus to baptize "In THE NAME (And of the Son,
                              (And of the Holy Spirit,

                              (LORD
is to baptize "In THE NAME of the (JESUS
                              (CHRIST.

Lucy P. Knott, in "The Triune Name," Nazarene Publishing House, p. 30, 31, writes concerning the Name of the Lord Jesus Christ saying:

     "Only the Triune God could conceive such a name; presenting the Persons of the Trinity in three names--Father, Son and Holy Ghost; and then in the New Testament showing forth the Trinity in one Name--the Lord Jesus Christ.

     Let us give a brief resume of the introductions of the previous chapters.

          (1) The Name "Lord," shows forth the wisdom, foreknowledge and love of the Father. This wisdom, foreknowledge and

love, He hides in the Son for the execution of all His plans and purposes. The Name "Lord" also identifies the Son as the Jehovah of the Old Testament.

(2) The Name "Jesus," shows forth the <u>humility</u>, <u>humanity</u>, <u>sufferings</u> and <u>example</u> of the <u>Son</u> who is made the <u>visible</u> active agent of the Godhead.

(3) The Name "Christ," shows forth the <u>power of the Holy Ghost</u>. This power was poured out upon the Son "without measure," for the execution of the Father's eternal plans and purposes."

CHAPTER VI

THE DUAL APPLICATION OF THE TRIUNE NAME

A careful study of "The Name" in the New Testament revelation shows that there is a twofold application of the Triune Name.

(1) The Triune Name of the Lord Jesus Christ is the Name of the Triune God. It is the Name of the Father, Son and Holy Spirit, the Godhead Name.

(2) The Triune Name of the Lord Jesus Christ is also the Name of the Fulness of the Godhead Bodily.

Much misunderstanding can arise through failure to recognize this truth. Therefore under this subheading, we consider the dual aspect of the Triune Name.

(1) THE NAME OF THE ETERNAL GODHEAD

As has been seen in the previous chapter, the Name of the Lord Jesus Christ, by interpretation, is the Name which involves the Godhead as Father, Son and Holy Spirit.

The Triune God	and	The Triune Name
The Father		LORD
The Son		JESUS
The Holy Spirit		CHRIST

It is impossible to use this Name without involving the Godhead. This Triune Name is a compound Name. It is the greatest compound Redemptive Name of God ever to be revealed because it comprehends the greatest, even each Person in the Eternal Godhead.

As to the Name "LORD" --

> The Father is LORD. Joel 2:32. Exodus 3:14-15. Psalms 110:1.
> The Son is LORD. I Corinthians 12:3. Acts 2:36.
> The Holy Spirit is LORD. II Corinthians 3:17.

This was especially noted in the revelation of "The Name" of ELOHIM to Moses at the burning bush. The declaration of the Name YAHWEH, or I AM THAT I AM, was the expression of the Name of the Godhead. Exodus 3:14-16.

The Aaronic blessing of "putting the Name" of the LORD upon the nation of Israel also attested to this. The Three-fold invocation of the Name "LORD" was an allusion to the Godhead, Three-in-one and One-in-three implied in that Name. Numbers 6:24-27.

It is also seen in Israel's national tenet of faith. "Hear, O Israel, the LORD our GOD is ONE LORD." Deuteronomy 6:4. That is, a compound LORD; Father, Son and Holy Spirit. One Name yet compounded in Three Divine Persons.

In Matthew 28:19 the Greek construction is "into the Name." It is singular and implies only one Name for Three Divine Persons. The one Name is to be equally and contemporaneously borne by all Three Persons. Matthew's Gospel is the only Gospel written to the Jews and they would know what that Name was as it had been revealed in the Old Testament. Refer again to Numbers 6:24-27 with Deuteronomy 6:4. In the Old Testament YAHWEH (LORD) was the Name of the Triune God. It is the Name of each member of the Godhead.

This is "THE NAME" of the Father, Son and Holy Spirit. This is the ONE NAME spoken of in Matthew 28:19. The New Testament is consistant in retaining the Name "LORD." However, it finds its fullest expression when the Name "LORD" is used in the Triune Name of the "LORD Jesus Christ," or in that COMPOUND NAME.

It was the association of the Name "LORD" (the Name of Deity) with the Name of Jesus Christ that caused the unbelieving Jews to react so violently when anyone called on the Name of the LORD in and through the Name of the LORD Jesus Christ. Acts 7:54-60 with 9:14-16. It was the use of this ONE NAME in the TRIUNE NAME which brought great opposition in the Early Church, as evidenced in the Book of Acts.

Thus the Name "LORD" involves the Godhead as Father, Son and Holy Spirit, but in the order of redemptive revelation and manifestation it is firstly the Father's Name. This Name interpreted reveals Covenantal and Redemptive ministry.

As to the Name "JESUS" :

The Name was quite a common Name amongst the Jews up to the beginning of the second century, A.D. It is the Greek derivation of the Hebrew word "Yahweh." The Name "Jesus" means "Bringing or having salvation," "to save," or "Saviour." "Joshua" or "Jehoshua" is the equivalent, these also meaning "Yahweh is salvation." Joshua 10:12. Acts 7:45. Hebrews 4:8.

As to the Name of Jesus having its derivation in the Name "Yahweh," the significance points us to the truth that the Son came forth from the bosom of the Father God. John 16:27, 28. It shows forth also His union with the Self-existent One, the Eternal Jehovah Elohim.

The Name "JESUS" is the Name of the Son. Luke 2:11. Matthew 1:21-23. Luke 2:26,27. It is the Name of the Son of Man. It is His personal Name, the Name of His sinless humanity. It is the Name the angels used at the ascension. Acts 1:11. It is the Name spoken to Saul on the Damascus road Acts 9:5, 22:8. It is the Name Stephen spoke as he was being stoned. Acts 7:55.

It is not the Name of the Father, nor the Name of the Holy Spirit. It cannot be used for any Person in the Godhead but the Man, our Saviour, Jesus of Nazareth. This Name interpreted reveals His ministry, "He shall save His people from their sins."

As to the Name "CHRIST" :

The Father God is the Anointed (Chrio). Luke 4:18. Acts 10:38.
The Son of God is the Anointed (Christos). Acts 2:36.
The Holy Spirit of God is the Anointing (Chrisma). I John 2:20,27.

This Name involves the Godhead in that which pertains to the Anointing. The Father anointed His Son with the Holy Spirit, the Divine Chrisma, thus constituting Jesus of Nazareth as the Christ of God. That is, the

Lord's Anointed by reason of that Anointing. This Name sets forth the ministry or work of the Spirit upon the Blessed Son of God.

The Name of the LORD - JESUS - CHRIST is the Name of the Godhead.

"The Name" as it relates to the Godhead is complex, each Person being involved. Consider these Scriptures in relation to the Godhead Name.

1. The Father sent the Son in His Name. Jesus said, "I am come in My Father's Name." John 5:43.

2. The Son worked and ministered in the Father's Name. "The works I do in My Father's Name." John 10:25.

3. The Son declared the Father's Name to the disciples. "I have declared unto them Thy Name." John 17:6, 11, 12, 26.

4. The Father gave a Name to His Only Begotten Son before His birth. "Thou shalt call His Name Jesus." Matthew 1:21-23.

5. The Holy Spirit is sent from the Father in the Son's Name. "But the Comforter, which is the Holy Spirit, whom the Father will send in My Name ...." John 14:26.

The Father sent the Son in His Name. The Son ministered in the power of the Father's Name, revealing it to His disciples. The Holy Spirit is sent by the Father in the Name of the Son. The Godhead is totally involved in that which pertains to the Name.

The final commandment of the Saviour is to baptize disciples into THE NAME of the Father, and of the Son and of the Holy Spirit. Matthew 28:19.

The Triune Name of the Lord Jesus Christ is interwoven in compound glory, each part expressing the Divine Persons in God, sharers and partakers together in the same Divine Triune Name. It is in this way that "The Name" is to be understood when invoked in baptism.

(2) THE NAME OF THE GODHEAD BODILY

The other aspect of the Triune Name is that it is also the Name of the Godhead Bodily, the Name of God manifest in the flesh. The Son of God is God manifest in the flesh. I Timothy 3:16. John 1:14-18.

In His Deity He was always LORD and CHRIST. He is the Eternal WORD. It was in His Deity as God the Son that Jesus could proclaim all the "I AM's as seen in the Gospel of John. John 8:56-58; 18:5-8. (Refer to Appendix)

In His Humanity He is made both LORD and CHRIST. The Eternal Son of God laid aside His reputation, emptying Himself, veiling His Deity in Humanity, and taking upon Himself the form of a Servant, becoming a Man subject to the Father. Philippians 2:5-8.

God the Son became MAN for the purpose of redemption. There is One God and One Mediator between God and men, THE MAN Christ Jesus. I Timothy 2:5-6.

Hence it is from the Manward side that we see the majesty of the Triune Name upon the Son. It is the MAN - THE GOD-MAN - who is made both LORD and CHRIST at the set times appointed by the Father.

It is God the Father who made this "JESUS both LORD and CHRIST." Acts 2:36. This Triune Name is given to the Son, and it is the Son's full Name since His exaltation.

It has pleased the Father that in the Son all fulness should dwell. Col. 1:19. The Son of God is the Fulness of the Godhead Bodily.

"For in Him dwelleth (Tabernacles) all the fulness of the Godhead bodily." Col. 2:9.

Because this is so, it has pleased the Father that all the fulness of the GODHEAD NAME dwell in Him also.

In the Mystery of the incarnation Jesus said that the Father indwelt Him. Also the Scripture clearly tells us that He received not the Spirit by measure.

Thus: The Father indwelt the Son. John 14:10-11. II Corinthians 5:19. Hebrews 1:2.

The Son is God manifest in the flesh. John 1:1-3, 14-18. I Timothy 3:16.

The Holy Spirit indwelt the Son. John 3:34, 35.

If the Fulness of the GODHEAD dwells bodily in the Son, so also the Fulness of the GODHEAD NAME dwells in Him. The Church, His Body, is also to be filled with the Fulness of God. John 14:21-26. Ephesians 3:19-21. Ephesians 4:13.

Again this does not make the Son to be the Father or the Holy Spirit. The Father, the Son and the Holy Spirit are eternally distinguished as Father, Son and Holy Spirit, but in the Mystery of Godliness (I Timothy 3:16) the Fulness of the Godhead dwells BODILY in the Son.

The Fulness of the Godhead NAME is given to the Son of God, THE GOD-MAN.

The second aspect of the Triune Name is that the Name of the LORD JESUS CHRIST is the Name of the Godhead BODILY.

The dual application of the Triune Name then is summarized as follows:

1. It is the Name of the Eternal Godhead, the Name of the Father, and of the Son, and of the Holy Spirit.

2. It is the Name of the Godhead BODILY, as given to the Son of God, the Kinsman Redeemer.

This brings us to the consideration of the reception of this Triune Name in the Ministry and Exaltation of the Son of God.

THE REVELATION OF THE TRIUNE NAME AT PENTECOST

The first declaration of the Triune Name was that which was revealed to Peter, the Apostle on the Day of Pentecost in Acts Chapter Two.

It is significant that the revelation of the Triune Name was given under the initial Outpouring of the Holy Spirit at the foundation of the New Testament Church.

An analysis of Acts Chapter Two is set out here:

1. The Outpouring of the Spirit at Pentecost upon the 120 Disciples. vs. 1-13. The gathering of the amazed multitude.

2. Peter's Pentecostal Sermon to the people. vs. 14-36.

3. The first converts added to the Church after fulfilling the condition of membership. vs. 27-47.

The climax of Peter's sermon is the declaration of the Triune Name of the LORD JESUS CHRIST. "Let all the House of Israel know assuredly that God hath made this same JESUS both LORD and CHRIST." Acts 2:36. In other words, God has made His Son, THE LORD JESUS CHRIST.

This is the first declaration or first use of the Name in its Triune form in the New Testament. It came by revelation of the Holy Spirit. The Triune Name is never used in the four Gospels. The full glory of this Triune Name could not be given until the work of redemption was accomplished.

The question arises, "When was Jesus made Lord and Christ?"

Although the Angel declared to the shepherds in the field that "Unto you is born this day in the City of David, a Saviour, which is Christ the Lord" (Luke 2:11), this was prophetic of that which was involved in the reception of the Triune Name in the appointed times.

The revelation of the Name under the Ministry of the Holy Spirit is prophesied of in the Old Testament.

God sent an Angel before Israel to bring them into the Land of Promise. Of this Angel it is said, "Behold, I will send an Angel before thee, to keep thee in the way, and to bring thee into the place which I have prepared. Beware of him and obey his voice, provoke him not, for he will not pardon your transgressions for MY NAME IS IN HIM." Exodus 23:20,21.

The Ministry of this Angel is typical of the Ministry of the Holy Spirit leading and directing the Church into Rest and the Spiritual Land of Promise.

Believers are warned not to transgress against the Holy Spirit or to provoke Him. We are to obey the voice of the Spirit. Blasphemy against the Holy Spirit will not be forgiven. And it is the ministry of the Holy Spirit to bring the revelation of "THE NAME" of God as in the LORD JESUS CHRIST, for "My Name is in Him."

So it was the Holy Spirit who brought to Peter at Pentecost the revelation of the Triune Name of the Triune God. The Holy Spirit is the One who takes of the things of Jesus and makes them known to us. John 16:12-15. On the Day of Pentecost the Holy Spirit brought "The Name" to the Church and used the Apostle Peter to declare this Triune Name, that Jesus had been made both Lord and Christ!

Let us follow the Scriptures which show the application of each part of the Triune Name upon the Son of God.

1. The Name at His Incarnation

   There is no doubt about the Name of the Son of God which He received at His Virgin Birth or the Incarnation. It was the Name "JESUS." "Thou shalt call His Name JESUS." Luke 1:30-31. Matthew 1:21-25.

   For thirty years He was simply known as "JESUS of Nazareth!" He was eternally THE WORD but when The Word was made flesh, He was named "JESUS." This is the Name of His sinless humanity.

2. The Name at His Manifestation

   Though the Name "CHRIST" was declared at His birth (Luke 2:11,26) it was at His Baptism in water in Jordan and the Anointing with the Holy Spirit which qualified Him to function in His Ministry as the Christ or the Messiah.

   Though born of the Spirit and led of the Spirit for thirty years as the Son of God, He did not receive that Anointing of the Holy Spirit for ministry until His inauguration at Jordan's water.

   It was then and there that He was manifested as "The CHRIST" or "The MESSIAH," The Saviour Anointed, publicly and officially. This was the fulfilment of the prophecy of Daniel concerning "Messiah the Prince" being manifested in Israel. Daniel 9:24-26.

   Here God the Father anointed Him with the Holy Spirit, Who is the Anointing, thus making Him the Anointed One. Matthew 3:16,17. Hebrews 1:9. Acts 10:38.

   It was after this that Jesus said, "The Spirit of the Lord is upon Me because He hath anointed Me ..." i.e., made Him the CHRIST. Luke 4:18.

   From now on JESUS of Nazareth is more especially known as JESUS CHRIST! The Saviour Anointed!

   He could not be "THE CHRIST" (The Anointed) without, "The CHRISMA" (The Anointing). Whenever they called Him "Christ" or "Jesus Christ" it always meant, by interpretation of the Name, that He had been anointed with the Holy Spirit, the Divine Oil.

   Peter, by revelation received from the Father, confessed that He was indeed THE CHRIST, the Son of the Living God. Matthew 16:16.

It was at the River Jordan that Jesus was manifested as Messiah Prince. John 1:41.

He was thus declared CHRIST by the Holy Spirit's Anointing upon Him.

3. The Name at His Exaltation

The final part of the Triune Name is "LORD." When was Jesus Christ made "LORD?" When did He receive this part of the Triune Name?

Again it should be remembered that the Name "LORD" was declared in a Titular way at His birth. Luke 2:11, 26. But in realistic way He was made "LORD" in His exaltation. In His Deity He always was "LORD." However, we are looking at the MANHOOD of the Son of God and the glorification and exaltation of THE MAN of Galilee was in the reception of this Name "LORD."

The Scriptures are clear on this fact. The declaration that He was made "LORD" is after His Death, Burial, Resurrection, Ascension and Exaltation to the Father's Right Hand.

He was raised from the dead that He might be "LORD of both the dead and the living." Romans 14:9.

Because He made Himself of no reputation, but took upon Himself the form of a servant, being made in the likeness of men, humbling Himself to the death of the Cross, "God also hath highly exalted Him and given Him A NAME which is above every Name that at the Name of Jesus every knee should bow, of things in heaven, and things in earth, and things under the earth; and that every tongue should confess that JESUS CHRIST is LORD, to the Glory of God the Father." Phil. 2:7-11.

Kittel's Theological Dictionary of the New Testament has a splendid section on JESUS AS LORD (pages 1088-94), from which we quote several statements.

> "Further light is shed by the well known and inexhaustible passage in Phil. 2:6-11 ... The name, which is characterised as a very specific one by the repetition of the article, can only be the name 'kurios.' It is thus given to Jesus as the divine answer to His suffering of death in obedience ....
>
> The name 'kurios' implies a position equal to that of God ....
>
> The name of 'kurios' thus designates the position of the risen Lord.
>
> ... brought out especially in Psalms 110:1. This verse is the only basis for the idea of session at the right hand of God. There is no reference. In this Psalm, however, session is linked with Lordship, and specifically with David's Lord .... Session at the right hand of God means joint rule. It thus implies Divine dignity, as does the very fact of sitting in God's presence."

On the Day of Pentecost, the Apostle Peter declared to the multitude, the Death, Burial and Resurrection of Jesus of Nazareth. He climaxes his address by quoting Old Testament Scriptures which showed that the crowning glory and seal of God upon His Son's redemptive work was in His Ascension, Exaltation and Glorification.

The actual exaltation of the Son of God was in the reception of "The Exalted Name." Acts 2:29-34.

"God hath __made__ that same JESUS who ye have crucified both __LORD__ and CHRIST" Acts 2:36.

The Prophet David in the Psalms, from which Peter quotes, says, "The __LORD__ said unto my __LORD__, Sit Thou at My Right Hand until I make Thine enemies Thy footstool." Psalms 110:1.

This whole Psalm should be particularly noted for it is one of the most important Messianic Psalms quoted in the New Testament.

It is quoted by Jesus Himself (Matthew 22:41-46), by Peter at Pentecost (Acts 2:34-36) and by Paul (Hebrews 10:12,13). All quote the same to confirm the LORDship of Jesus Christ.

Some may ask why Psalms 110:1 uses the Name "ADONAI" after the use of "JEHOVAH." That is, "The LORD (Jehovah, The Father) said unto my LORD (Adonai, The Son), Sit Thou at My Right Hand until I make Thine enemies Thy footstool."

By this is meant that "JEHOVAH" is undoubtedly the Father's Name, but "ADONAI" (translated "LORD") simply means that the Son has been made "Master, or Ruler" over all. Not that He has received the Father's Name, or been made JEHOVAH, or LORD.

However, the Psalm relates to the Priesthood of Jesus Christ after the Order of Melchizedek, and it is to be noted in verse 5 of the same Psalm that the "ADONAI" at the Right Hand of the Father in verse 1 becomes "JEHOVAH" at the Right Hand who will strike through Kings in the Day of Wrath.

Thus the Father is __LORD__ (Jehovah), and He makes His Son "LORD," ADONAI, JEHOVAH.

Worthy of repetition is that paragraph which has been quoted in an earlier section from "The Companion Bible."

The Companion Bible states: "ADONAI is the Lord in His relation to the earth, and as carrying out His purposes or blessing in the earth. With this limitation it is almost equivalent to JEHOVAH. Indeed, it was from an early date so used, by associating the vowel points of the word Jehovah with Adon, thus converting Adon into Adonai."

"A list of 134 passages where this was deliberately done is preserved and given in the Massorah." (Appendix 4. VIII 2.)

And again we quote from The Companion Bible: "Out of extreme (but mistaken) reverence for the Ineffable Name, "Jehovah," the Ancient custodians of the Sacred Text substituted in many places "Adonai." These in the A. V., and R. V., are all printed 'Lord'. In all these places we have printed it ... marking the word ... to inform the reader." (Appendix 32)

Whenever the New Testament Scriptures quote Old Testament passages with the Name "Lord" therein, they use the equivalent (though inadequate) Greek word "KURIOS," meaning "Sir," "Master," "Lord."

If the reader will bear the repetition of this point, it is worthy to remind ourselves that many if not all, of the New Testament Scriptures would become empty and meaningless, robbed of their full significance, if the "LORD Jesus" simply means "Sir," or "Master Jesus."

"Whosoever shall call on the Name of the LORD (Sir, Master?) shall be saved." Romans 10:13. Acts 2:21.

"God has made this same Jesus both LORD (Sir, Master?) and Christ." Acts 2:36.

Jesus is spoken of as "LORD" numerous times in the New Testament. To undervalue or minimize this Name to a mere title is to rob Him of His Deity and exaltation as the God-Man.

To the Jew the Name "LORD" was the Name of Deity. Thousands of Jews would rather die than call Caesar "LORD," as many of the Roman Emperors were acknowledged to be. To ascribe LORDship to a man was utter blasphemy and idolatry. It was ascribing the Name of Deity to mere man.

It was for this reason that Saul persecuted all who "called (invoked) on this Name." Acts 9:14. It was not the Name "JESUS," but it was the association of the Name "LORD" in "LORD JESUS" which was counted as blasphemy and idolatry to the Jew. This was attributing the Name of Deity to A MAN, Jesus of Nazareth.

It was certainly not a meaningless title to the Jew. This meant far more than simply calling Jesus "Sir, Master." It was making Jesus "LORD."

Saul actually believed it was a manifestation of the God of the Old Testament appearing to him on the Damascus Road when he cried, "Who art Thou LORD?"

To a Pharisee, like Saul, he knew that there was but "One Lord" (Deut.6:4) and to call Jesus of Nazareth "Lord" was blasphemy indeed.

Hence his trembling in amazement when the voice answered, "I am JESUS whom thou persecutest." Saul responded by asking, "LORD, what wilt thou have me to do?"

He called Jesus "LORD," or "LORD JESUS," recognizing that THE MAN of Galilee was Deity and had received the Name of Deity.

"LORD" in the Name of the "LORD Jesus Christ" is the Name of Deity. It is the Name of the Father in the Old Testament and when the Father made Jesus "LORD," it was the giving to THE MAN Christ Jesus His own Name!

Every earthly son partakes of his father's Name. Every son has his own personal Name and every father puts his Name on his son.

128

The Son of Man has His own personal Name given to Him by His Heavenly Father and the Father has also put His own Name upon the Son, in exaltation.

Thus wherever we see the Name "LORD" in the New Testament, it is either the Father's Name directly, or else it is the Father's Name upon the Son.

Father and Son are partakers together of the same Name in the Name "LORD." Compare Genesis 19:24; Zech. 3:1; Psalms 110:1, 5; Acts 2:34-36; 3:19.

The Old Testament emphasized "The LORD God," The Father's Name. The New Testament emphasized "The LORD Jesus," The Father's Name upon the Son.

This is what is meant in Hebrews 1:1, that "the Son by inheritance obtained a more excellent Name" than the angels.

God gave the Angels their Names, but He never gave an Angel His own Name. No Angel ever received the Father's Name. It was the Son of Man, the Son of God, who, by right of birth and accomplished redemptive ministry, INHERITED His Father's Name, even as every earthly son inherits his father's Name.

What is "this more excellent Name?" It is the Father's Name, "LORD." The Psalmist, in another of the great Messianic Psalms cries out "O LORD, our LORD, how excellent is Thy Name in all the earth." Psalms 8:1,9.

This is the Name which is above every Name, both in this world and in the world to come. Ephesians 1:17-23.

There is no Name higher or above the Father's Name. The Father could not give to the Son a greater Name than His own. Therefore every tongue will be made to confess that "Jesus Christ is LORD to the Glory of God the Father" because that is the Father's Name upon the Son!

All will confess the Glory of the Triune Name, the Name of the Lord Jesus Christ.

Nothing could be plainer than this, that it is THE MAN Christ Jesus who has been exalted by the Father and made the LORD Jesus Christ. This is why the Holy Spirit brought the revelation to Peter on the Day of Pentecost, the birthday of the New Testament Church, which is the Body of Christ.

The Fulness of the Divine Name, the Godhead Name, is upon the Son, even as the Fulness of the Godhead dwells in Him. Col. 1:19; 2:9.

The Triune Name is a compound Name involving the Godhead. It is the greatest Name because it comprehends the greatest, even the Fulness of the Godhead, the Father, the Son and the Holy Spirit.

In Summary:

Interpret the Name "LORD" and behind that Name is Jehovah, The Self-Existent One, the Father God.

Interpret the Name "JESUS" and behind that Name is the Saviour, The Redeemer, the God-Man, The Son of God.

Interpret the Name "CHRIST" and behind that Name the work of the Holy Spirit is seen upon the Son of God, as the Holy Anointing Oil, the Divine Chrisma.

The Name is always significant of the Nature and here the very Nature of God is revealed in the Triune Name. It is significant also of the Divine manifestations.

When we say "LORD" it is the Father's Name directly or it is the Father's Name upon the Son.

When we say "JESUS" it is the Son's Name always, ever only and eternally His Name.

When we say "CHRIST" it is the Son anointed with the Holy Spirit or it is that same anointing upon the Church which is His Body, the Body of Christ. I Cor. 12:12.

The Triune Name is a compound Name of the Triune God. It is the Name of the Eternal Godhead and the Name of the Godhead Bodily. Matt. 28:19. II Cor. 13:14. It is the greatest compound REDEMPTIVE NAME in the whole Bible.

<u>This may be illustrated as follows:</u>

1. Illustration of the Triangle with the Triune Name. Compare these Scriptures with the illustration given. Luke 2:11,26,27. Acts 2:36.

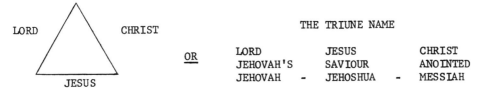

LORD / CHRIST

JESUS

OR

THE TRIUNE NAME

LORD	JESUS	CHRIST
JEHOVAH'S	SAVIOUR	ANOINTED
JEHOVAH -	JEHOSHUA -	MESSIAH

2. The Triune Name given to the Son.

    (1) In His Incarnation - "JESUS")
    (2) In His Anointing - "CHRIST")   JESUS CHRIST, The LORD. Acts 2:36.
    (3) In His Exaltation - "LORD".)

He was called JESUS in His incarnation, in the Virgin Birth.

He was manifested as the CHRIST in Jordan by that Holy Spirit anointing upon Him.

He was made LORD in Heaven by the Father exalting Him to His Throne.

He is indeed the LORD - JESUS - CHRIST.

130

3.

<u>THE OLD TESTAMENT REVELATION</u>

(TRIUNE GOD IN ONE NAME)

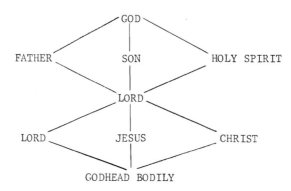

<u>THE NEW TESTAMENT REVELATION</u>

(TRIUNE GOD IN A TRIUNE NAME)

CHAPTER VII

THE GREAT COMMISSION CONSIDERED IN THE BOOK OF ACTS

In this Section we consider the Great Commission in the light of the Book of Acts.

The following Scriptures should be read in order to get the full comprehension of that which is involved in the Commission of the Risen Lord to His Disciples.

1. Matthew 28:18-20   )
2. Mark 16:15-20   )   Acts 1:8
3. Luke 24:44-49   )   All these Scriptures together
4. John 20:21-23, 30, 31   )   constitute the Commission.

This Commission was given AFTER the death, burial and resurrection of Jesus, and BEFORE His ascension to the Throne of the Majesty on High, and BEFORE the Outpouring of the Holy Spirit on the Day of Pentecost.

The Commission closes off the Gospel story.

When we study the Book of Acts, we find exactly how the Disciples understood what Jesus meant in the commandments given in the Great Commission, which Commandments were given by the Holy Spirit through Him (Acts 1:2).

The general content of these Scriptures tell us how Jesus commanded His Disciples to preach the Gospel of repentance and remission of sins to every creature. He instructs them that they are to teach all nations, make disciples and baptize the converts into the Name of the Father, and of the Son and of the Holy Spirit. The Lord promised that signs and wonders would follow in His Name, and as the believers went forth, the Word of the Gospel was confirmed accordingly.

The Gospel was to be preached first at Jerusalem, then Judea, then Samaria and finally unto the Uttermost parts of the earth.

We will note the fact that, stamped upon each Gospel-Commission, there is "THE NAME" by which all is to be accomplished.

Let us see the emphasis in each Gospel pertaining to the "THE NAME."

1. In Matthew's Gospel, Water Baptism is commanded to be "Into THE NAME of the Father, and of the Son and of the Holy Spirit."

2. In Mark's Gospel, Jesus promised that signs and wonders would be done "In MY NAME."

3. The emphasis in Luke's Gospel is that "repentance and remission of sins is to be preached in HIS NAME" to all nations beginning at Jerusalem.

4. John's Gospel emphasizes the facet of life through "believing in HIS NAME."

Thus the whole of the Great Commission centers around the power of "THE NAME" in some way or another.

Now, if we desire to know how the Disciples obeyed the Commission of Jesus, as set forth here, then where do we go to find this out? The answer is to the Book of Acts and NOT to the history books or the traditions of men.

The Book of Acts is the only Divinely infallibly inspired Book that we have of Early Church beginnings and how they understood what Jesus said. The Acts of the Apostles stands in its own Divine light as a demonstration of the Great Commission. The Acts of the Apostles are really the Acts of the Holy Spirit in and through the Church, the Body of Christ. It is recorded for us as infallible Scripture.

Thus, if we want to understand what is meant in Luke's Gospel by "preaching repentance and remission of sins in HIS NAME," we must study the Sermons in the Book of Acts and see how they fulfilled this Command.

Let the Student read and compare Luke 24:44-49 with Acts 2:38; 26:20; for there we see the message of repentance and remission of sins preached in the Name of the Lord Jesus Christ.

If we desire to know what Jesus meant in Mark's Gospel when He said that "these signs shall follow them that believe; IN MY NAME they shall cast out devils; they shall speak with new tongues, they shall take up serpents, and if they drink any deadly thing, it shall not hurt them; they shall lay hands on the sick, and they shall recover," then to which Book shall we turn?

The answer is evident. We turn to the Book of Acts. In the Book of Acts we find what is meant in this part of the Commission.

There they spoke with other tongues. Refer to Acts 2:4; 10:46; 19:6.
There they laid hands on the sick. Refer to Acts 9:17, 18; 28:8.
There Paul unknowingly took up a serpent and was unharmed. Acts 28:3-6.
There they cast out devils in His Name. Acts 8:6-8; 16:16-18; 19:11-12.
There is no account of any one drinking any deadly thing recorded.

Thus, the Book of Acts gives clear and unmistakable demonstration of the part of the Commission as recorded in Mark's Gospel and the power and use of the Name of Jesus.

The same can be applied to that which John's Gospel recorded concerning those receiving life through believing in the Name of the Lord Jesus Christ. Acts 11:18.

Thus, Mark, Luke and John are clearly understood in the Book of Acts, relative to obedience to the Commission.

CONSISTENCY OF INTERPRETATION requires that if we desire to understand what Jesus meant in Matthew 28 and verse 19 concerning "Baptizing into THE NAME of the Father and of the Son and of the Holy Spirit," then we must again turn to the Book of Acts.

The Book of Acts is indeed the fulfillment of the very words of Jesus. The Commandments He gave were given by the Holy Spirit. Compare Acts 1:2 with Matthew 28:19.

How the Disciples understood the commands of Jesus is recorded for us in the Acts of the Holy Spirit.

Both the Gospels and the Acts go together. The Gospels cannot be used against the Book of Acts nor the Book of Acts against the Gospels. The words of Jesus cannot be used against the words of the Apostles or the words of the Apostles against the words of Jesus.

Unbelieving believers (?) may argue and disagree as to what Jesus means by speaking with new tongues, healing the sick, casting out devils, preaching the Gospel of repentance and remission of sins, but THE BOOK OF ACTS stands in its own Divine light and is recorded for us as infallible Scripture.

There is no chance for mistake! Both the Gospels and the Acts mean what they say and say what they mean!

And so, when we come to the Book of Acts and see how the Disciples obeyed the command of Matthew's Gospel in Chapter 28:19, concerning baptism "into the Name" of the Eternal Godhead, then we find that in every case recorded, Water Baptism was administered in THE NAME of the LORD - JESUS - CHRIST, or abbreviations of the full Name, as noted in various translations.

The use of THE NAME, in part or parts, often involved the full Triune Name. It is inconsistent to think that several different formulas were used in Water Baptism or that the Apostles contradicted each other as well as contradicting Jesus.

Endless strife and divisions have arisen in the Church over its history concerning the method and formula in Water Baptism. If God's people would accept both the Gospels and the Acts as well as that which is given to us in the Epistles concerning Baptism, then the Divine answer would be seen. The Gospels, the Acts and the Epistles need to be considered together in order to gain the full truth pertaining to Water Baptism. None should be used against each other or used to contradict each other, for all complement the other.

THERE IS NOTHING WRONG WITH MATTHEW 28:19. This command was given by the Spirit. Acts 1:2.

THERE IS NOTHING WRONG WITH ACTS 2:36-38. This was also given by the Spirit. Acts 2:4.

BOTH Scriptures can be rightly used. Peter by the Spirit declares the TRIUNE NAME in Acts Chapter 2 and verse 36 and then commands Water Baptism on the basis of that Name in verse 38.

Perhaps if we had a written record in the Book of Acts stating that the Apostles used Matthew 28:19 as a Baptismal Formula, then all controversy would cease. However, it should be recognized that one does not fulfill a command by QUOTING it but only by OBEYING it.

Let it be noted clearly here that everything is to be done in "HIS NAME," but Water Baptism is to be administered in "THE NAME." That is, into the TRIUNE NAME, A Name in which the Godhead as Father, Son and Holy Spirit is revealed.

It is for this reason that <u>no single part, or parts of the Triune Name fulfill the Command</u> of Matthew 28:19 which implies the use of the TRIUNE NAME. Therefore, just the singular Name "Jesus," or even "Jesus Christ" or "Lord Jesus" does not fulfill the requirements laid down in the Gospel of Matthew.

It must be THE TRIUNE NAME of the LORD - JESUS - CHRIST that Water Baptism is administered in, for only the TRIUNE NAME fulfills the requirements for Baptism into THE Name of Father, and of the Son and of the Holy Spirit.

It is to be A TRIUNE NAME for the TRIUNE GOD. This is THE NAME to be invoked in Baptism, and it is this Name which was first revealed on the Day of Pentecost.

In the light of these things, it will be profitable to look at the various Scriptures in the Gospels on Baptism, then at the accounts of Baptism in Acts, and also at that which is recorded in the Epistles, thus gaining a full view and interpretation of "The Name" used in this Ordinance.

In the passage context of the accounts of Baptism in Acts we find that everything centers about the ministry and power of that Name.

WATER BAPTISM "IN THE NAME"

IN THE GOSPELS

There are two specific references to Water Baptism as commanded in the Commission given in the Gospels by Jesus to His disciples.

These references are to be found in the Gospels of Matthew and Mark. No references to Baptism are given in the Commission as recorded in the Gospels of Luke and John.

The Commission in the Gospel of Matthew.

After the resurrection of the Lord Jesus Christ, He gave His disciples the Great Commission as recorded in Matthew 28:19.

He declared to them that all power (Greek "authority") in heaven and earth had been given to Him. Because of this, He told them "Go ye therefore, and teach (Greek "disciple") all nations, baptizing them in the Name of the Father, and of the Son and of the Holy Ghost."

"Go ye therefore, and teach all nations, baptizing them in the name of the Father, and of the Son and of the Holy Spirit." A.V.

"Go ye therefore, and teach all nations, baptizing them into the name of the Father, and of the Son and of the Holy Spirit." R.V.

"Poreuthentes oun mathateusate panta ta ethne, baptizontes autous eis to onoma tou Patros kai tou huiou kai tou Agiou Pneumatos." Nestle-Arland Greek Text.

The emphasis in Matthew's Gospel is upon baptism INTO THE NAME of the Eternal Godhead, the Name of the Father, and of the Son and of the Holy Spirit.

It is not merely that baptism is "on the authority of" Jesus Christ, but "INTO THE NAME of the Father, and the Son and the Holy Spirit" that is to be understood in the Baptismal command.

The Commission in the Gospel of Mark.

"Go ye into all the world, and preach the Gospel to every creature. He that believeth and is baptized shall be saved; but he that believeth not shall be damned." Mark 16:15, 16.

"Ho pisteusas kai baptistheis sothasetai, ho de apistesas katakrithasetai." Nestle-Arland Greek Text.

The emphasis in Mark's Gospel pertaining to baptism is believing. It is he that believeth and is baptized...and he that believeth not... ."

It is believer's baptism. Refer to Acts 8:12, 13, 36, 37; Mark 1:15; Acts 16:31-34; 18:8; 19:4.

IN THE ACTS OF THE APOSTLES

It will be noted in the full context of each of the accounts of Baptism in the Book of Acts that the Name of the Lord - Jesus - Christ is used, and then out of such arises Baptism in that Triune Name.

(1) <u>In Jerusalem</u>.

The first reference and record of Water Baptism in the Book of Acts is found in the chapter of events which took place on the Day of Pentecost, Acts Chapter 2.

It cannot be overemphasized that that which took place here pertained to the birth of the New Testament Church.

The disciples numbered about one hundred and twenty, and as they continued in one place of one accord unto the Day of Pentecost, the Feast of the fiftieth day, the Scripture tells us that the Holy Spirit descended suddenly from heaven as a mighty rushing wind, filling the house where they were sitting. Cloven tongues like as of fire appeared and sat upon the head of each of the disciples, both men and women. All were filled with the Holy Spirit and began to speak with other tongues as the Spirit gave them utterance.

As the multitude gathered together, Jews out of every nation under heaven were made to realize that the supernatural manifestations seen and heard were evidences of the risen and exalted Lord. He had received the Promise of the Father and had poured forth this upon the waiting disciples.

The speaking in tongues ceased as Peter stood with the eleven other Apostles and began to preach the first "Pentecostal Sermon." This Sermon laid down for all times the prerequisites for the full establishment of a New Testament Church.

After declaring the death, burial and resurrection of Jesus Christ, the Son of God, conviction settled upon the crowd. They were pricked or thoroughly stabbed in their heart and cried out, "Men and brethren, what shall we do?"

Peter said, "<u>Repent, and be baptized everyone of you in the Name of Jesus Christ</u> for the remission of sins, and ye shall receive the gift of the Holy Ghost." Acts 2:38.

"...<u>Metenoasete, kai baptistheto ekastos humon epi to enomati Iesou Christou</u>... ." Nestle-Arland Greek Text.

The Egyptian Sahidic Version, translated about A.D. 350 gives the full Name of the Lord Jesus Christ in Acts 2:38. Refer to Table of Scriptures on Translations, p. 131. (William Phillips Hall, p. 72.)

That is, they were to repent and be baptized "upon, over and on" the Name of Jesus Christ.

It is to be remembered that Peter has just declared that "God hath made this same _Jesus_ both _Lord_ and _Christ_." Acts 2:36. The Jew knew the full implication of this in Baptism.

The response was immediate. About three thousand souls received the Word of the Gospel and were baptized after repentance. Thus the Lord added to His Church.

The three outstanding things to be seen here in this vital "foundation Sermon" for the New Testament Church are as follows:

1. The Call to repentance.
2. The Command of Baptism, that is, Water Baptism.
3. Baptism in or upon the Name of Jesus Christ, or Lord Jesus, or Lord Jesus Christ.

   (Egyptian Sahidic Version, A.V. and Lamsa Translation.)

The argument of silence does not always prove anything, but its worthy to note that we do not have written record of any Baptismal Formula mentioned here, neither the quoted command of Jesus from Matthew 28:19 or any other Formula. We would ask why this is not mentioned? It is a most important sermon, the inaugural sermon for the New Testament Church. Had Peter but quoted Matthew 28:19 and this had been recorded for us then it could have settled forever all controversy over whether a Formula is to be used in administering Baptism or not. Then again, the Gospel of Matthew has not been written as yet and the transition from the Old Covenant order into the New Covenant order is still in its earliest formative period.

(2) _In Samaria._

The next account of Water Baptism is found in Acts Chapter 8 which records that which took place under the Evangelist Philip's ministry in Samaria.

The Church at Jerusalem came under a period of persecution which caused the disciples to be scattered everywhere, scattering the Seed of the Word.

Philip, one of the original 7 deacons, went down to Samaria and preached Christ unto them. Signs and wonders followed the preaching of the Word according to the Lord's promise in the Gospel of Mark (Mark 16:15-18).

The Scripture tells us, "When they believed Philip preaching the things concerning the Kingdom of God, and the Name of Jesus Christ, they were baptized, both men and women." Verse 12.

Here the prerequisites of acceptance of the Word and faith were followed by Water Baptism. Further, the Scripture adds that they were "baptized in the Name of the Lord Jesus." Verse 12, 16.

   "...only they were baptized in the Name of the Lord Jesus." A.V.
   "...only they had been baptized into the Name of the Lord Jesus." R.V.
   "...monon de bebaptismenoi uperchon eis to onoma tou Kuriou Iesou."
   Nestle-Arland Greek Text.

In the context of verse 12 and 16 we find the Name of the Lord Jesus Christ mentioned.

Again it is to be noticed that there is no mention of the Command of Jesus as in the "Great Commission." The Baptismal Command is not referred to. They were baptized in the Name of the Lord. No written record of a Formula is found here.

In summary of the account:

1. Water Baptism followed faith, and was by immersion.
2. Water Baptism was administered into the Name of the Lord Jesus. The whole context deals with the Name of the Lord Jesus Christ.

Philip preached the death, burial and resurrection of the Lord Jesus Christ. The Samaritans believed it, embracing it into their lives and entered into fellowship by being baptized in the Name of the Lord Jesus Christ. It was not an outward sign of an inward cleansing, but they became partakers of the Lord.

They had called upon the Name of the Lord for salvation. "Whosoever shall call upon the Name of the Lord shall be saved." Acts 2:21. This is the only Name given under heaved whereby men can be saved. Acts 4:10-12. It was the "saving Name." Only as they truly called upon this Name in salvation could they be qualified to be baptized in that same Name. Philip administered baptism into that Name.

Indeed without proper believing and invocation of that Name there is no salvation, and Water Baptism in that Name becomes ineffectual in bringing any benefit to the one baptized. Simon, the sorcerer, is a case in point.

Water Baptism is believer's Baptism, administered by calling upon the Name and having that Name invoked upon the repentant and believing candidate.

(3) In Gaza Desert.

Philip's ministry extended beyond Samaria. In Acts Chapter 8:26-40 the details of Philip's personal evangelism are given.

The Angel of the Lord directed Philip to leave Samaria and go toward the desert of Gaza. As he travelled, there was a man from Ethiopia, a man of great authority under Candace, Queen of the Ethiopians, returning in his chariot from Jerusalem to his own country.

Having been to Jerusalem, he was returning home, hungry of heart after the knowledge of the God of Israel.

The Spirit told Philip to join himself to the chariot. The Ethiopian, as was the custom, was reading the Scriptures out loud, reading the great Messianic Chapter of the Prophet Isaiah, Chapter 53.

Philip asked him whether he understood what he read. He gave Philip a negative answer, inviting Philip to join him in the chariot. As they journeyed on, "Philip preached unto him Jesus."

This preaching of Jesus must have included the whole Gospel, for, as they came to certain water, the Eunuch asked Philip if there was anything to hinder him from being baptized. Upon the Eunuch's confession of faith in Jesus Christ as the Son of God, both he and Philip went down into the water, and he was baptized.

Once again there is no mention of the Formula as given in "The Great Commission." Baptism is administered here:

1. By immersion in water, and
2. Upon confession of faith in Jesus Christ as the Son of God. This was administered by Philip, who had previously baptized the Samaritans "into the Name of the Lord Jesus."

We note the emphasis in this account of Baptism is upon <u>confession of faith</u> in Jesus Christ as the Son of God.

(4) <u>In Damascus</u>.

In Acts Chapter 9 we have the account of Saul's conversion on the Road to Damascus. In due time he would be known as the Apostle Paul.

The Lord arrested Saul in the midst of his mad persecutions against the believers. As he was enroute to Damascus with letters of authority from the High Priest to bind many that were of "The Way," both men and women; a supernatural light shone from heaven. This light was the very outshining of the glorified Son of God, Jesus Christ. As Saul fell to the earth he heard the voice of the Lord calling to him, "Saul, Saul, why persecutest thou Me?" Saul, recognized that this was a Divine visitation, that the Lord was appearing to him. As God appeared to Moses in the burning bush and called to him, so the Lord was appearing here and calling to Saul. "Who art Thou, <u>LORD</u>?", Saul replied.

Undoubtedly Saul thought he was speaking to the God of the Old Testament, that is, <u>the LORD God</u>.

No wonder he began to tremble with astonishment when the voice said, "I am <u>JESUS</u> whom thou persecutest: it is hard for thee to kick against the pricks."

At this moment Saul was converted, born from above, for he called <u>Jesus</u> "<u>LORD</u>," and "no man can say that <u>JESUS is THE LORD</u> but by the Holy Spirit."

Blinded by the Shekinah Glory of the risen and exalted Lord Jesus, Saul is led by the hand into Damascus, there to await instructions and directions as to the will of the Lord for his life.

As he was fasting 3 days and 3 nights without food or water, he received a vision of a man, Ananias, coming in and laying his hands on him in order that he might receive his sight. The Lord always works by His Spirit at both ends, and thus we find that Ananias receives a corresponding vision.

Ananias came in obedience to the vision, laid hands on Saul, and as he did so, scales fell from Saul's eyes and his sight was restored. He received the Holy Spirit, and in the process Ananias called on Saul to be baptized.

In the account of Saul's conversion in Acts Chapter 22 and verse 16, he recalled the words of Ananias, "And now, why tarriest thou? Arise and be baptized, and wash away thy sins, <u>calling on the Name of the Lord</u>."

In prayer Saul called on the Name of the Lord. Again confirming Acts 2:21, that "whosoever shall call on the Name of the Lord shall be saved." This is the only "saving Name." Saul knew that this Name "LORD" was now to be called upon in and through the Name of the "LORD Jesus Christ," as in his experience on the Damascus Road.

Thus again, the emphasis is placed upon obedience to the command for Water Baptism. Saul is baptized as a believer. Once more there is no written record of any particular Formula for Baptism. However, the whole context of the Scriptures under consideration center about the Name of the LORD in and through the Name of the LORD JESUS CHRIST.

> "And why tarriest thou? Arise, and be baptized, and wash away thy sins, <u>calling on the Name of the Lord</u>." Acts 22:16. A.V.

> "...<u>calling on His Name</u>." R.V.

> "...<u>anastas baptisai kai apolousai tas amartias sou, epikalesamenos to onoma autou</u>." Nestle-Arland Greek Text.

Here it is clearly shown that the Apostle Paul in his conversion was brought to acknowledge JESUS as LORD (Acts 9:5, 6 with 22:10) and was then baptized calling on the Name of the Lord (Acts 22:16).

Indeed, if that Name brings salvation to us through the death, burial and resurrection of the Lord Jesus Christ, it would be consistent to say that this is the Name called upon in Baptism, for there the believer is identified with Him in His death, burial and resurrection.

It also shows how the believer may call upon that Name in Baptism.

In summary of this account:

1. Saul is converted by calling Jesus "LORD."
2. Saul is then baptized in water by immersion.
3. As he is baptized he called upon the Name of the Lord. Acts 22:16. Later on he writes to the Roman believers concerning being baptized in Jesus Christ, into his death and resurrection. Romans 6:3,4. All centers around the glory of that Triune Name of the Lord Jesus Christ.

(5) In Caesarea.

The next account of Baptism is found in Acts Chapter 10. Here the Holy Spirit through Luke the beloved physician records that which took place under Peter's ministry to the Gentiles in the house of Cornelius. It was to Peter that the Lord Jesus committed "the keys of the Kingdom" when He foretold the building of His Church.

It was Peter who was expressly and specifically chosen as the channel in the Book of Acts to use these "keys of the Kingdom" to open the Door of Faith, first to the Jews (Acts 2), and then to the Gentiles (Acts 10-11). Once again the risen Head of the Church, working by His Spirit at both ends, brought both ends together in due time.

As Cornelius, a Centurian of the Italian Band, was praying to God, an angel appeared to him in a vision assuring him that his prayers had been heard. The Angel gave him exact instructions and details by which he was to send men to Joppa and bring the Apostle Peter to his house, telling him that Peter would give them "words, whereby he and all his house would be saved."

He obeyed immediately. At the other end, in Joppa, the Lord was working through a vision given to Peter. In the vision Peter saw a sheet let down from heaven to earth with all sorts of unclean creatures on it. A voice commanded him to rise, kill and eat. Peter, steeped in Hebrew food-laws, refuses to do so. He did not as yet perceive the mind of the Spirit. This vision was repeated three times, for, "in the mouth of two or three witnesses shall every word be established."

As Peter meditated on the vision, "The Spirit said unto him, Behold three men seek thee, arise therefore and get thee down, and go with them, doubting nothing, for I have sent them."

Peter accompanied the men with six of his own Jewish brethren to the house of Cornelius. The Lord had to deal with his nationalistic sectarian attitude as he stood before the Gentiles. Hence, as Peter preached the Word of the Gospel, the Holy Spirit fell on all who heard the Word, and the evidence was seen and heard, as at Pentecost on the Jews, in that the Gentiles began to speak with other tongues.

The Scripture account records, "Then answered Peter, Can any man forbid water that these should not be baptized, which have received the Holy Spirit as well as we? And he <u>commanded</u> them to be <u>baptized in the Name of the Lord</u>." Acts 10:48.

Peter had to admit that as the Lord Jesus had baptized the Gentiles in the Spirit, then he could not refuse to baptize them in water, for one was the completeness of the other.

However, this was the exception, not the rule, in the Acts. God did this in order to deal with the nationalistic, sectarian attitude and spirit of the early believers and bring the Gentiles in the One Church, the Body of Christ.

> "...And he commanded them to be baptized <u>in the Name of the Lord</u>." A.V.
> "...And he commanded them to be baptized <u>in the Name of Jesus Christ</u>." R.V.
> "...And he commanded them to be baptized <u>in the Name of the Lord Jesus Christ</u>." Syriac Peshitta, Lamsa, and Douay Translation.
> "...<u>prosetaxen de autous en to onomati Iesou Christou baptisthenai</u>." Nestle-Arland Greek Text.

Here baptism was <u>in</u> the Name of the Lord, or Jesus Christ, or Lord Jesus Christ, as in the various translations noted. Again, the whole context of the passage centers about the Name of the Lord Jesus Christ in His Person and His redemptive work.

Remember that it was Peter the Apostle, the one who received the revelation of the Triune Name for Baptism at Pentecost who was ministering Baptism here also.

In this manner they entered into full fellowship with other Christians who had been baptized in the Name of the Lord Jesus Christ from the Day of Pentecost to that time.

The invocation of that Name on their part and on the part of the one baptizing them, with the reception of the Gift of the Holy Spirit, constituted them in full accord and fellowship with the apostolic believers, as later on expressed by Peter to the Church at Jerusalem (Acts 11:13-18).

Thus God had sealed that both Jew and Gentile were to constitute One Body, baptized in water and in the Holy Spirit in the Name of the Lord Jesus Christ, thus entering into full fellowship with Him, His Name resting in and over and upon them. They had entered "into" that Name. They were baptized by "<u>calling upon</u>" that Name, and they were baptized "in" or "by" the power and authority in that Name.

In summary, the same facts are seen here as in each of the previous accounts:

1. Baptism for the Gentiles, as for the Jews, was by immersion in water; and
2. Baptism was not an "optional," but a command; and
3. Water Baptism was administered in the Name of the Lord Jesus Christ. Again there is no reference to the Baptismal Formula of Matthew 28:19, nor is there a written record of the exact Formula used here by Peter.

(6) <u>In Philippi.</u>

Acts Chapter 16 furnishes us with the next account of Water Baptism.

Paul and Silas came from Troas into Philippi, a city of Macedonia, after a vision from the Lord. In the course of ministry there, a damsel with a spirit of divination (python) was delivered in the Name of Jesus Christ. The business men who used the damsel were aroused, causing an uproar in the city, the end result being that Paul and Silas were cast into prison. However, "all things work together for good," according to Romans Chapter 8 and verse 28. At the midnight hour, they prayed and sang praise to God. God sent an earthquake to the prison; the foundations were shaken. All the prisoners bands were loosed, and all the doors were opened. The penalty of death was upon any Prison-keeper who lost his prisoners.

The keeper of the prison was about to kill himself thinking that all the prisoners had escaped. Paul and Silas assured him that they were all there. The jailor, under conviction, cried out, "Sirs, what must I do to be saved? And they said, Believe on the <u>LORD JESUS CHRIST</u> and thou shalt be saved, and thy house."

What was the result?   The jailor and all his house <u>believed</u> and were <u>bap-tized</u> straightway. (vs. 31-34)

"...kai ebaptisthe autos kai oi autou apantes parachrema."   Nestle-Arland Greek Text.

<u>They believed on the Lord Jesus Christ and were baptized in water, believing in God.</u>

So far, in Acts, Peter the Apostle, Philip the Evangelist, Ananias the disciple, and now the Apostle Paul, have not referred to or quoted the Command of Jesus recorded in the "Great Commission." They simply baptized repentant, believing persons in water by immersion in the Name of the Lord Jesus, or Jesus Christ, or the Lord.

Water Baptism stood out very clearly in Apostolic preaching and practice. When real conversion and salvation was evidenced by those hearing and embracing the Word, they were ready for Water Baptism as a part of entering into and embracing Christianity.

Thus the Philippian jailor and his household were:

1.   Baptized by immersion,
2.   Believing in God, by
3.   Believing in the Lord Jesus Christ.
4.   Again we have no written record of a Baptismal Formula, however, the account centers around God as revealed in the Lord Jesus Christ.

(7) <u>In Corinth.</u>

The seventh particular reference to Water Baptism is found in Acts Chapter 18, under Paul's ministry at Corinth.

After Paul left Athens, he came to Corinth. He reasoned in the Synagogues with the Jews and Greeks out of the Scriptures, persuading them that Jesus of Nazareth was indeed the Christ of God, the Saviour of the World.

After being opposed by the blasphemy of the Jews, he shook his raiment, declaring to the unbelieving Jews that their blood would be upon their own heads, and that from then on he would go to the Gentiles. Paul then entered into the house of Justus whose house was joined to the Synagogue. Crispus, the Chief Ruler of the Synagogue, believed on the Lord with all his house, and the Scriptures declared, "Many of the Corinthians hearing <u>believed</u>, and were <u>baptized</u>." Acts 18:8.

Though no details beyond this are given in Acts, in the Epistle to the Corinthians Paul reminded them of his coming to Corinth and the establishment of the Church there. He reminded them that they should not be divided over names and personalities, beseeching them by the <u>Name</u> of the <u>LORD JESUS CHRIST</u> to speak the same thing, and have one mind, and one judgment. Then he referred them to their Baptism by saying, "Is Christ divided? Was Paul crucified for you? <u>Or were ye baptized in the name of Paul</u>? I thank God that I baptized none of you, but Crispus and Gaius; lest any should say that I had <u>baptized in mine own name</u>."

The implications of this will be considered later on. It is sufficient for the present to note the main points in this record of Baptism, which are as follows:

1. Water Baptism was by immersion in water,
2. It was administered to those who believed, and
3. Paul later on reminds the Corinthians that they had not been baptized in his name. This implies that they had been baptized into the Name which they as saints were to be gathered around in unity, that is, in the Name of our Lord Jesus Christ.
4. It is to be recognized again that there is no written record of a Formula of Baptism here.

(8) <u>In Ephesus.</u>

The final record of Baptism in the Acts is that which took place in Ephesus, and again this is under the ministry of the Apostle Paul. The details are supplied for us in Acts Chapter 19, and verses 1 through 7.

Paul found certain disciples at Ephesus. As he began to minister to them, in the spirit he sensed that something, someone, was absent. He immediately questioned them as to the matter of their Baptism. He asked them if they had received the Holy Spirit? They replied that they had not even known that the Holy Spirit had been given.

Paul continues, "Unto what (Greek--"<u>eisti oun ebaptisthete</u>") were ye baptized? And they said, Unto John's Baptism." Then Paul declares to them the difference between John's Baptism and Christian Baptism. (vs. 3-4)

These disciples had not experienced any form of Christian Baptism; only the Baptism of John. This difference will be explained in the proper section. When the Ephesians heard this "they were <u>baptized in the Name of the Lord Jesus</u>." "<u>Akousantes de ebaptisthesan eis to onoma tou Kuriou Iesou.</u>" Nestle-Arland Greek Text. (vs. 5)

The Holy Spirit sealed this act of Paul and Baptism in the Name of the Lord Jesus by coming upon these Ephesians in the laying on of hands, for "they spake with tongues and prophesied."

They experienced that "one baptism." Ephesians 4:5.

(NOTE: Textual criticism on these passages show that Papyri number 38 (P. 38) which was discovered in Egypt and Manuscript "D" also use all three Names "Lord Jesus Christ" in Acts 19:5. Both of these Manuscripts, P. 38 being a fragment, are later than Codex Sinaiticus and Codex Vaticanus. Hence, although these two do not use the full Triune Name of "Lord Jesus Christ" P. 38 and MSS "D" are relatively early compared to the copious amount of later uncials. Therefore, in analyzing scientifically through Textual Criticism there is some evidence of Acts 19:5 having employed all three Names in reference to Water Baptism.)

In summary of this section presently under consideration, it is to be seen that there was something inadequate, something lacking in John's Baptism even though it was by immersion. Under Paul the Apostle, these Ephesian believers were re-immersed to complete that which was insufficient in the Baptism of John.

Once again we conclude:

1. Water Baptism is by immersion, and
2. Water Baptism is administered in the Name of the Lord.
3. Water Baptism is for the repentant and believing.
4. No reference is given to the Triadic Formula of Matthew 28:19, nor is there any written record of a Baptismal Formula. The whole account once again centers around the Person and Name of the Lord Jesus Christ.

In concluding our findings on Water Baptism in the Book of Acts, let us bring into focus that which each record reveals.

1. <u>In Jerusalem</u>. Baptism was for the repentant and by immersion in the Name of Jesus Christ.

2. <u>In Samaria</u>. Baptism was for the believing by immersion in the Name of the Lord Jesus.

3. <u>In Gaza Desert</u>. Baptism was for the believing upon confession of faith in the Lord Jesus as the Son of God.

4. <u>In Damascus</u>. Baptism was by immersion for the believing Saul, calling on the Name of the Lord.

5. <u>In Caesarea</u>. Water Baptism was by immersion, and was commanded to be administered in the Name of the Lord.

6. <u>In Philippi</u>. Baptism was by immersion, as the jailor and his house believed in the Lord Jesus Christ, believing in God.

7. <u>In Corinth</u>. Baptism was by immersion, not in the Name of Paul but by implication in I Corinthians 1:10-17 they were baptized in the Name of the Lord Jesus Christ.

8. <u>In Ephesus</u>. The Baptism of John was redundant, lacking that which was vital to the New Testament Church, and so the Ephesians were re-immersed under Paul and in the Name of the Lord Jesus.

Therefore, the eight accounts of Baptism in Acts show that Baptism was by immersion, and not by sprinkling. They also show that there is no written record of the exact Formula used in Baptism. No written record is given of the Apostles quoting the Triadic Formula of Matthew 28:19. The records generally pertain to Baptism in the Name of the Lord, or the Lord Jesus, or Christ Jesus. Baptism was only for those who had experienced the necessary prerequisites of repentance from dead works and faith toward God through Christ.

148

(NOTE: Various translations as the Revised Version, the King James, the Lamsa
Translation, the Douay Version and others show Baptism to be in the
Name of the "Lord Jesus," "Jesus Christ," "Lord," and some have the
full Triune Name of the "Lord Jesus Christ."

Original Manuscripts are not to be found. The Earliest Manuscripts
provide the same information as in the above Translations.)

IN THE EPISTLES

Having considered Water Baptism in the Gospels and in the Acts, we proceed to understand the revelation of Baptism as in the Church Epistles.

It is appropriate at the beginning of this Section to recognize the difference in the significance of Baptism as laid out in the Gospels, the Acts and the Epistles. As in other fundamental Doctrines of the Faith "once delivered to the saints" (Jude 3) so it is with regard to the Doctrine of Baptisms. There is a progressive revelation and unfolding of the truth in the Gospels, the Acts and the Epistles; and in order to receive the complete view and perceive the fulness of truth, all these groupings are necessary to each other.

We cannot understand the full significance or truth of Baptism only by that which is supplied in the Gospels.

Nor can we get the full truth of Baptism only by that set forth in the Acts of the Apostles. The same holds true as to the Epistles. The Gospels, the Acts and the Epistles are all needed to give to us a full and balanced outlook on this subject. The difference is seen in the following brief remarks.

1. The Gospels especially record the <u>Commands</u> of Jesus.

2. The Acts particularly give the <u>fulfillment</u> of these Commands by the Baptism of the repentant and believing.

3. The Epistles especially bring out the very essence and the <u>inner spiritual truth</u> of Baptism. This is not to be found expressly in the Gospels or the Acts as clearly as it is set forth in the Epistles. This same principle holds true as pertaining to the Lord's Table. In the Gospels we see the Lord instituting the Table by His own Body and Blood of the New Covenant. In the Acts we see the Early Church meeting together and "breaking bread" the first day of the week. In the Epistles is given the true essence of Communion, the inner and spiritual truth of the Table, which is not found in the Gospels and the Acts.

All of this is given to the Church by the Apostle Paul, and without it there would be lacking much truth concerning the Table as well as Baptism.

The same is true as to the death, burial and resurrection of the Lord. These things are recorded for us <u>factually</u> in the Gospels. These things are <u>preached</u> in the Book of Acts. However, it is in the Epistles that these things are <u>interpreted</u> for us, as to the very heart, the very essence, the inner and spiritual significance of that which took place at Calvary. This is also true of many other things, as it is of Water Baptism.

Without the Epistles we would not have the inner and spiritual reality of Baptism as commanded by Christ in the Gospels and obeyed in Acts.

The Epistles could represent the <u>spirit</u>, the Acts could represent the <u>soul</u> and the Gospels could represent the <u>flesh-body</u>, as it relates to the truth progressively unfolded in the Gospels.

150

Let us consider the references to Baptism in the Epistles and see how all confirm that which is commanded in the Gospels and obeyed in the Book of Acts.

(1) The Epistle to the Romans.

Paul, in writing to the Romans reminds them of that which took place in their Baptism.

"Know ye not that so many of us as were baptized into Jesus Christ were baptized into His death...we are buried with Him in baptism..." Romans 6:3, 4. A.V.

"e agnoeite oti osoi ebaptisthemen eis Christon Iesoun, eis ton thanaton autou ebaptisthemen; sunetaphemen oun auto dia tou baptismatos eis ton thanaton..." Nestle-Arland Greek Text.

Thus the person who belongs to Jesus Christ by reason of the new birth is baptized into the Name of the Lord Jesus Christ.

Is it possible to separate "The Name" from "The Person" in this transaction? It is not. When we are baptized into Jesus Christ we are baptized into His Name. He and His Name are inseparable. To be baptized into His Person is to be baptized into His Name. This is strongly portrayed in Romans 6.

Paul did not say, "As many of us as have been baptized into the Name of the Father, and of the Son and of the Holy Spirit," but uses what which the Holy Spirit had revealed to the Apostle Peter on the Day of Pentecost, the birthday of the New Testament Church.

Certainly the believer does enter into a marvelous fellowship with the Father, and with the Son, and with the Holy Spirit, but this is through Christ's death, burial and resurrection and THE NAME of the GODHEAD BODILY, in THE NAME OF THE LORD JESUS CHRIST. The Fulness of the Divine Name dwells in Him. Philippians 2:6-11. Colossians 1:19; 2:9.

The Lord Jesus Christ humbled Himself and became identified with our humanity, taking our sin and death into Himself at Calvary in that three days and three nights pertaining to the Atonement. The believer becomes identified with Him in Water Baptism in this same death, burial and resurrection.

In fact, Christ refers to His own death as "a Baptism," as seen in the use of the Greek word Baptisphanai. Thus Baptism is linked with His death, burial and resurrection.

The "going down" of the candidate into the water is the symbol of the "going down into death," identification with Christ's death. The immersion, submersion of the candidate "beneath the water," is identification with His burial. This is why sprinkling cannot fulfill the significance of Baptism. Only Baptism by immersion, or submersion demonstrates or illustrates this truth. The "rising up" out of the water signifies the believer's resurrection rising up to walk in newness of life. In Christ. It is identification with the resurrection of Christ.

This is seen in the Scriptures under consideration here, all of which show that the believer is identified with the Lord Jesus Christ in His death, burial and resurrection.

1. The believer is identified with His Death:
    "Know ye not that so many of us as were baptized into Jesus Christ have been baptized into His DEATH?" Romans 6:3.
2. The believer is identified with His Burial:
    "Therefore we are BURIED with Him by baptism into death..." Romans 6:4.
3. The believer is identified with His Resurrection:
    "That like as Christ was RAISED UP from the dead by the glory of the Father, even so we also should walk in newness of life." Romans 6:4,5.

The teaching of Paul in the Epistle of Romans declares that Baptism is into Jesus Christ. Thus the believer is identified with Him in His death, burial and resurrection. This is the very essence of the meaning of Baptism. This distinctive emphasis is not brought out by simply quoting the Baptismal command of Matthew 28:19. It is there by implication. The invocation of the Triune Name of the Triune God identifies the One whose death, burial and resurrection the believer is identified with.

(2) The Epistle to the Corinthians.

As noticed already in the accounts of Baptism in the Acts, Paul had been preaching at Corinth that Jesus was the Christ and as a result numbers had been brought to believe on the Lord Jesus Christ and were baptized.

> "And Crispus, the chief ruler of the synagogue, believed on the Lord with all his house; and many of the Corinthians hearing believed, and were baptized." Acts 18:8.

> "Krispos de ho archisunagogos episteusen to kurio sun olo to oiko autou, xai polloi ton Korinthion akouontes episteuon xai ebaptizonto." Nestle-Arland Greek Text.

No details are mentioned beyond this in the account in Acts. However, when Paul writes the Epistle to them, it is interesting to note his reproof to them for the divisions among them.

He said, "Now I beseech you, brethren, by the Name of the Lord Jesus Christ that there be no divisions among you; but that ye be perfectly joined together in the same mind and in the same judgment... Now this I say, that every one of you saith, I am of Paul; and I of Apollos; and I of Cephas; and I of Christ. Is Christ divided? Was Paul crucified for you? Or were ye baptized in the name of Paul? I thank God that I baptized none of you... lest any should say I had baptized in mine own name." I Corinthians 1:10-16.

From the context of these verses, it is implied that Paul baptized the Corinthians into the Name of the Lord Jesus Christ. He beseeches them by THE NAME of the LORD JESUS CHRIST to speak the same thing, to have the same mind and be joined together in the same judgment. He then appeals to them on the basis of their Baptism. He kindly reminds them they had not been baptized into (Greek--"eis") the Name of Paul. Paul did not want any

152

to say that they had been baptized in the Name of an Apostle. He asks them, "Was Paul crucified for you?" and again, "Were ye baptized into the Name of Paul?"

The answer to these questions should be evident to any thoughtful student. It was the LORD JESUS CHRIST who had been crucified for them. And seeing that Water Baptism is identification with Him in His death, burial and resurrection, into whose Name should they have been baptized? The very passage context under consideration implies that they had been baptized into the Name of the Lord Jesus Christ, the Name of the Person who had been crucified for them.

Therefore, upon this foundation, the fellowship and unity of that NAME should be a rebuke to the divisions over personalities and names mentioned among them.

Christ is one and they were one in Him.

This is the Divine standard as contained in the Word of the Lord. To be truly Apostolic in faith and practice, we must believe and obey.

It is also worth noting another reference to Water Baptism in Paul's Epistle to the Corinthians.

In the tenth Chapter (I Corinthians 10:1-2) Paul takes the experience of Israel as a Nation and their crossing of the Red Sea after the deliverance from Egypt by the Blood of the Passover Lamb as a type of the Baptism of a Nation.

> "...I would not that ye should be ignorant, how that all our fathers were under the cloud, and all passed through the sea; and were all baptized unto Moses in the cloud and in the sea." I Corinthians 10:1,2.

> "...and were all baptized into Moses..." R.V.

> "...kai pantes eis ton Mousen ebaptisanto en te nephele kai en te thalasse..." Nestle-Arland Greek Text.

Here we have a wonderful picture of the Christian life in its beginning. Deliverance from Egypt by the Blood of the Passover Lamb, Jesus Christ. Then the next step is to follow Him in Water Baptism and follow the Cloud of the Holy Spirit.

Israel, as a Nation, was baptized "unto" or "into" Moses, the Mediator of the Old Covenant; the one who had brought them deliverance.

Moses was preached in every city in Acts. Acts 15:21.

The Church is baptized into the Lord Jesus Christ, the Mediator of the New Covenant, the One who brought deliverance from sin.

He it was who was crucified for us, and it is into His Name, into the Godhead Name, that we are baptized in Water and in Spirit.

(3) <u>The Epistle to the Galations</u>.

When writing to the Galatians, Paul refers again to the subject of baptism.

"As many of us as were <u>baptized into Christ</u> have put on Christ." Galatians 3:27. A.V.

"<u>osoi gar eis Christov ebaptisthete, Christov evedusasthe</u>." Nestle-Arland Greek Text.

To be baptized into Christ is to be baptized into His very nature and Person, into His Name.

The Name of the Lord Jesus Christ cannot be separated from His Person. His Name and His Person are one.

This is the very essence and spiritual meaning of Water Baptism.

(4) <u>The Epistle to the Ephesians</u>.

There is but one reference to Baptism in Ephesians.

"There is...one baptism." Ephesians 4:5. In the Early Church both Water Baptism and Holy Spirit Baptism were counted as "one baptism," the one pointing to and being the completion of the other.

(5) <u>The Epistle to the Colossians</u>.

The Epistle to the Colossians confirms the same facet of truth as brought out in the Epistle to the Romans.

"<u>...buried with Him in baptism.</u>" Colossians 2:12.

Thus Water Baptism involves death, burial and resurrection with HIM; that is, the Lord Jesus Christ. It is not merely quoting a Baptismal Command over a person, but it is immersion into the Name of the Godhead as expressed in the Name of the Lord Jesus Christ. It is identification with the work of Calvary and the three days and three nights of the Atonement.

While in the Epistle to the Colossians, let us refer to another facet of truth pertaining to Baptism which is brought out in the same verse as noted above. This is the matter of "New Covenant Circumcision."

Water Baptism is the New Testament antitypical fulfillment of the Old Testament Rite of Circumcision. Abraham was given "The Covenant of Circumcision." Acts 7:8.

There were three particular things involved in the rite, each of which pointed first to the work of the Cross, and then on through the Cross to the believer's experience in Water Baptism, which is New Covenant Circumcision. These things were:

1. The cutting away of the <u>flesh</u>, which also involved the shedding of <u>blood</u>. It pointed to the DEATH of the Lord Jesus Christ, for, when His Flesh and Blood were offered in sacrifice for us to God, He was indeed "cut off" out of the land of the living for our sins and transgressions. Isaiah 53:8.

2. The second thing was that this rite took place on the <u>eighth</u> day. Eight is significant of the number of resurrection. It pointed to the RESURRECTION of the Son of God on the eighth day, or, the first day of a new week. Matthew 28:1.

3. The third thing involved was the <u>invocation of the Name</u> of the child. This took place at the circumcision of the child. Though the Name was given at birth, it was not invoked until the day of his circumcision. Genesis 17:12; 21:3.

   This pointed to THE NAME of the Godhead Bodily, the Fulness of the Divine Name as given to Jesus when He was made both Lord and Christ, or, the LORD JESUS CHRIST. Acts 2:36.

Each of these points are implied in Genesis chapter 17. Only when a Hebrew child had especially experienced these things involved in the rite were they counted in Covenant relationship with God, and thus entitled to the blessings, the promises, the privileges and responsibilities of the Abrahamic Covenant.

The New Testament antitypical fulfillment of this is in New Testament or New Covenant Circumcision, Water Baptism. Paul in writing to the Colossians tells them, "In whom also ye are circumcised with the circumcision made without hands, in putting off the body of the sins of the flesh, by the circumcision of Christ ...."

In Water Baptism, the believer is identified with Christ's death. He is "cut off" from the old life of sin, and this old life is buried with Christ. Water Baptism speaks of a circumcision of the heart, and spirit, and not of the flesh.

In Water Baptism the believer has A NEW NAME invoked upon him, the Name of the Father, Son and Holy Spirit which is interpreted in the Name of the Lord, in the Lord Jesus Christ, the Name of the Godhead Bodily.

In Water Baptism the Holy Spirit comes upon the candidate so that he may rise to walk in newness of life. This is resurrection. The believer comes into New Covenant relationship with God through Christ, and is now entitled to all the blessings, promises, privileges and responsibilities of that Covenant.

All of this is inwrought by FAITH in the operation of God. The Holy Spirit working <u>in us</u> what was done <u>for us</u> at Calvary.

Thus the Epistle to the Colossians confirms the truth that Baptism is into the death, burial and resurrection of the Lord Jesus Christ.

There "The New Name" for "The New Nature" is invoked, and there New Covenant Circumcision is operative.

(6) <u>The Epistle to the Hebrews</u>.

There is but one reference to the matter of baptism in the Epistle to the Hebrews. Hebrews 6:2.

"...the doctrine of baptisms." A.V. It is the doctrine of "washings."

To the Hebrew Nation this was seen in the numerous ceremonial washings of the Law, all of which pointed to New Testament Water Baptism in its full meaning and significance once the Messiah had come.

In New Testament sense "the doctrine of baptisms" covers all of the teaching pertaining to the subject.

Read the following Scriptures in connection with these remarks:

Exodus 29:4; Leviticus 8:6; 14:8,9; Numbers 19; Exodus 30:18, 19; Leviticus 16:4; Hebrews 9:13.

The ceremonial washings (baptisms) of the Law primarily prophesied (Matthew 11:13) of the inner spiritual washing by the water of the Word under the ministry of Messiah. Titus 3:5; I Corinthians 6:11; Acts 22:16; John 3:3-5.

Secondarily, they pointed to Water Baptism as set forth in the New Testament. Acts 22:16; Matthew 28:19; Acts 2:38.

(7) <u>The Epistle of James</u>.

In this Epistle, James, in writing to the Twelve Tribes scattered abroad, alludes to the matter of baptism.

"Do not they blaspheme <u>that worthy Name by the which ye are called</u>?" James 2:7. A.V.

"Do they not blaspheme <u>the good Name which was called upon you</u>?" Literal translation of Nestle's Greek Text.

"ouk autoi blasphemousin to kalon <u>onoma to epiklethen eph umas</u>?" Nestle-Arland Greek Text.

The Amplified New Testament amplifies this verse: "Is it not they who slander and blaspheme <u>that precious Name</u> by which you are distinguished and called (<u>the Name of Christ invoked in baptism</u>)?" James 2:7. Amp. N.T.

<u>Jamieson, Fausett and Brown Commentary</u> has an interesting amplification of this verse.

"<u>that worthy Name</u>" -- which is "good before the Lord's saints" (Psalms 52:9; 54:6); which ye pray may be "hallowed" (Matthew 6:9), and "by which ye are called, "lit., which was invoked (or called upon) by you (cf. Genesis 48:16; Isaiah 4:1, Margin; Acts 15:17), so that at your baptism "<u>into</u> the Name" (so the Greek, Matthew 28:19) of Christ, ye became Christ's people (I Corinthians 3:23)."

This verse would lose its full significance if the above remarks were not so. The "precious Name" had been invoked upon them in baptism. The Name of the LORD in the LORD Jesus Christ is that "worthy Name," that "precious Name." They were baptized into His Name, the Name of the Eternal Godhead. They called upon that Name and that same Name was called upon them.

(8) The Epistle of Peter.

The final reference to Baptism in the Epistles is given by the Apostle Peter himself. Peter is the one who received the Keys of the Kingdom of Heaven. Peter is the one who received the revelation of the Triune Name on the Day of Pentecost and commanded Baptism into that Triune Name.

It is Peter who commanded Baptism into the Name of the Lord for both Jews and Gentiles under the sovereign outpourings of the Spirit on both. Acts 2:38; 10:47-48.

In referring to Baptism, Peter writes, "The like figure whereunto baptism doth also now save us, not the putting away of the filth of the flesh, but the answer of a good conscience towards God by the resurrection of Jesus Christ." I Peter 3:20, 21.

Water Baptism, in its proper interpretation, cannot be separated from the work of Jesus Christ at Calvary. It involves His death, burial and resurrection, and the believers identification with the same.

We are buried with Him in baptism, and we rise to walk in newness of life in Him.

SUMMARY

In bringing to a close our comments on Baptism in the Name as seen in the Gospels, the Acts and the Epistles let us gather together the main points brought to our attention.

It is evident from the commands concerning Baptism as given in the Gospels and the accounts of the fulfillment of those commands as in the Book of Acts that there seems to be a great discrepancy. The discrepancy is particularly centered around "the Formula" to be administered in Baptism.

Why did the Lord Jesus command the disciples to "Baptize in the Name of the Father, and of the Son, and of the Holy Ghost," yet nearly every record or reference to Baptism--both in the Acts and in the Epistles--is spoken of as Baptism "in or into the Name of the Lord, the Lord Jesus, or Jesus Christ, or the Lord - Jesus - Christ?," depending on various translations.

We are forced to ask some pertinent questions in order to find some reconcilable answer. Did the disciples disobey the command of Jesus? Did they misunderstand His command? Why is there no written record of the disciples quoting Matthew 28:19 in Acts? Why is Baptism generally associated with "The Name" in some form or another? Why is there no exact "Formula" used in the New Testament? Is there some mistake? Is there some contradiction between the Gospels and the Acts? Does it really matter what the disciples did in Acts, or should we really just quote the Command of Jesus from the Gospel of Matthew? Do words really matter at all, if the person who is being baptized has a <u>heart that is right</u> before God and is in obedience to the Word? Is the <u>act of obedience</u> in Baptism by immersion more important than any <u>words of a Formula</u>?

These and other related questions naturally arise as one studies the Doctrine of Baptisms both in the Gospels and Acts. Can these things be reconciled? Endless strife and division has resulted out of an endeavor to reconcile the Gospels with the Acts.

The Gospels have been pitted against the Acts and the Acts against the Gospels. Jesus has been made to contradict Peter and Peter to contradict Jesus. The Apostles have been made to contradict each other. All of this need not be so. The writer believes that there is no contradiction between the Command of Jesus and the obedience of the Apostles. Both the Gospels and the Acts belong to each other.

The writer believes that the Book of Acts is that which gives us understanding, by the Spirit, of that which was intended in the Great Commission and the commands of Jesus as in the Gospels. That is to say, the Great Commission ought to be considered in the light of the Book of Acts.

(Refer again to these Scriptures: Matthew 28:18-20; Mark 16:15-18; Luke 24: 47-49; John 20:21-23, 30, 31; and Acts 1:2, 8.)

The Commission as given in these Scriptures was given <u>after</u> the DEATH, BURIAL AND RESURRECTION of the Lord Jesus and just <u>before</u> His ASCENSION, EXALTATION to the Father's Right Hand and <u>prior</u> to the Day of Pentecost when the Holy Spirit was poured out on the disciples waiting to fulfill the Commission.

As we considered the Book of Acts we discovered how the disciples obeyed the Commission and commandments of Jesus.

The only TRIUNE NAME in the whole revelation of God is that revealed in the New Testament, THE NAME of the LORD JESUS CHRIST.

It is unthinkable that the Apostles disobeyed the Command of the Lord Jesus.

No Doctrine of Scripture can be established on <u>one verse only</u>, but in the mouth of two or three witnessing Scriptures. Scripture must interpret Scripture.

We have before us the <u>one</u> Scripture command of Jesus to baptize into the Name of the Father, Son and Holy Spirit, and then we have about <u>twelve</u> Scriptures which show baptism in the Name of the Lord, or Lord Jesus, or Jesus Christ. Therefore, the twelve Scriptures ought to be taken as the fulfillment of the one Scripture. The declaration of Peter in Acts that Jesus had been made both Lord and Christ and then his command for baptism in that Name gives us insight as to the interpretation of the command of Jesus for baptism into the Name of the Godhead. The writer believes it is in this way it is to be understood when invoked in water baptism.

The reason that Matthew 28:19 is not specifically used or even quoted in the Acts is this. <u>One does not fulfill a command by merely quoting it!</u> The Apostles did not <u>quote</u> the Command; they <u>obeyed</u> it!

There seems to be no reconciliation between the Gospels and the Acts if this is not so. If the record of Acts be mistaken here and does not mean this, then what do words mean?

As it has pleased the Father that in the Son all fulness should dwell, so the fulness of the GODHEAD NAME is in the Son. It is not that the Son is the Father, nor the Holy Spirit, for, the Father is eternally the Father, the Son is eternally the Son, and the Holy Spirit is the Holy Spirit eternally. But in the redemptive plan it has pleased God that in the Son all the Fulness dwell. The Son is the FULNESS of the GODHEAD - BODILY! Colossians 1:19; 2:9.

Because this is so, the Fulness of the Godhead Name dwells in Him; that is, "The NAME of the FATHER, and of the SON, and of the HOLY SPIRIT" is completely expressed in Him. This is seen in the Name of the Lord Jesus Christ. It is "The Family Name" of which Paul writes, "For this cause I bow my knees unto the Father of our LORD JESUS CHRIST of whom the whole family in heaven and earth is Named." Ephesians 3:14-15.

The Name is always significant of the Nature in Bible days. To be baptized into the Name of the Father, Son, and Holy Spirit is to be baptized into the Name of the Eternal Godhead and all that belongs in the redemptive plan. To be baptized into the Name of the Lord Jesus Christ is to be baptized into the Family Name and into the Name of the Fulness of the Godhead Bodily. It is being baptized into the New Nature which belongs by right of New Birth to the New Creature.

"IN OR INTO THE NAME"

What does the expression "into the Name" ("eis to onoma") mean as used in the New Testament with reference to Water Baptism?

"In the Name" has created great difficulties because of the Greek preposition "eis" as used in the various accounts. The meaning has been keenly debated. Generally speaking the theological bearing of the preposition can only come from the context.

In the Old Testament this formula "in the Name of" is used many times.

> David came "in the Name of" the LORD. I Samuel 17:45.
> Elijah built an altar "in the Name of" the Lord. I Kings 18:32.
> Israel set up their banners "in the Name of" the Lord. Psalms 20:5.
> "In the Name of" the Lord Israel would tread down their enemies. Psalms 44:5.
> The Prophet like unto Moses was to speak "in the Name of" the Lord. Deuteronomy 18:18, 19.
> False Prophets often spoke using the formula "in the Name of" the Lord to give authority to their false utterances. Deuteronomy 18:20 with Jeremiah 14:14, 15; 23:25.

This does not always mean "with the invocation of" the Name of Yahweh, though many times it involves this. The following meanings or senses to this formula have been presented in various Commentaries, as to the expression in the Old Testament.

"IN THE NAME OF" means:

1. "On the commission of;"
2. Often signifies "the mention or invocation or utterance of;"
3. Acting on the commission with appeal to the Name of Yahweh; or
4. It signified the Presence of Yahweh with the Person.
5. Also "in virtue of," or "on the basis of" the Name (Person) of the Lord.

In the New Testament, various Commentaries and Greek Lexicons present two broad general ideas or a dual meaning of the preposition "eis," these being the linear and the static sense. The word "eis" is a very versatile preposition and suggests many possibilities and variations.

The following usages help us to gain some insight concerning the formula "into the Name" as used in the New Testament.

1. "Into the Name" (Greek--"eis to onoma")

   Used in Matthew 28:18; Acts 8:16; 19:5; I Corinthians 1:13; 10:2; Galations 3:27; Romans 6:3, 3. Compare these with Matthew 10:41; 18:20.

   "Into the Name" or "Unto the Name" is suitable in the translation of these verses.

   It has the meaning of:

   (a) "with respect or regard to;"
   (b) "in relation to;"

(c) "with reference to;"

(d) "entrance into"--that is, motion towards;

(e) "to or towards"--that is, approach;

(f) "unto or upon"--that is, of a limit reached.

(Refer to G. Abbott-Smith. "A Manual Greek Lexicon of the New Testament," pp. 133-134, for a fuller development of the three main areas pertaining to this preposition.)

2. "In the Name" (Greek--"epi to onomati") Acts 2:38

Here it implies the meaning as being "upon the Name, upon this as the basis or ground for the ceremony."

3. "In the Name" (Greek--"en to onomati") Acts 10:48

Here it implies in its meaning "within the limits of, with relation to it and it alone."

G. Kittel in "Theological Dictionary of the New Testament" (pp. 242-283) gives a number of various ways in which the formula "in the Name" is used in the Old and New Testaments. The following references demonstrate this:

1. Prayer "in His Name" is to pray according to His will and at His commission in fulfillment of the mission given to the disciples.

2. To believe "in His Name" (John 2:23) is to believe in His Messianic mission, to believe that He is the Son of God.

3. To do works "in His Name" is to act on His commission and in His power Luke 10:17; Mark 9:38, 39.

4. Baptism "in the Name" is mentioned as the Name of the One to whom the candidate is made over. It is baptism on the basis of the Name of Jesus.

5. "In the Name" also means with the invocation of His Name. John 14:13.

Thus, Baptism, as many other things in the Church, is to be "in the Name" of the Son of God, our Lord Jesus Christ.

It involves both the linear and static sense of the word "eis" or "into." The person is baptized because he is already in the Lord Jesus Christ. It is because the candidate is already "in" the Lord Jesus Christ that he is baptized "into" His Name, which is the Name of the Eternal Godhead.

Baptism involves the repentant person calling "upon" the Name of the Lord Jesus Christ and the calling "upon" or "over" the candidate that same Name by the one baptizing them.

Baptism is also baptism "into" the Name, into the Person of the Lord Jesus Christ, into a new sphere of walk and life for the believer. It is with distinct and exclusive reference to Him. It is into the fellowship of the Father, Son and Holy Spirit. It is with reference to His Name. It is upon the basis of that Godhead Name.

Water Baptism is on the authority of the Lord Jesus Christ and is administered by calling upon His Name and His Name being called over the baptized one, as well as being immersed into the Name of the Godhead. It includes them all. Baptism is not just a "matter of words and names" (Acts 18:15) but there is power in the invocation of that Name if entered into in true faith. Water Baptism is the only ordinance ordained in the Church where "The Name" in its Triune glory is to be actually called upon the believer. Therefore it is not a meaningless ceremony.

Meditation on this chapter will help us to understand more fully what the formula "into the Name" or "in the Name" truly means.

Jamieson, Fausset and Brown Commentary.

Commenting on Matthew 28:19. "Baptizing them in the Name...it should be, "into the Name" as in I Corinthians 10:2, "And were all baptized unto (rather, 'into') Moses;" and Galatians 3:27, "For as many of you as have been baptized into Christ."

Baptizing them into the Name; i.e., into the whole fulness of the grace of "The Father, and of the Son and of the Holy Spirit," as belonging to those who believe.

INVOKING "THE NAME"

It has already been considered in the previous section that one of the various uses of the expression "in or into the Name" was the invocation of that Name.

Paul wrote to the Colossians saying, "And whatsoever ye do in word (Greek--"lego") or deed (Greek--"ergo"), do all in the Name of the Lord Jesus..." Colossians 3:17. Thus whatever we say or do is to be done in His Name.

It is to be admitted that there is no written record of any exact formula in Scripture concerning water baptism. However, it is also to be admitted that the expression "into the Name of" is a formula, part of its meaning being "the invocation of the Name."

Should the Godhead Name be invoked or called upon in baptism by the candidate or by the one baptizing, or by both? The Scripture implies the answer in the affirmative. The Godhead Name is called upon in this as in other areas of life.

"The Name" is actually invoked in salvation, in repentance, in the healing of the sick and in casting out of devils. "The Name" is actually called upon in prayer, worship and praise. The true believer does not go through meaningless rite in the invocation of "The Name" in these things. Nor is the believer silent in the fulfillment of the ministry involved in these things. "The Name" is invoked, it is called upon, either by the one in need or the one in ministry, or by both.

When "The Name" is invoked it is not done as in the use of some magic formula. It is not done as the heathen do by invoking or calling on the names of their gods in some superstitious way. This is not what is meant when the believer invokes or calls upon "The Name."

G. Kittel's "Theological Dictionary of the New Testament" (pp. 255) writes concerning the expression "calling on the Name:"

> The Hebrew expression "calling on the Name of the Lord" originally signified "To invoke (the deity) with the Name Yahweh," still bears traces of the idea of a magical constraint which can be exercised by the utterance of the Name.
>
> In the Old Testament, of course, the invocation bears the weaker sense of "calling on Yahweh;" i.e., worshipping Him (Genesis 4:26; 12:8; 26:25; Zephaniah 3:9 with I Kings 18:24) and the magical notion disappears. Indeed, misusing the Name of God in magic and incantation is expressly forbidden in the Decalogue (Exodus 20:7; Deuteronomy 5:11). Yahweh refuses to be conjured up by the utterance of His Name. He promises His coming at the appointed shrines when He is called upon there... . Thus the Name of Yahweh is not an instrument of magic; it is a gift of revelation. This does not rule out the fact that uttering or calling on Yahweh's Name implies faith in His power; this is true also of use not directly connected with the cultus.

The seven sons of Sceva, who were Jewish excorcists, tried to use "The Name" in some magical form. Acts 19:13-17. They uttered or mentioned "The Name." They had the right words, the right formula, but that Name was powerless on their lips because they were not in spiritual union with the One whose Name it was. The demon spirits knew this. They had no legal right to use His Name for they were not His. John 16:23-28.

Thus we see that it is not merely pronouncing a set formula, but through the Lord working with His Name in response to those who are in union with Him and who call or invoke His Name in faith.

The Name represents the Person. What is done to His Name, is done to Him. To reject His Name is to reject Him. To believe on His Name is to believe on Him. To call upon His Name is to call upon Him. One cannot separate the Name from the Person. His Name is Himself. Romans 2:24; I Timothy 6:1; James 2:7; Revelation 13:6; 16:9. His Name is not to be desecrated or blasphemed.

"Let every one that nameth the name of Christ depart from iniquity."
II Timothy 2:19; Matthew 7:21-23.

Kittel continues to comment on "The Name" (pp. 252, 253, 262, 272) by saying that the Hebrew phrase "on or in the Name of the Lord" is often combined with the verbs "to invoke," "to speak," "to prophecy," "to bless," but we also find "to walk," "to serve," "to tread down enemies," "to raise banners," etc., in isolated instances.

"Yahweh gives the stars their names as Creator and Lord. Psalms 147:4.
He calls Israel by Name and thereby establishes His claim to it.
Isaiah 43:1.
Conversely, Yahweh's Name is named over Israel and it thus becomes the people of His possession. Isaiah 63:19; II Chronicles 7:14.
The Name of Yahweh is named over the Temple (Jeremiah 7:10),
over the Ark (II Samuel 6:2),
over Jerusalem; this makes the city holy.
(Jeremiah 25:29; Daniel 9:18)."

"In the Name" in Old and New Testament does not always mean "with the mention of," or "with the utterance or invocation of the Name." Sometimes it simply means "on the commission of."

"The most general meaning of "en to onomatai" ("In the Name of") is "with the invocation of." He who says or does something in the name of someone appeals to this one, claims his authority. This gives us the various nuances according to the context. It may mean "with calling upon" or "with proclamation of the Name," or "on the commission," or "in fulfillment of the will," or "in obedience." But "en onamati" ("In the Name of") can also mean "in the sphere of power," or "in the power," or "in the presence."

There are several words used in the New Testament which involve the utterance of invocation of "The Name." These words are "Name," "Surname," and "Call." The word "call" has a variety of uses in the New Testament.

W. E. Vine in "An Expository Dictionary of New Testament Words" gives the Greek definition and explanation of these several words.

1. <u>KALEO</u> - To "call" or "clamour."

    It is used (a) with a personal object, to call anyone, invite, summon; e.g., Matthew 20:8; 25:14. Particularly of the Divine call to partake of the blessings of redemption; e.g., Romans 8:30; I Corinthians 1:9.
    (b) of nomenclature or vocation, to call by a name, to name; in the Passive Voice, to be called by a name, to bear a name.

Thus it suggests either vocation or destination; the context determines which.

2. <u>EPIKALEO</u> - "<u>epi</u>," upon; "<u>kaleo</u>," call.

    This word denotes (a) to put a name on, to surname (Acts 10:18; 11:13; Luke 22:3).
    (b) to be called by a person's name; used of being declared to be dedicated to a person, as to the Lord (Acts 15:17 with Amos 9:12; James 2:7).
    (c) to call a person by name by charging him with an offence (e.g., Matthew 10:25; 12:24).
    (d) To call upon, invoke; in the Middle Voice, to call upon one for oneself (i.e., on one's behalf), Acts 7:59, or to call upon a person or a witness, II Corinthians 1:23, or to appeal to an authority, Acts 25:11.

<u>Thayer's Greek English Lexicon</u> on the Greek word "<u>epikaleo</u>" writes concerning a number of uses of the word:

    (a) The name of one is named over someone; i.e., he is called by his name or declared to be dedicated to him. Acts 15:17 with Amos 9:12.

    (b) Hebraistically, "To call upon by pronouncing the Name of Jehovah." Genesis 4:26; 12:8; II Kings 5:11.
    Prayers addressed to God ordinarily began with an invocation of the Divine Name. Psalms 3:2; 6:2; 7:2; Acts 2:21 with Joel 2:32; Romans 10:13; II Timothy 2:22.

    (W.F. Arndt & F.W. Gingrich in "A Greek-English Lexicon of the New Testament" confirm the same as above.)

Thus "<u>To call upon the Name</u>," or "<u>To Name</u>," is to "<u>invoke the Name</u>," or "<u>to call upon the Name</u>."

It includes the sense of "by the command and authority of Christ," and "in the use of the Name by the power of His Name being invoked for assistance."

William Phillips Hall in "<u>A Remarkable Biblical Discovery</u>" (American Tract Society, 7 West 45th Street, New York, 1929), pp. 100-104 confirms the fact that the "calling on the Name of the Lord" in both Old and New Testaments was the calling upon or invocation of that same Name.

"So that he who through faith invokes the Name Lord, as the Name of God, not only invokes that Name, but he also invokes that Name upon himself; and he who so invokes that Name upon himself, invokes, and so puts, the Lord, the Spirit, upon himself. For according to the thought and word of the Lord, as is clearly shown in Numbers 6:22-27, R.V., and Jewish Version, by going forth against Goliath "in (or, with, that is, with the invocation of) the Name of the Lord of Hosts," David invoked, or called, that Name upon himself. In other words, he put on that Name through invocation of, and so confessed trust in, that Name; and so clothed in that Name he was victorious. That was why he did not require any armour. He was clothed, in a spiritual sense, with and in the Name of the Lord of Hosts, which to him, as a Hebrew, was like a strong tower (see Proverbs 18:10) in which he was safe, and through which he prevailed."

Refer to these Scriptures where men "called on the Name of the Lord" or where they acted "in the Name of the Lord." Genesis 4:26; 12:8; 13:4; 21:33; 26:25; I Samuel 17:45; Psalms 20:1, 5, 7; 63:4; 129:8; Exodus 20:7.

Hence the calling on the Name was the invocation of the Name; it constituted the putting upon themselves His Name, assuring the blessing of the Lord there. It signified in spiritual significance a clothing of themselves in and with that Name. There is no other way. Scripturally, to put that Name on a person than by the way God has commanded and that is by "calling upon" or "invoking the Name."

The believer has "the worthy Name <u>called</u> upon" him. James 2:7. That is, the Name of the Lord Jesus Christ has been invoked upon him designating that he belongs to the Lord Jesus Christ; that he is in fellowship with the Father, the Son and the Holy Spirit.

In Water Baptism performed in or with the invocation of the Name, the believer is clothed with that Name, they put on that Name, the Name surrounds them as a strong tower. Thus the believer fulfills spiritually Romans 13:14 where Paul commands us to "put ye on the LORD JESUS CHRIST and make no provision for the flesh..."

In Water Baptism "into the Name of the Godhead" this glorious Name is called upon the believer as he also called upon that Name in salvation. Acts 2:21. Old and New Testament confirm the truth that the Name of God is called or named upon God's people. Isaiah 56:5; 62:2; 65:15; Revelations 3:12; 14:1; 22:4. The child of God will bear the Name and nature of God.

In Water Baptism Saul washed away his sins "calling on the Name of the Lord." Acts 22:16.

R. E. O. White, in "<u>The Biblical Doctrine of Initiation</u>" (Wm. B. Eerdmans Publishing Company, Grand Rapids, Michigan, 1960), pp. 148-153, when dealing with "The Use of The Name" writes:

"All types of New Testament writing characterize baptism as in or into the Name of (Jesus) Christ, or the Lord, or of the Lord Jesus, or as into Christ (Jesus; we read of one baptized "calling upon the Name of the Lord," and again of "that worthy Name which was called upon you," and "those upon whom My Name is called."

166

"Whether the calling on the Name of the Lord was done by the one baptizing or the one baptized, the implication is plain that the baptized is passing into a new relationship in which the distinctive and constitutive feature is the Name -- Kurios -- now acknowledged as belonging to Jesus as of right."

Acts 2:38; 10:48; 8:12, 16; 10:5; Galations 3:27; Romans 6:3, Acts 22:16 (cf. I Corinthians 1:13); Romans 10:8, 9; James 2:7; Acts 15:17; 9:14, 21; I Corinthians 1:2; Acts 15:14 (cf. II Timothy 2:22).

On page 150 he writes: "At the same time, with most interpreters we must avoid oversimplifying the significance of the Name: the baptismal phrase comes to imply much more than change of ownership. For one thing it must be recalled that "baptism...involved a twofold recognition of the Name...a confession of it--i.e., an avowed acceptance--on the part of the baptized, and an invocation of it on the part of the baptizer, which at once suggests a double intention."

Thus the believer calls on "The Name" and "The Name" is called upon him. This is the teaching of Old and New Testament as pertaining to the invocation of "The Name."

"For this cause I bow my knees unto the Father of our LORD JESUS CHRIST, of whom the whole family in heaven and earth is NAMED." Ephesians 3:14, 15. This is the family Name. All who are born into the family of God shall indeed bear this Name.

As "The Name" is actually invoked in repentance and salvation, in prayer and worship, in healing the sick, excorcism and all other functions in the Church, so it is that "The Name" is called upon, invoked, in Water Baptism. It is not a magic formula, or empty meaningless words, but there is authority and power and blessing when that Name is invoked in true faith and union with Him whose Name it is.

On Matthew 28:19 Kittel writes (pp. 274): "(Matthew 28:19 combines the Name of the Father and Son and Holy Ghost. Only through this link with the Name of the Son and the Holy Ghost does the Name of the Father acquire its fulness. The common Name ("onoma" occurs only once) also expressed the unity of being. Baptism into the Name means that the subject of baptism, through fellowship with the Son who is one with God, receives forgiveness of sins and comes under the operation of the Holy Spirit."

The Triune Name of God belongs to the believer by right of new birth. In new birth he becomes a new creature having a new nature. The Name of this new nature is in the Triune Name. God has ordained that the believer have this Godhead Name "called upon" him in the ordinance of baptism. This is the only distinctive ordinance in which the Triune Name of God is invoked according to Matthew 28:19. Baptism is in the Name of the Godhead, calling upon that all-glorious Triune Name as revealed in the Name of the LORD - JESUS - CHRIST.

TABLE OF SCRIPTURES ON WATER BAPTISM

We bring into concentrated focus a Table of Scriptures on Water Baptism into
the Name of the Lord, or Lord Jesus, or Jesus Christ with the various Translations and Versions of the Scriptures that are available.   The Translations
listed are at the close of this section.

(1) THE GOSPELS

    a. Matthew 28:19 - The Command of Jesus.

       "Baptizing them in the Name of the Father, and of the Son, and of the
       Holy Ghost." A.V.
       "Baptizing them into the Name..." R.V.
       "Baptizing them into the Name..." Amp. N.T.

    b. Mark 16:15.

       "He that believeth and is baptized shall be saved..." A.V.

(2) THE BOOK OF ACTS

    a. Jerusalem--Acts 2:36-41 (Peter).
       Baptized in the Name of Jesus Christ. A.V.
       Baptized into the Name of Jesus Christ. R.V.
       Baptized in the Name of the Lord Jesus. L.
       Baptized in the Name of Jesus Christ. D.
       Baptized in the Name of the Lord Jesus. S.P.

    b. Samaria--Acts 8:12-16, 35-38 (Philip).
       Baptized in the Name of the Lord Jesus. A.V. R.V.
         Into The Name of... L. D. (Note vs. 12, Lamsa)

    c. Ceasarea--Acts 10:48 (Peter).
       Baptized in the Name of the Lord. A.V.
       Baptized in the Name of Jesus Christ. R.V.
       Baptized in the Name of our Lord Jesus Christ. L.
       Baptized in the Name of the Lord Jesus Christ. D.
       Baptized in the Name of the Lord Jesus Christ. L.V.
       Baptized in the Name of the Lord Jesus Christ. S.P.

    d. Damascus--Acts 9:5-18; 22:16 (Ananias).
       Baptized, calling on the Name of the Lord. A.V.
            calling on His Name. R.V. D.
            calling on the Name of the Lord. L.

    e. Philippi--Acts 14:14-15, 31-34 (Paul).
       Believe on the Lord Jesus Christ and be saved...and was baptized...be-
       lieving in God. A.V.

    f. <u>Corinth</u>--Acts 18:8 (Paul) I Corinthians 1:10-17.
        <u>Believed on</u> the <u>Lord</u>...and were baptized. A.V.
        Were ye baptized <u>in the name</u> of Paul? A.V.

    g. <u>Ephesus</u>--Acts 19:1-6 (Paul).
        Baptized <u>in the Name</u> of the <u>Lord Jesus</u>. A.V. R.V.
        Baptized <u>in the Name</u> of our <u>Lord Jesus Christ</u>. L.
        Baptized <u>in the Name</u> of the <u>Lord Jesus Christ</u>. D.
        Baptized <u>in the Name</u> of the <u>Lord Jesus Christ</u>. L.V.
        Baptized <u>in the Name</u> of the <u>Lord Jesus Christ</u>. S.P.

(3) <u>THE EPISTLES</u>

    a. <u>Romans</u> (Paul) -- Romans 6:3-4.
        As many of <u>us</u> as were baptized <u>into Jesus Christ</u> were baptized into
        <u>His</u> death...buried <u>with Him</u> by baptism. A.V.

    b. <u>Corinthians</u> (Paul)--I Corinthians 1:10-17.
        Were ye baptized <u>in the Name</u> of <u>Paul</u>? Lest any should say I baptized in
        mine own name. A.V.
        <u>Into</u> the Name of Paul? R.V.
        All baptized <u>unto</u> Moses. A.V.
        <u>Into</u> Moses. R.V. I Corinthians 10:1-3.

    c. <u>Galatians</u> (Paul) -- Galatians 3:27.
        As many as were baptized <u>into Christ</u>. A.V.
        Those of us...baptized <u>in The Name</u> of <u>Christ</u>...L.

    d. <u>Ephesians</u> (Paul) -- Ephesians 4:4; Hebrews 6:2.
        There is...<u>One Baptism</u>.)
        Doctrine of <u>Baptisms</u>.) Acts 19:5

    e. <u>Colossians</u> (Paul)--Colossians 2:12.
        Buried <u>with Him</u> in Baptism. A.V.

    f. <u>The 12 Tribes</u> (James)--James 2:7.
        That <u>worthy Name</u> by which you are <u>distinguished</u> and <u>called</u> (<u>The Name</u>
        of <u>Christ invoked</u> in <u>Baptism</u>). Amp. N.T.

    g. <u>The Strangers</u> (Peter)--I Peter 3:20-21.
        The like figure whereunto <u>Baptism</u> doth also now save us, not the put-
        ting away of the filth of the flesh...but the answer of a good con-
        science towards <u>God by the resurrection</u> of <u>Jesus Christ</u>.

(TRANSLATIONS used in the above Table of Scriptures)

    1. Authorized King James Version. (A.V.)
    2. Revised Version. (R.V.)
    3. The Lamsa Translation. Authorized Bible of the East (The Peshitta). (L.)
    4. The Douay Version. (D.)
    5. The Amplified New Testament. (Amp. N.T.)
    6. The Syriac Peshitta. (S.P.)
    7. The Latin Vulgate (Douay Version translated from this). (L.V.)

CHAPTER VIII

THE GODHEAD REVEALED IN BAPTISM

1. IN RELATION TO THE SON OF GOD:

At Water Baptism
(Matt.3:13-17)

1. THE FATHER	2. THE SON	3. THE HOLY SPIRIT
The Father's Voice, "This is My Beloved Son."	The Lamb of God buried in the waters of Jordan and raised from the same in full obedience to the will of the Father.	The Holy Spirit Descending and remaining on Him as the Dove, and the Anointing.

At the Crucifixion

1. THE FATHER	2. THE SON	3. THE HOLY SPIRIT
God gave His Son. John 3:16. Put the Son to death. Made Him the Sacrifice. Isaiah 53:6, 10.	Went to the Cross voluntarily. "I lay down My life." John 10:17.	Enabled and empowered by the Holy Spirit to go to the Cross. Hebrews 9:14.

At the Resurrection

1. THE FATHER	2. THE SON	3. THE HOLY SPIRIT
God raised His Son. "Thou art My Son, this day have I begotten Thee." Psalms 2:7. Acts 13:33. Romans 1:4. Rev. 1:5. Col. 1:18. Acts 2:32. Gal. 1:1.	Jesus raised Himself. John 10:18. "I have power to lay down My life and I have power to take it again. Phil.2:8. Matt. 26:39, 42, 44.	The Holy Spirit quickened and raised the Body of Jesus from the dead. I Peter 3:18. Heb. 9:14. Romans 8:11.

172

2. IN RELATION TO THE CHURCH:

At Our Water Baptism

1.	2.	3.
THE FATHER	THE SON	THE HOLY SPIRIT

BAPTIZING INTO THE NAME

Of the Father   And of the Son   And of the Holy Spirit

INTO THE NAME OF THE

LORD   JESUS   CHRIST

INTO THE
DEATH, BURIAL AND RESURRECTION

Thus, as the Godhead is revealed in the Baptism of the Son of God, the Head of the Church, as also in His Crucifixion and Resurrection, so the Godhead is revealed and involved in the Water Baptismal Ordinance in the Church which is His Body and in identification with His Death and Resurrection. Romans 6:3-4.

This is the Atonement, wrought in the three days and three nights of Calvary. Matthew 12:38-40.

The whole Godhead was involved.

The Father gave His Only Begotten Son. The Son was offered upon Calvary as the Lamb of God taking away the sin of the world. And the Holy Spirit raised Him from the dead to live in the power of an endless life.

The Father, the Son and the Holy Spirit were each involved in the work of the Cross and in the Death, Burial and Resurrection of the LORD JESUS CHRIST. Thus in Water Baptism the believer is linked with the Eternal Godhead, being baptized into THE TRIUNE NAME of the TRIUNE GOD, even THE NAME OF THE LORD JESUS CHRIST.

A FORMULA OF SCRIPTURE

In the light of the Doctrine of Baptism in the Gospels, the Acts and the Epistles, we bring together a Formula of Scripture which the writer believes will fulfill that which is contained in each of these sections of the New Testament.

The Apostolic interpretation of Baptism then is as follows:

AS TO FORM OR MODE:

> Water Baptism is by immersion, not sprinkling. Immersion, or submersion only sets forth properly the significance of Baptism as identification with the Lord Jesus Christ in His death, burial and resurrection.

AS TO FORMULA:

> The following is a Formula composed of three verses of Scripture; one from the Gospels, one from the Book of Acts and one from the Epistles. It is only as the doctrine of baptism is considered in the Gospels, the Acts and the Epistles that one gains the full truth on the subject. This has been done in the course of this compilation of notes. We have looked at the Scriptures pertaining to Baptism in the Gospels, the Acts and the Epistles. By bringing together a verse from each we present a Formula made up of Scripture verses from each section.

A FORMULA OF SCRIPTURE VERSES is as follows:

> "I baptize you INTO THE NAME:
>   Of the Father,
>   And of the Son,
>   And of the Holy Spirit:
>   Into the Name of the Lord Jesus Christ,
>   That like as Christ was raised up from the dead by the glory of the
>   Father, even so you also shall arise to walk in newness of life."

This is simply placing three verses of Scripture together in a Formula composed of Scripture which fulfills that which is set forth in the Gospels, the Acts and the Epistles.

Surely one cannot violate that which constitutes a Formula when using the very Scriptures themselves as a Formula! There is power in the Word of God. His words are spirit and life when spoken in true assurance of heart and not used as mere ritual or form just to fulfill a ceremony.

1. It quotes the Command of Matthew 28:19, the words of Jesus, from the Gospel.

2. It invokes the Triune Name as declared and invoked in Acts 2:36,38.

3. It declares the spiritual truth of Baptism as set forth in Romans 6:3 and 6:4 and in the New Testament Epistles.

    Thus we allow Scripture to interpret Scripture.
    The Tri-unity of God is revealed in Water Baptism.

This Formula of Scripture, setting forth the TRI-UNITY of God is similar to that which is seen in the Creation of man in the Book of Genesis.

"And GOD (Elohim) said, Let US make man in OUR image after OUR likeness .... So GOD (Elohim) created man in HIS own image, in the image of GOD created he him...." Genesis 1:26,27.

Thus verse 26 sets forth GOD in His TRIUNE Being, His Threeness of Being, and verse 27 sets forth GOD in His UNITY of Being, Three in One and One in Three.

GOD is revealed in His TRI-UNITY in Genesis 1:26, 27 in the creation of man in the image of God. God is revealed in His Tri-Unity in the redemption of man as testified in Water Baptism.

To those who believe that there is power in the invocation of "The Name" this will not be a mere form of words. It will not be simply quoting a few verses of Scripture over the candidate. One cannot go wrong or be unScriptural when using the Scriptures themselves in proper faith and understanding. The invocation of the virtues and power of the Godhead as Father, Son and Holy Spirit is in the invocation of the Godhead Name. Baptism takes on rich and full meaning as one enters into New Covenant relationship with the Godhead through our Lord Jesus Christ.

Matthew Henry's Commentary, Volume V comments on Matthew 28:19:

(1) "It is into the Name of the Father, believing Him to be the Father of our Lord Jesus Christ (for that is principally intended here), by eternal generation, and our Father, as our Creator, Preserver, and Benefactor, to whom there we resign ourselves, as our absolute owner and proprietor, to actuate us and dispose of us; as our supreme rector and governor, to rule us, as free agents by His law; and as our chief good, and highest end.

(2) It is into the Name of the Son, the Lord Jesus Christ, the Son of God, and correlate to the Father. Baptism was in a particular manner administered in the Name of the Lord Jesus, Acts 8:16; 19:5. In baptism we assent, as Peter did, Thou art the Christ the Son of the living God (Matthew 16:16), and consent, as Thomas did, My Lord and my God (John 20:28). We take Christ to be our Prophet, Priest and King, and give up ourselves to be taught, and saved, and ruled, by Him.

(3) It is into the Name of the Holy Ghost. Believing the Godhead of the Holy Spirit, and His agency in carrying on our redemption, we give up ourselves to His conduct and operation, as our sanctifier, teacher, guide and comforter."

In the invocation of the TRIUNE Name we have the New Testament fulfillment of that which was set forth in the invocation of a Threefold Name in the Old Testament.

(1) There was a Threefold Name called upon the sons of Joseph as they were adopted into the Twelve Tribes of Israel. Genesis 48:13-16.

Verse 16 says, "... and let my Name be named on them, and the Name of my fathers Abraham and Isaac...."

Thus the Name of "Abraham, Isaac and Jacob" (A Threefold Name) was called or invoked upon Ephraim and Manasseh as they were adopted into the Tribes of Israel. By the invocation of this Name they were in Covenant relationship. This Threefold Name brought them into the Israel of God, entitling them to the promises, privileges and blessings of the Abrahamic Covenant.

It has pleased God to call Himself "The God of Abraham, the God of Isaac and the God of Jacob." Exodus 3:6.

Abraham, Isaac and Jacob illustrate typically certain characteristics of the Godhead as Father, Son and Holy Spirit. Let the student refer back to the Types of God in Chapter One.

The believer today is adopted in the True Spiritual Israel of God through the Triune Name invoked upon him.

(2) There was a Threefold invocation of the Name of JEHOVAH upon the Nation of Israel in the Aaronic blessing commanded by the Lord through the lips of Moses. Numbers 6:22-27. Note especially verses 24-27.

> "The LORD bless thee and keep thee:
> The LORD make His face shine upon thee, and be gracious unto thee
> The LORD lift up His countenance upon thee, and give thee peace.
>
> And they shall PUT MY NAME upon the children of Israel; and I will bless them."

Thus the Nation of Israel had the invocation of a Threefold (yet One) Name upon them. This Name "Jehovah" is the Name of the Triune God. Thus Israel had the Name of God called upon them. This is why He speaks of His people who are "called by My Name." II Chronicles 7:14.

Israel had the Threefold Name called upon them and this was the source of all blessing. It was because of their iniquities that the Name of the Lord was blasphemed among the Gentiles. The Gentiles asked whether these were the people called by the Name of the Lord by the way they lived. Ezekiel 20:39; 39:7,25; 43:7,8. Romans 2:24.

This is why the believer who names the Name of Christ and has that worthy Name called upon him must depart from iniquity. II Timothy 2:19. James 2:7. Otherwise the believer "takes the Name of the Lord his God in vain" if his life does not correspond with the Name he has called upon him. Exodus 20:7.

Thus, just as Israel had a Threefold Name called upon them in blessing from the Lord, by Aaron the High Priest, so the believer has a Threefold Name called upon him according to the commandment of our Great High Priest, the Lord Jesus Christ. For Israel it was the Threefold invocation of THE NAME of the LORD. For the believer it is the Triune Name of the LORD in and through THE NAME of the LORD JESUS CHRIST.

(3) The New Testament command of Jesus for Baptism into THE NAME of the Father and of the Son and of the Holy Spirit now fulfills that which was demonstrated in the Old Testament in the two accounts given above.

The believer has the <u>Threefold Name</u> of the Father, Son and Holy Spirit called upon, fulfilling that which was illustrated in the adoption of Joseph's sons into Natural Israel.

The believer has the <u>Threefold Name</u> of the LORD as finding its fulness in and through the Name of the LORD JESUS CHRIST called upon him, thus fulfilling that which Natural Israel had put upon them under the Aaronic Priesthood. The believer is under the Melchisedec Priesthood and thus finds greater blessing as found in the all-glorious Name of the Eternal Godhead.

There should be great joy in believing and obeying the command of the Lord in Water Baptism and having THE GODHEAD NAME called or invoked upon those who are already His by new birth. What greater Name in heaven or earth could the believer be called by?

Undoubtedly, this is why there has been so much controversy in the area of Water Baptism as to mode, formula and interpretation. "The Name" may be invoked or called upon for any other activity in the life of the Church or the believer, but when it comes to the use of that same Name in Baptism there arises great controversy. In the light of all that pertains to "The Name" in Old and New Testaments, what other ordinance has so much meaning to it, relative to His Name, as Baptism when the believer takes that Name upon himself.

It is this Name upon the believer which fulfills all that is typified in "The Name" in the Tabernacle of Moses, in the Temple of Solomon, upon the children of Israel, and incorporated into many of the personal names of the Israelites.

AS TO APOSTOLIC INTERPRETATION:

Water Baptism is clearly taught to be identification with the Son of God in His death, burial and resurrection.

It is also New Covenant Circumcision of the heart, an operation of God which takes place by faith in the Word and the Spirit of God.

Baptism involves the establishment of a Covenant of grace between God and the person baptized.

Finally, Water Baptism in all its related areas must be obeyed, so that the believer will have "<u>the answer of a good conscience towards God</u>." That is, not governed by itself, or the traditions of men, but a conscience which lines itself up by submission and obedience to the infallible Word and will of God. I Peter 3:21.

QUOTABLE QUOTATIONS

The following quotations are taken from various sources and are worthy of our consideration as it relates to Water Baptism in the Name of God. It will be seen that both Matthew 28:19 and the Name of the Lord, or Jesus Christ is used or else one or the other is referred to.

Some of the quotations are rather full. One of the reasons for this being that some of these reference books are out of print or not within the reach of the average layman.

1. The Writings of the Church Fathers.

Although these writings are not accepted as inspired and infallible Scripture, nor are they as authoritative as the Bible, yet they give record concerning that which pertains to Water Baptism.

It seems that the Early Church Fathers did not recognize any special or set formula but used either Matthew 28:19 or the Name of the Lord, or the Name of Jesus Christ.

(1) The Didache, or Teaching of the Twelve Apostles. Didache 7:1.

The Didache was one of the earliest writings of the early post-apostolic Church. It held great authority in the early Church. It writes on baptism:

"Concerning baptism, baptize in this way. Having first rehearsed all these things, baptize in the Name of the Father and the Son and of the Holy Spirit in living water ...."

"Let none eat or drink of your Eucharist save such as are baptized into the Name of the Lord."

(2) Irenaeus, one of the Ante-Nicene Fathers, was a disciple of Polycarp, who was a disciple of the Apostle John, the disciple of the Lord Jesus Christ. Irenaeus lived between A. D. 120 - 202. The following quotation from "Fragments from the Lost Writings of Irenaeus," which will be found in "The Ante-Nicene Fathers," Vol I, page 574, also bears testimony to the use of the Name of the Lord Jesus Christ in Christian baptism shortly after the close of the apostolic age.

(William Phillips Hall, p. 74. "A Remarkable Biblical Discovery.")

(3) Justin Martyr, A.D. 139, Apology 61.

These quotations from chapter 61 read "... for in the Name of God the Father of all and Lord, and of our Saviour Jesus Christ, and of the Holy Ghost, they then receive the bath in water."

And again "... he who is illuminated is washed (baptized) in the Name of Jesus Christ."

(4) Tertullian, who died about A.D. 245, in a tract, "Concerning Baptism" (De Baptismo), written against Quintilla of Carthage, states:

"The law of immersion has been imposed, and the form has been prescribed. 'Go' said He, 'teach the nations, immersing them in the Name of the Father, and of the Son, and of the Holy Ghost' Matthew 28:19." (De Baptismo, C 13)

Also in the same tract he says, "He (Christ) gave as His last command that they should immerse into the Father and the Son and the Holy Ghost, not into one person."

It is to be remembered that Tertullian was the greatest early theologian of that Century and he was in the midst of the great Arian controversy concerning the Trinity of the Godhead. Hence he emphasized a Triune Baptism by being baptized three times, each with reference to the three Persons of Matthew 28:19.

(5) Cyprian, in Writings of Cyprian, A. D. 200-258, writes concerning Baptism and quotes Acts 2:38 from a manuscript or version antedating by many years the Vulgate and Greek manuscripts from which the Douay and English versions were translated. Cyprian was a spiritual son and pupil of Tertullian.

"Repent and be baptized every one of you in the Name of the Lord Jesus Christ for the remission of sins, and ye shall receive the gift of the Holy Spirit." (Epistles of Cyprian, Epistle 72, ch. 17, "Ante-Nicene Fathers," American Edition.)

Thus Cyprian confirms the use of the Name LORD in the Name of the LORD Jesus Christ as in the Baptismal command of Peter on the Day of Pentecost, after he had declared that God had made this "Jesus both Lord and Christ." Acts 2:36,37,38.

(6) Clement, in the Recognition of Clement (Schaff Philip, History of the Christian Church, Volume II, New York: Charles Scribner's Sons, 1844, p. 436) gives full instructions for performing the rite. (Book III, chapter 67)

"But everyone of you shall be baptized in ever flowing waters, the Name of the Triune Beatitude being invoked over him."

The Triune Beatitude was the command of Matthew 28:19, following the prominant example of Tertullian of Triune Baptism in respect of Matthew 28:19.

(7) Jerome, who gave to us the translation, from the Latin Vulgate, known as the Douay Version records the Triune Name of the Lord Jesus Christ in the records of Baptism in Acts 8:16; 10:48 and 19:5.

(8) The Constitution of the Holy Apostles.

This source purports to date from apostolic times, but probably is of Syrian origin and a compilation of ancient sources during the fourth century. Its value is in the compiling of much ancient sources. (Ante-Nicene Fathers. Roberts and Donaldson, American reprint of the Edinburgh edition. New York: Charles Scribner's Sons, 1905. Introduction, p. 388.)

Section 3 of Book III states, "After that, either thou ... or a pres-
byter that is under thee, shall in the solemn form name over them the
Father and Son and Holy Spirit, and shall dip them in the water ...."

Book VII contains ancient material traced back to the second century
Didache. Book VII, chapters 43 and 44 give further detail of the Baptismal rite where it is stated, "Look down from heaven and sanctify
this water and give it grace and power that so he that is to be baptized according to the command of Thy Christ, may be crucified with
Him, and may die with Him, and may be buried with Him, and may rise
with Him ...."

(9) Testimony from the Fathers.

B. F. Smith, in Christian Baptism (Nashville, Tennessee: Broadman
Press, 1970) pp. 74-76 lists a number of the names of the Church Fathers who admit that the customary mode of baptism in 3rd and 4th
centuries was by immersion and all listed testify to immersion with a
trinitarian formula.

Cyril, Bishop of Jerusalem. A. D. 315-85.
Ambrose. A. D. 340-97.
Jerome. A. D. 340-420.
John Chrysostom. A. D. 345-407.
Augustine. A. D. 354-430.
Pelagius. A. D. 363-65.

During some of the period the great heresies concerning the Godhead
were raging and thus the trinitarian formula of Matthew 28:19 was
used as a powerful verse in its value against the heresies of that
era.

Some commentators have expressed the opinion that the Church of the Apostolic
age used the Name of the Lord Jesus Christ in baptism, and that the Church
afterwards substituted the words "the Name of the Father, and of the Son, and
of the Holy Ghost" in place thereof. As a matter of historical record such
appears to have been the case.

It seems evident then that from the close of the first century Baptism was
regularly administered in the threefold Name according to Matthew 28:19. This
is particularly evident in the 2nd, 3rd and 4th Centuries when the Church was
torn by various heresies concerning the Godhead and the Person of Christ.

The writer of these notes believes that the above evidence, not only shows the
validity of Matthew 28:19, but it also shows how the Church over the centuries
following the Apostolic period neglected to invoke the Godhead Name as revealed in the Triune Name of the Lord Jesus Christ. As the Church declined in its
glory, so there was a departure from "The faith once delivered to the saints"
(Jude 3) in the area of Water Baptism as in many other areas of truth.

The revelation of the glory in that Triune Name was almost lost, as were so
many other truths given to the Early Apostolic Church. The Lord has been recovering "lost truth" to the Church since the time of the Reformation and
among these truths is the recovery of "the Name" of the Eternal Godhead, the
Name of the LORD as in the LORD Jesus Christ relative to water Baptism.

2. **F. B. Meyer**

Lange dissents from Meyer when he maintains that the passage (Matthew 28:19) is "improperly termed the <u>baptismal formula</u>," assigning as reason that Jesus does not, assuredly, dictate the <u>words</u> which are to be employed in the administration of baptism.

He does quote Meyer as further saying that "No trace is to be found of the employment of these words by the Apostolic Church...."

(Lange, John Peter. "<u>The Gospel According to Matthew</u>." Translated from the Third German Edition, with additions by Philip Schaff. New York: Charles Scribner's Sons, 1899.)

3. **Professor George T. Purves, D. D.**

In his book, <u>Christianity in the Apostolic Age</u>, p. 56, he says: "The first record of their use (that is the use of the word, "the Name of the Father and of the Son and of the Holy Spirit") in baptism is in The Teaching of the Apostles (about A. D. 100)." This has already been noted in the Didache.

4. **Professor John Alfred Faulkner, D. D.**

In <u>Crisis in the Early Church</u>, p. 13 f., writes: "There is not the least doubt that the baptisms in the Acts were in the Name of Jesus only, but that does not necessarily mean that Jesus never spoke, Matthew 28:19."

5. **Professor Kirsopp Lake, D. D.**

In <u>Dictionary of the Apostolic Church</u>, Vol. I, p. 29, says: "There is no doubt that the writer of Acts regarded baptism as the normal means of entry into the Christian Church. There is also no doubt that he represents baptism at an early stage of Christian practice in which baptism was 'in the name of the Lord Jesus' (or 'of Jesus Christ'), not in the triadic formula (Acts 2:38; 8:16; 10:48; 19:5)."

(William Phillips Hall, p. 61. "A Remarkable Biblical Discovery.")

6. **Dr. A. C. Gaebelein**

A Trinitarian and noted Bible expositor writes: "I rather think inasmuch as baptism is into the death of Christ, that the formula 'In the Name of the Lord Jesus Christ' is the correct one."

7. **The Wonderful Name of Jesus**, by E. W. Kenyon (Kenyon's Gospel Publishing Society. 528 West Amerige, Fullerton, California. 1927.)

Kenyon says, concerning Baptism into the Name of the Father and of the Son and of the Holy Spirit:

"When we are baptized into the Name of the Father it gives us the place of a child and all the privileges of a child, all the inheritance and wealth of the child. We are baptized into the protection and care and fellowship of the God of the universe as our Father. We take on all that union means.

We have the standing of a Son, the privilege of a Son, the responsibilities of a Son. We have become by that baptism a joint heir with Jesus, and an heir of God .... When we are baptized into the Name of the Holy Spirit, we are baptized into the Name, wealth, power, wisdom, and glory of God's representative on the earth - all the Spirit has we are baptized into." Page 57.

Again we would ask, "What does it mean to be baptized into the Name of the Lord Jesus Christ?"

Once more we quote from E. W. Kenyon. He writes:

"When a believer is baptized into the Name of the Lord Jesus he puts on the Lord Jesus .... Baptizing into the Name of the Lord Jesus Christ is even richer and fuller than either of these -- it comprehends all that is in them with additions. When I am baptized into Christ, I put on Christ .... Baptism in this sense is equivalent to marriage. When the wife puts on marriage she takes her husband's name and enters into her husband's possessions and has legal right to her husband's home. When the believer is baptized into the Name of Christ, he puts on all that is in Christ. He not only puts on the Name but takes his legal rights and his privileges in Christ." Page 59.

8. <u>Names and Titles of the Holy Spirit</u>, from <u>Jones Catholic Doctrine of the Trinity</u>, Page 57, 83, Vol. II.

"The disciples of Christ were commanded to baptize in the Name of the Father, and of the Son and of the Holy Ghost." And without doubt, the Baptism they administered was in all cases agreeable to (with) the prescribed form. Nevertheless, we are told of some who were commanded to be baptized in the Name of the Lord (Acts 10:48), and particularly in the Name of the Lord Jesus (Acts 8:16), so that there was a strong defect either in the Baptism itself, or in the account we have of it; or, the mention of One Person in the Trinity must imply the Presence, Name and Authority of Them All; as the passage is understood by Iranaeus, i.e.;

> "By Baptism in the Name of Christ, is to be understood,
> He who anointed,
> He who was anointed,
> And the anointing itself by which He was anointed;
> in other words, FATHER, SON AND HOLY SPIRIT."

(Irenaeus. 50.3 and 100.20)

9. <u>William Phillips Hall</u>, in "A Remarkable Biblical Discovery," or "The Name of God according to the Scriptures" (pp. 61, 63, 64, 76-78) says:

"For some eighteen hundred years the Church in its various branches has ministered the rite (of baptism) with the use of the words "I baptize thee ... in The Name of the Father, and of the Son and of the Holy Spirit." But <u>those words were never used in baptism by the original apostles or by the Church during the early days of its existence according to the record of the Acts of the Apostles and the Epistles of the New Testament</u>. According

to that record in the earliest manuscript readings and versions, all baptisms in those early days were commanded to be or stated to have been performed in, or with the invocation of, the Name of the Lord Jesus Christ."
Page 61.

"The Church of the apostolic age used the Name of the Lord Jesus Christ....
All Manuscripts and versions of Matthew's Gospel, without exception contain
the words as recorded in Matthew 28:19." Page 63.

"Assuming therefore, that the words of Matthew 28:19 were actually spoken
by the Lord Jesus Christ, how can that be reconciled with the obvious fact
that, according to the Acts and the apostolic Epistles, Christian baptism
in the apostolic age was invariably commanded and performed in the Name of
the Lord Jesus Christ." The answer to this question, which has remained unanswered for some 1800 years, will be found in the original apostolic interpretation of the words, "The Name of the Father and of the Son and of
the Holy Spirit." Page 63.

"Although the Lord Jesus Christ commanded His original disciples to "disciple all nations, baptizing them in the Name of the Father and of the Son
and of the Holy Spirit (Matthew 28:19, Greek Text), neither they nor the
Church of the apostolic age ever literally repeated the words of that command in baptizing anybody, so far as the New Testament bears witness. So
far as the New Testament shows, the rite of baptism during the apostolic
age was commanded, and took place, "in" and "into" the Name of "the Lord"
(A. V. and D. V.) or "Jesus Christ" (A. V., R. V. and D. V.), or "the Lord
Jesus" (A. V., R. V. and D. V.), which, as we shall show, are in each case
and every instance but abbreviations of the full Name of the Lord Jesus
Christ, or of the Lord Jesus, the Christ. There are no exceptions recorded.
Any person can verify the accuracy of this statement by reading Acts 2:38,
8:16, 10:48 and 19:5. A. V., R. V., and D. V." Page 64.

"And now may it be distinctly noted that the Lord Jesus Christ did not command His disciples to baptize in the Names (plural) of the Father, and of
the Son, and of the Holy Spirit, but in the Name (singular) - "Father, Son,
and Holy Spirit." The Spirit of truth according to the Scriptures, revealed
to those apostles and disciples and to the church of the apostolic age the
fact that "the Name of the Father, and of the Son, and of the Holy Spirit"
is the Name Lord, revealed to mankind, and therefore invokable in prayer
and otherwise primarily and always for salvation by mankind only in and
through the Name of the Lord Jesus Christ, the Son of God.

Baptism was never commanded nor performed during the apostolic age, in, (or
with that is, with the invocation of) any other Name than the Name LORD, IN
AND THROUGH THE NAME OF THE LORD JESUS CHRIST, the Son of God.

Saul persecuted the Christians in those days because he believed them to be
guilty of idolatry and blasphemy in calling on or invoking in prayer for
salvation the Name ("Lord") of God the Father, IN AND THROUGH THE NAME OF
THE LORD JESUS CHRIST." Pages 76-78.

10. The Exalted Name, by Lucy P. Knott (Nazarene Publishing House, 2923 Troost
Avenue, Kansas City, Mo., 1937.)

From this beautifully written work we quote several portions taken from pp.
224-229, and 234, 245, 257, relative to the Triune Name.

The Mystery of the Godhead

"The Exalted Name shows forth the Godhead. In the Name 'Jehovah' three persons are veiled in one name: in the name 'Lord Jesus Christ' one person is expressed by three names while through these names, as we shall find, the Father, Son, and Holy Ghost show forth. The mystery of the Godhead is presented in the Exalted Name which is so full of mystery that it alone is enough to declare the authorship of the Bible. With all its hidden mystery, nevertheless it is given to us as a revelation. No man-made book could present such a name. In the Lord Jesus Christ "dwelleth all the fulness of the Godhead bodily." The Exalted Name must needs show forth the Father and the Spirit as well as the Son. While the Son bears the Exalted Name, the Father and the Spirit are equally exalted for they are all one in essence." (pp. 226, 227)

The Name "Lord"

"In the name 'Lord' the first person of the Godhead shows forth. In the Old Testament name 'Jehovah,' the Godhead is veiled: in the New Testament name 'Lord Jesus Christ,' the Godhead shows forth. This Name does not infringe upon the names of the blessed Trinity nor upon the office work. As before observed the Father is the 'everlasting Father,' the Son is 'the same yesterday, today and forever' and the Holy Ghost is 'the eternal Spirit.' Just as the name, 'Jehovah' could be known and worshipped only by Israel, so the name, 'Lord Jesus Christ," can be known and worshipped only by the true Church ...." (page 224)

"The name 'Lord' shows forth the majesty, will and foreknowledge of the Father. The New Testament identifies the name 'Lord' with the Name 'Lord' (Jehovah). Every quotation from the Old Testament where the name Jehovah (Lord) is used, is applied to the Lord Jesus." (page 229)

The Name "Jesus"

"In the name 'Jesus' the second person of the Godhead shows forth. We could have no conception of the meaning of the Exalted Name but for the name 'Jesus.' Indeed it is this name which has caused the Son to be so exalted in the Godhead. It is because of the name 'JESUS' that God hath made Him both 'Lord' and 'Christ.' (page 245)

The Name "Christ"

"In the name 'Christ' the third person of the Godhead shows forth. Not only has the Godhead made Jesus 'Lord,' He has made Him 'Christ.' While the name 'Lord' shows forth the knowledge and will of the Father, the name 'Christ' shows forth the Holy Ghost." (page 234)

The Name "Lord Jesus Christ"

"In the Old Testament Scriptures the 'fullness of time' had not come for the Godhead to reveal Himself through the fullness of the name 'Lord Jesus Christ.' In those Scriptures the revelation He gives of Himself is through the first part of the Exalted Name 'Lord' (Jehovah). In this name the Son appears, speaks and acts, directed by the Father and empowered by the Holy Spirit. In Jehovah, the names of the triune God are veiled. In the Exalted Name - Lord Jesus Christ - they show forth. And "His name is one" (Zech. 14:9). (page 257)

"Like the mystery of the triune God, our finite brains will never be able to compass the mystery of its meaning, doubtless through eternity we shall be learning it. Though divided into three parts it is so harmonious that the full name is an unbroken whole; yet each part is perfect and distinct in itself as is every combination of its parts. It is the Exalted Name given to the Son." (page 225)

11. Strong's Exhaustive Concordance.

On the Name "Christ," we quote from Strong's Concordance and the Greek Section.

5548	Chrio	- Luke 4:18. Acts 4:27. Acts 10:38. Through the idea of contact; to smear or rub with oil. i.e., to consecrate to an office or religious service: Anoint.
5547	Christos	- from 5548. Anointed: i.e., Messiah, an epithet of Jesus: Christ.
5545	Chrisma	- An unguent, or smearing; i.e., the special endowment ("Chrism") of the Holy Spirit- Anointing, unction. I John 2:20,27.

On this we comment:

Thus showing the Anointer (the Father),
the Anointed (the Son), and
the Anointing (the Holy Spirit).

SUMMARY AND CONCLUSION

The only proper reconciliation of all the Scriptures pertaining to Baptism in the Gospels, in the accounts in the Book of Acts and the teaching in the Epistles, is the following:

> Baptism into the Name of the Father, and of the Son and of the Holy Spirit is Baptism into THE NAME of the LORD JESUS CHRIST. The Triune Name of the Triune God.

> This was Apostolic fulfillment of the command of Jesus for this ordinance.

No wonder Malachi (1:6) declares, "O Priests, that despise MY NAME. And ye say, wherein have we despised THY NAME?" For the Priests in Malachi's time, the Name of God was despised by the behavior of the Priests in Temple ministrations. For the believer today, the Name of God is often despised when it comes to the truth of that Name as pertaining to Baptism.

And again, Malachi (3:16) gives us a wonderful word of assurance for meditating on the Name of God, by saying: "Then they that feared the LORD spake often one to another, and the LORD hearkened and heard it, and A BOOK OF REMEMBRANCE was written before Him for them that feared the LORD and that THOUGHT UPON HIS NAME."

It is the greatest Name we can think upon. In the closing days of this Age, the Name of God is to take great prominence. This is seen in the Book of Revelation.

The Name in the Book of Revelation

1. The Lord commended the Church at Pergamos for "holding fast His Name." Revelation 2:13.

2. The Church at Philadelphia was also commended because they had "kept His Word and not denied His Name." It is to this same Church that the Lord promised that He would give to the overcomer, "The Name of God ... The Name of the City of My God ... and My New Name." Revelation 3:7-13.

3. In the period of Antichristal reign, he "opens his mouth in blasphemy against God and His Name ..." while all the world is caused to receive "The Name, the Number or the Mark of the Beast." The whole world will be divided over A NAME in the Last Days. Revelation 13:6, 16-18.

   This will either be the Name of the Lord Jesus Christ, the Name of God, or else the Name of the Beast, the Antichrist, the Name of Satan. The choice of the Name depends on ourselves. In the Name we take is our eternal nature and destiny. II Thessalonians 2:4. I John 2:18. Revelation 13:16-18.

4. The Great Harlot Church has "the Names of blasphemy" written in her forehead. It is the Name of Mystery, declaring her nature and characteristics. Revelation 17:1-5.

5. The Book of Revelation closes with a promise for the redeemed, " ... they shall see His face and HIS NAME shall be in their foreheads." Rev. 22:4.

What greater Name would any believer desire to have upon his forehead for all eternity? Though in this world we shall be hated for His Name's sake there is no greater Name ever to be revealed. Mark 13:13. Acts 9:13-16.

THE NAME of the LORD JESUS CHRIST is the most comprehensive NAME OF GOD ever to be revealed to mankind. It is the greatest REDEMPTIVE NAME in this world and in the world to come, because it comprehends the greatest, even THE FATHER, THE SON, and THE HOLY SPIRIT. It comprehends the Fulness of the Godhead Bodily in the Lord Jesus Christ. What a privilege to have that Name called or invoked upon us.

The Book of Genesis opens with, "In the beginning GOD ...." Genesis 1:1. It is the declaration of the Triune God.

The Book of Revelation closes with, "The Grace of our LORD JESUS CHRIST be with you all. Amen." Revelation 22:21. It is the declaration of the Triune Name.

-- AMEN --

APPENDIX I

REDEMPTIVE NAMES

1. The Redemptive Name, YAHWEH, or Jehovah, I Am what I Am, I will be who I will be. Exodus 3:14-16.

2. Jehovah Elohim.   Genesis 2:4.   The Lord, our Creator.

3. Jehovah El Elyon.   Genesis 14:22.   The Lord, the Most High God, the Owner.

4. Jehovah Adonia.   Genesis 15:2.   The Lord, the Master.

5. Jehovah El Olam.   Genesis 21:33.   The Lord, the Everlasting.

6. Jehovah Jireh.   Genesis 22:14.   The Lord, the Provider.

7. Jehovah Rapha.   Exodus 15:26.   The Lord, the Healer.

8. Jehovah Nissi.   Exodus 17:15.   The Lord, the Banner.

9. Jehovah MakaddeshKem.   Exodus 31:13.   The Lord, our Sanctification.

10. Jehovah Shalom.   Judges 6:24.   The Lord, our Peace.

11. Jehovah Shaphat.   Judges 11:27.   The Lord, the Judge.

12. Jehovah Saboath.   I Samuel 1:3.   The Lord of Hosts.

13. Jehovah Zidkenu.   Jeremiah 23:6.   The Lord, our Righteousness.

14. Jehovah Raah.   Psalms 23:1.   The Lord, the Shepherd.

15. Jehovah Elyon.   Psalms 7:17.   The Lord, the Blesser.

16. Jehovah Hosenu.   Psalms 95:6.   The Lord, the Maker.

17. Jehovah Gibbor.   Isaiah 42:13.   The Lord, the Mighty.

18. Jah- Jehovah.   Isaiah 12:2; 26:4.   The Lord, the Jehovah.

19. Jehovah Shammah.   Ezekiel 48:35.   The Lord, the Everpresent.

20. Jehovah Jehoshua Messiah. Matthew 1:21. Acts 2:36. The Lord Jesus Christ

A study of the Compound Redemptive Names of JEHOVAH in the Old Testament unfold the glories of this Covenantal and Redemptive Name of God. Each of these Names, relative to man's need, find their ultimate fulfillment in the greatest Compound Redemptive Name ever revealed and as unfolded in the New Testament, this Name is the LORD JESUS CHRIST. It is Divinely suitable that the Redemptive Names of God find their consummation in the Redeemer Himself. This Triune Name embodies in itself all the previous Compound Redemptive Names.

"For His Name's Sake"

Thus when the Lord speaks of doing things "for His Name's sake," it stands for all that He is to and for His people in Covenantal and Redemptive revelation. The Name stands for His Person. Jehovah dwells in Heaven (Deuteronomy 4:36; 26:13) but He chooses a PLACE or a PERSON for His Name to dwell and thus sets it there. Deuteronomy 12:11; 14:23; 16:11; Exodus 20:24-26; Isaiah 30:27. It is the Name which guarantees His Presence there in the Temple in clear distinction from Jehovah's Throne in Heaven. Deuteronomy 18:3-7 with I Kings 8:13.

All that JEHOVAH does is "for His Name's sake" - His REDEMPTIVE NAME's sake as in the LORD JESUS CHRIST. Psalms 54:1; Jeremiah 14:7, 21; Malachi 1:11,14; 2:5; Psalms 106:8, 109:21, 143:11; Ezekiel 20:9, 14, 22; Romans 15:30; III John 7.

APPENDIX   II

THE "I AM's" of JESUS

1.   I AM THAT I AM.   The Name of the Eternal Godhead.   Exodus 3:14,15.

2.   Before Abraham was, I AM.   John 8:58.   cf.   Leviticus 24:16.

3.   Jesus saith unto them, I AM.   John 18:5,6,8.

4.   If ye believe not that I AM, ye shall die in your sins.   John 8:24.

5.   I AM from above ... I AM not of this world.   John 8:23.

6.   When ye shall have lifted up the Son of Man, then shall ye know that I AM.
     John 8:28.

7.   Messiah ... I that speak unto thee AM.   John 4:26.

8.   I AM the Bread of Life.   John 6:35.

9.   I AM the Living Bread which came down from heaven.   John 6:51.

10.   I AM the Light of the world.   John 8:12.   John 9:5.

11.   I AM the Door.   John 10:9.

12.   I AM come that they might have life.   John 10:11.

13.   I AM the Resurrection and the Life.   John 11:25.

14.   I AM the Son of God.   John 10:36.

15.   That ye might believe that I AM.   John 13:19.

16.   Ye call Me Master and Lord ... and so I AM.   John 13:13.

17.   I AM the Way, the Truth and the Life.   John 14:6.

18.   I AM the True Vine.   John 15:1.

19.   That they may be with Me where I AM.   John 17:24.

20.   Take courage, I AM.   Matthew 14:27.   Amp. N. T.

21.   Lo, I AM with you alway.   Matthew 28:20.

22.   Fear not, I AM the First and the Last.   Revelation 1:17. cf. Isaiah   44:6.

23.   I AM Alpha and Omega.   Revelation 1:11.

24.   I AM the Root and Offspring of David.   Revelation 22:16.

25.   Jesus said, I AM.   Mark 14:62.   Amp. N. T.

26. Where two or three are gathered together in My Name, there I AM in the midst. Matthew 18:20. Amp. N. T.

27. Whatever you ask in My Name (presenting all I AM). John 14:13,14. 15:16. 16:23,24. Amp. N. T.

28. Many shall come in My Name saying I AM. Mark 13:6. Luke 21:8.

29. I AM He that liveth. Revelation 1:18.

30. As I was with Moses, so I will be (I AM) with thee. Exodus 3:12-15, cf. Joshua 1:5,9.

31. I AM the Good Shepherd. John 10:14.

32. From Him which is, which was and which is to come. Revelation 1:8. That is, I AM.

BIBLIOGRAPHY

1. Amplified New Testament, Grand Rapids, Michigan: Zondervan Publishing House, 1958.

2. Ante-Nicene Fathers, Robert & Donaldson, American Reprint of the Edinburgh Edition, New York: Charles Scribner's Sons, 1905.

3. Brumback, Carl, God in Three Persons, 922 Montgomery Avenue, Cleveland, Tennessee: Pathway Press, 1959.

4. Hall, William Phillips, A Remarkable Biblical Discovery, or "The Name" of God According to the Scriptures, 45th Street, New York: American Tract Society, 1931.

5. Henry, Matthew, Commentary on the Whole Bible, New York: Fleming H Revell Company, 1710.

6. Jamieson, Fausett & Brown, Commentary Critical & Explanatory on the Whole Bible, Grand Rapids, Michigan: Zondervan Publishing House.

7. Kenyon, E. W., The Wonderful Name of Jesus, 528 West Amerige, Fullerton, California: Kenyon's Publishing Society, 1927.

8. Kittel, Gerhard, Theological Dictionary of the New Testament, Vol., Grand Rapids, Michigan: Wm. B. Eerdman's Publishing Company, 1969.

9. Knott, Lucy P., The Triune Name, and The Exalted Name, 2923 Troost Ave., Kansas City, Missouri: Nazarene Publishing House, 1937.

10. Lange, John Peter, The Gospel According to Matthew, Translated from the Third German Edition, with additions by Philip Schaff, New York: Charles Scribner's Sons, 1899.

11. Nestle-Arland Greek Text, Printed in Germany, 1968.

12. Obermann, Julian, Journal of Biblical Literature, 68:305, The Divine Name YHWH in the Light of Recent Discoveries, December, 1949.

13. Offiler, W. H., God and His Name, Bethel Temple, Inc., Seattle, Washington, 1932.

14. Offiler, W. H., Harmonies of Divine Revelation, Bethel Temple, Inc., Seattle, Washington, 1946.

15. Smith, William, L. D., A Dictionary of the Bible, Philadelphia, PA., Universal Book and Bible House, 1884.

16. Smith, B. F., Christian Baptism, Nashville, Tennessee: Broadman Press, 1970.

17. Strong, Names, Exhaustive Concordance, New Jersey, Madison, 1890.

18. Thayer, Joseph Henry, D. D., <u>Thayer's Greek-English Lexicon</u>, Grand Rapids, Michigan: Associated Publishers & Authors Inc., 1885.

19. <u>The Companion Bible</u>, 72 Marylebone Lane, London: W. I. Samuel Bagster & Sons, Ltd., 1972.

20. Thompson, Frank Charles, <u>The New Chain Reference Bible</u>, Indianapolis, Indiana: B. B. Kirkbride Bible Co. Inc., 1964.

21. Vine, W. E., <u>An Expositionary Dictionary of the New Testament. Words</u>, Old Tappan, New Jersey: Fleming H. Revell Company, 1966.

22. Vos, Geerhardus, <u>Biblical Theology</u>, Grand Rapids, Michigan: Wm. B. Eerdman's Publishing Company, 1959, p. 129.

23. White, R. E. O., M. A., B. D., <u>The Biblical Doctrine of Initiation</u>, Grand Rapids, Michigan: Wm. B. Eerdman's Publishing Company, 1960.

24. William Arndt & F. Wilbur Gingrich, <u>A Greek-English Lexicon of the New Testament</u> & Other Early Christian Literature, Chicago: University of Chicago Press, 1969.

25. Young, Robert, L. L. D., <u>Analytical Concordance to the Holy Bible</u>, United Society for Christian Literature, London: Lutterworth Press, 1953.

ALSO FROM KEVIN J. CONNER

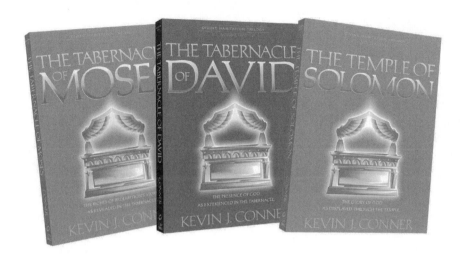

THE TABERNACLE OF MOSES

Redemption's Story Revealed through the Tabernacle

The Tabernacle of Moses is the first in this trilogy of books dealing with the intriguing topic of the dwelling places of God. A thorough and detailed study into the spiritual significance of every facet of Old Testament tabernacle worship, it sets forth redemption's story as typified in its furniture and construction.

Softcover, 119 pages
7" X 10", 0-914936-93-X

THE TABERNACLE OF DAVID

The Presence of God as Experienced in the Tabernacle

The Tabernacle of David is the second work in Conner's Divine Habitation Trilogy. This text answers many vital questions concerning the tabernacle in the Old Testament and its significance to New Testament revelation. It presents an exciting and stimulating challenge to the believer who is hungry to learn more about the move of the Holy Spirit today.

Softcover, 276 pages
7" X 10", 0-914936-94-8

THE TEMPLE OF SOLOMON

The Glory of God Displayed through the Temple

The Temple of Solomon completes the trilogy dealing with the dwelling places of God in the Old Testament. Kevin Conner's study yields rich and precious truths concerning Christ and His Church. These truths are tied into the New Testament as the Church is presented as the "Temple of God."

Softcover, 261 pages
7" X 10", 0-914936-96-4

FROM KEVIN J. CONNER & KEN MALMIN

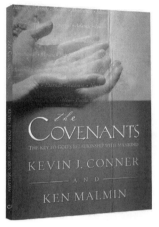

THE COVENANTS

God's Covenantal Plan Exposed

Kevin J. Conner & Ken Malmin

This textbook introduces covenant theology through a systematic study of the divine covenants found in Scripture. Perhaps better than any other subject, *The Covenants* give us a biblical framework for our understanding of the administration of God's dealings with mankind throughout all of human history. *Endorsed by Dr. C. Peter Wagner, Dr. Gary S. Greig, Ernest Gentile, and others.*

Softcover, 113 pages, 7" X 10"
0-914936-77-8

INTERPRETING THE SCRIPTURES

A Textbook on How to Interpret the Bible

Kevin J. Conner & Ken Malmin

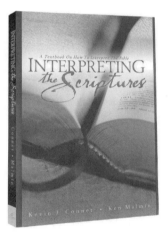

Interpreting the Scriptures introduces the reader to the science of hermeneutics by listing qualifications of an interpreter, the methods of interpreting, and a brief history of interpreting. The authors explore seventeen basic principles for interpreting any passage of Scripture. Any student of the Word will find this book to be a very helpful guide in his studies as well as a veritable gold mine of truth.

Softcover, 165 pages, 8 ½" X 11"
0-914936-20-4

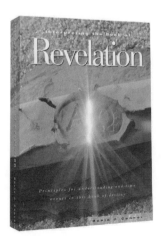

INTERPRETING THE BOOK OF REVELATION

Principles for Understanding End-time Events in this Book of Destiny

Kevin J. Conner

Discover how to interpret the book of Revelation for yourself, whether for use in developing your sermon or answering questions. *Interpreting the Book of Revelation* teaches you how to apply proper hermeneutical principles and unlock answers on your own. An invaluable tool to balance the varied interpretations of today.

Softcover, 203 pages, 7" X 9 ¾"
0-914936-10-7

ALSO FROM KEVIN J. CONNER

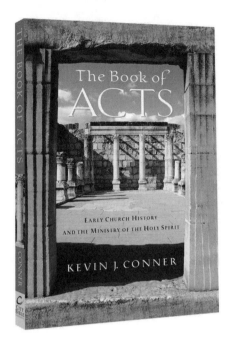

THE BOOK OF ACTS

*Early Church History and
the Ministry of the Holy Spirit*

In these days of renewed outpouring of the Holy Spirit, God's people are looking once again at the book of Acts. *The Book of Acts* is designed to give emphasis to early church history and the ministry of the Holy Spirit. This insightful text unlocks the keys to the success and impact of the early Christian church and its relevance today.

Biblical Studies

Softcover, 165 pages, 7" X 10"
1-886849-02-1

THE CHURCH IN THE NEW TESTAMENT

*A Comprehensive Study
of the New Testament Church*

Kevin J. Conner's comprehensive study of the Church and God's eternal plan for it is laid out in *The Church in the New Testament*. This encyclopedic reference work is designed to give a comprehensive biblical understanding of the universal and local New Testament Church.

Biblical Studies

Softcover, 328 pages, 7 ¼" X 10 ¼"
1-886849-15-3

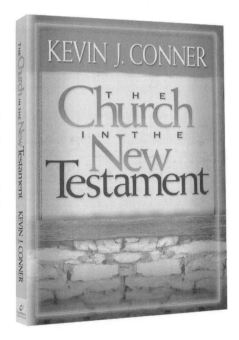

ALSO FROM KEVIN J. CONNER

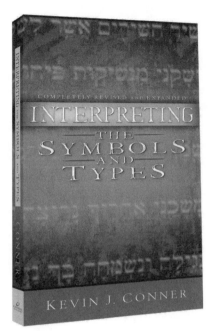

INTERPRETING THE SYMBOLS AND TYPES

Understanding the Use of Symbols and Types in God's Word

Interpreting the Symbols and Types is a comprehensive study unlocking the biblical language of the symbol & type, allowing for a greater understanding of scriptural truth. This language of divine origin reveals characteristics and shades of meaning that would be lost to the believer if he did not acquaint himself with this terminology.

Biblical Studies / Reference

Softcover, 199 pages, 5 ½" X 8 ½"
0-914936-51-4

THE FEASTS OF ISRAEL

A Comprehensive Study of Israel's Major Feasts

Kevin Conner presents a colorful picture of grace and redemption in this study of the feasts of Israel. He shows how Old Testament types find fulfillment in the new covenant and the church. Conner covers both Mosaic and post-Mosaic festivals. He also briefly covers the modern Jewish festivals and provides important spiritual lessons for the Church today.

Biblical Studies

Softcover, 111 pages, 8 ½" X 11"
0-914936-42-5

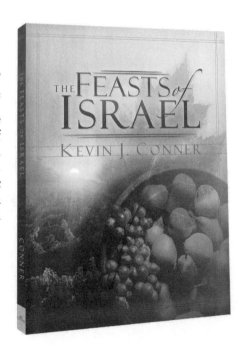

FROM KEVIN J. CONNER & KEN MALMIN

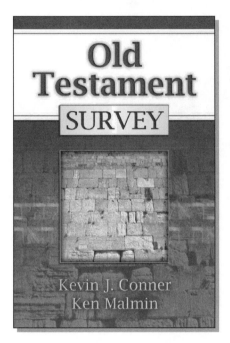

OLD TESTAMENT SURVEY

Kevin J. Conner & Ken Malmin

This introduction to the Old Testament is a guide that will acquaint Christians with the Bible in its entirety. It was written to help students understand the Bible by relating its many sections and books to the message of Scripture as a whole.

The format of this book is simple and concise. It is designed to give a patterned glimpse into the books of the Old Testament by applying these ten points to each: Titles • Author • Date • Key Words & Phrases • Key Verse • Purpose • Message • Outline • Summary • Christ Seen.

Biblical Studies

Softcover, 49 pages, 6" X 9"
0-914936-21-2

NEW TESTAMENT SURVEY

Kevin J. Conner & Ken Malmin

This introduction to the New Testament is a guide that will acquaint Christians with the Bible in its entirety. It was written to help students understand the Bible by relating its many sections and books to the message of Scripture as a whole.

The format of this book is simple and concise. It is designed to give a patterned glimpse into the books of the Old Testament by applying these ten points to each: Titles • Author • Date • Key Words & Phrases • Key Verse • Purpose • Message • Outline • Summary • Christ Seen.

Biblical Studies

Softcover, 36 pages, 6" X 9"
0-914936-22-0

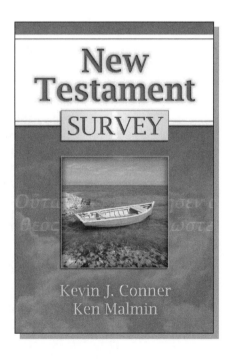

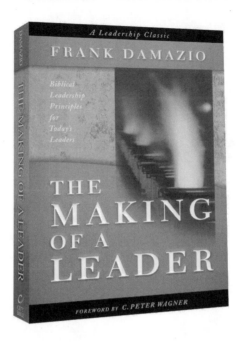

THE MAKING OF A LEADER

Biblical Leadership Principles for Today's Leaders

Frank Damazio

In *The Making of a Leader*, Frank Damazio lays a broad and deep discussion of what it means to be responsible for a group of "followers." This perennial best-seller presents a scriptural analysis of the philosophy, history, qualifications, preparation, and practice of Christian leadership. Charts, diagrams and illustrations enhance this well-tested and taught study on Christian leadership. *Endorsed by Dr. C. Peter Wagner, Joyce Meyer, and Dr. Joe C. Aldrich.*

Leadership

Softcover, 333 pages, 7 ¼" X 10"
0-914936-84-0

THE MAKING OF A LEADER: STUDY GUIDE

This study guide provides thought-provoking questions for each chapter of The Making of a Leader. It is an excellent resource to assist the reader in applying the truths and principles from this book to his own life and ministry.

Softcover, 50 pages, 7 ¼" X 10"
0-914936-57-3